TUNNEL PEOPLE

TUNNEL PEOPLE

Teun Voeten

First Published:
Tunnelmensen
Amsterdam: Atlas, 1996.

This book was published with the support of the Foundation for
the Production and Translation of Dutch Literature.

The 1996 edition was made possible with the support of the
Dutch Foundation for Special Journalistic Projects.

ISBN: 978-1-60486-070-2
LCCN: 2009912464

PM Press
PO Box 23912
Oakland, CA 94623
www.pmpress.org

Printed in the USA on recycled paper.

Cover: John Yates/Stealworks.com
Cover Photo: Frankie leaves the tunnel at the South End to start
a day of canning.
Interior design: Kersplebedeb

For Marieke and Sebastian

Map of the Tunnel

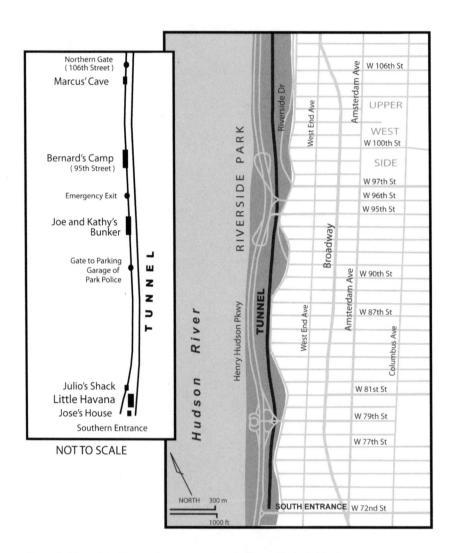

Figure 1. Map of double-track train tunnel under Riverside Park, Manhattan, New York City, 1994, with encampments shown (locations approximate).

CONTENTS

Part 3. Winter
January 1996

Part 4. Epilogue
September 2009

INTRODUCTION

In 1992, I was in New York to write an article about Malcolm X and racism in contemporary America. One of the people I spoke to was Terry Williams, at that time a very controversial ethnographer specializing in urban issues.

Williams told me about his latest project. After publishing provocative studies on crack houses and cocaine gangs in which he stated that crack dealers were just entrepreneurs who followed the American Dream, Williams was now focusing on the underground homeless. For the past few years, he had been studying people living in New York's tunnel system. "A new class of people who have been rejected by society and became in fact invisible," Williams formulated solemnly. "I want to give the invisible a human face."

Immediately, I was intrigued by the phenomenon of tunnel people. Williams was actually looking for a photographer so pretty soon we decide to cooperate. However, I found the tunnel people such an extremely fascinating subject that what initially was meant to be just an article to accompany my photos eventually turned into a book.

I was not the only one gripped by the subterranean dwellers. In the winter of 1989, Jim Dwyer, the special subway correspondent of *New York Newsday*, reported the first stories about homeless people living in the deserted tunnels at an abandoned subway station near Lafayette Street. New Yorkers became captivated with tunnel people when Dwyer reported that these mythical creatures were in fact just ordinary materialistic Americans. They had installed themselves quite comfortably, and by illegally tapping electricity, they had surrounded themselves with fridges, TV's, heaters, microwaves, and other luxurious appliances.

Soon more reports and articles saw the light. It was said that in the complicated labyrinth of hundreds of kilometers of subways and railroad tunnels, thousands of homeless people had found a home. And not only the relatively well settled group that were watching TV under Lafayette Street. There were also miserable cases, creatures abandoned by God who saw the tunnels as the final terminal in their failed lives, people who had gone underground just to wait until death took them away. There were cases of AIDS patients, whose bodies had been partially eaten by rats.

The subterranean world was painted as Dante's *Inferno*, making Dickens' gloomiest scenes seem just a picnic. The tunnel people became labeled with sensational names such as 'Mole People' and CHUDS: 'Cannibalistic Human Underground Dwellers.' There were urban legends about subway maintenance workers who had disappeared without a trace, having met their final destiny on the roasting spits of starving savages.

Apart from the numerous reports in the local papers and many documentaries on domestic and foreign channels, journalist Jennifer Toth published her book *The Mole People* in 1993. It was a gripping report of extensive research into a few underground colonies of homeless people: One group in the Amtrak tunnel (the one this book is about), one colony under Grand Central Station and several small groups and individuals living in the subway system.

Toth's book initially got rave reviews, but people in homeless advocacy groups, some journalists, and a few tunnel people accused her of sensationalizing and exaggerating her subject. Critics said her research was sloppy, impossible to confirm, and inaccurate. They pointed out that most of the so-called mole people were just the people in the Amtrak tunnel, a relatively safe and accessible location. Whatever critics have said, up to this point her book has been seen as the standard work on New York's underground homeless population.

At the end of 1995, photographer Margaret Morton published *The Tunnel*, a large coffee-table book with medium format photographs of the Amtrak tunnel alongside transcriptions of interviews. Some found her book too arty and conceptual. However, it provides meticulous documentation of the physical environment of the tunnel and its inhabitants. Terry Williams' book, *Voices from the Underground*, which he himself describes as creative non-fiction, was finished by 1994, but has not yet been published due to complications with the publishers. In 2001, Marc Singer presented his award-winning documentary *Dark Days*. Marc Singer spent months in the Amtrak tunnel and used its dwellers as film crew. Shot on 16 mm black-and-white film, the result is the ultimate tunnel documentary, with a shockingly honest portrayal of some of the people living there.

To add something new to the earlier studies, I decided to take the anthropological approach, using its favorite research method of participant observation. As the name implies, the researcher moves between a role of distant observer at certain times, to an involved actor at other times. While many associate cultural anthropology with the study of exotic tribes in faraway places, the U.S. has a long tradition of urban anthropology and ethnography, exemplified by the so-called Chicago School of Sociology. One of its most well known figureheads is Nels Anderson, who published *The Hobo* in 1923, a very detailed study of the life of the mobile class of itinerants and vagrant day laborers roaming the States in the early twentieth century. Other studies from around the same time focused on organized crime, prostitution, youth gangs, and poverty in the ghettos.

To get closer to the tunnel people, I asked to live in the tunnel myself and was offered a little bunker where I could stay. In total I spent about five months in the tunnel—two months at the end of 1994 and another three months in the summer of 1995—during which time I took part as much as possible in the daily life of the tunnel dwellers.

In the summer of 1995, the tunnel people were threatened with eviction by Amtrak. At the same time, however, there was also a federal program to offer the tunnel dwellers alternative housing. It was very interesting to see how the tunnel people reacted, both to their threatened existence as well as to the opportunity to start a new life. My old Dutch anthropology professor Speckmann would have called it a "laboratory situation." In January 1996, shortly before my book went to print, I returned to the tunnels to do a small update on the eviction and housing process.

Apart from my bunker in the tunnel, I also had a room in Brooklyn where I could escape after three or four days of tunnel life to wash up, develop my film, work out my field notes and ponder new research questions. This was not a luxury for a re-searcher, since in the tunnel I was constantly submerged in new information and bizarre events. "Never a dull moment," as one of the tunnel dwellers said.

I focused on one colony, the one living in the Amtrak railroad tunnel that runs under Riverside Park from 72nd to 125th Street on Manhattan's Upper West Side. This is the most approachable group of tunnel people; it is also the group most frequented by journalists.

I estimated that approximately thirty to fifty people lived in the Amtrak tunnel, scattered in small groups. My study focused on a dozen individuals within this population. The selection was more based on random meetings and chance instead of a well thought out research strategy.

I tried to place the stories of the tunnel people within a broader context, by interviewing outreach workers and authorities about their approach to the homeless and tunnel people phenome-non. I also give a brief summary of the homeless debate that has been going on in for the last few decades. It is a complicated discussion and for the sake of readability, I have kept most of the most technical details for the endnotes. Those who want to focus more on these issues will find useful literature mentioned in the works cited section at the end of the book.

In the end, my research did not result in an objective case study in a purely anthropological sense, but became instead more of a subjective, journalistic reporting on life in a dynamic community in which I became more and more involved.

From the outset, I made it very clear to those living in the tun-nels who I was, and what I was aiming at. I had the luck to come in contact with Bernard, a well-educated, reliable, and honest man with a great sense of humor, with whom I felt immediately at ease. Bernard was crucial as my guide, and in the course of my tunnel sojourn we became great friends.

Some people I showed some of my earlier publications as a form of reference letter. Others, for various reasons, were slow to understand the nature of my mission and only realized after months that I was not another homeless man but a reporter. Most people, however, accepted my presence, and the reasons for it, rather quickly. They were used to journalists but had never seen a reporter who would actually sleep in the tunnels and help with the daily—and dirty—chores of collecting cans, getting firewood, and carrying water. At first, some assumed I was crazy, but after a while most treated me with respect. A few people kept their hostile attitude throughout the five months, and closed themselves off to me. These were, however, primarily those heavily affected by substance abuse and mental illness.

The tunnel people portrayed in this book are therefore not representative of the tunnel population in general. At the time of my fieldwork in the mid 1990s, I estimate the total population of all of New York' s tunnel people to have been not a few thousand as some have claimed, but a few hundred at the most. Nor do the tunnel people represent the enormous group of people living on the streets. One of the principal differences is that most tunnel people had spent a considerable amount of time and energy in the creation of their own environment, and in this way showed a level of self-confidence and planning beyond the day-to-day that is nearly absent among street people. Most tunnel people did not even consider themselves to be homeless.

One of the most challenging things was reconstructing people's pasts and obtaining an accurate picture of how they had slid down into homelessness. For most, it was a sad succession of bad luck, mistakes, stupid choices and dramatic, sometimes embarrassing, events. In America, with its strong focus on social achievements and personal responsibility, failure is extra painful and not a favorite topic of conversation.

Many tunnel people had mental problems to some degree, had repressed or forgotten certain events, and mixed fantasy with wishes and reality as they pleased. Substance abuse often heightened these tendencies. A few people told me a different story every time I spoke with them.

Others loved to play games with the journalists who visited the tunnel. They realized what journalists wanted and performed a well-rehearsed script for their modest fee—ten bucks, a sandwich, a six-pack of beer, or a few packs of cigarettes.

With most people, it took many, many meetings and talks to gradually overcome the suspicion and feelings of shame to eventually win their confidence. I was able to confirm some life stories with official sources, others I double-checked with information from fellow reporters. Some I simply took at their word. With a few, I realized that they would never reveal to me their true life-story. Even so, the way they chose to portray themselves and their invented life stories were in themselves very interesting, so I kept some of these narratives.

In some cases, I had the names and addresses of family members of tunnel people. I did not knock on their door to confirm certain information. My respondents would have interpreted that as an unacceptable intrusion into their privacy and a breach of trust. Apart from ethical considerations, in my view some bits of confirmed data were not worth the sacrifice of a relation of trust.

The tunnel people loved to gossip about each other. Some of the gossip and tall tales were true, but for others I never managed to establish how much was truth and how much was hearsay. Again, I have mentioned these tales because they illustrate the cognitive world of the tunnel people in such a colorful way. By taking notes and working them out as soon as possible, I managed to transcribe most of the interviews and conversations literally. Thus I was able to save some of the vibrant tunnel slang. I gave a small remuneration to most of the tunnel people for their cooperation. In decent journalism you are not supposed to pay your informants, but in anthropology we have the law of mutual reciprocity. It seemed to me plainly impolite not to give the tunnel people some form of compensation for all their efforts.

Sometimes I gave cash, but I preferred to donate small presents like food (even pet food), beer, cigarettes, batteries, candles, clothes, dinner, and, in the end, my bike. Helping them with their work and providing extra labor was another way I could give the tunnel people something in return. I also gave them my photos; some put them on the walls of their dwellings, others turned them into a small album.

Another rule in journalism is that a journalist should not cover their fellow reporters as subjects so as to prevent incestuous meta-journalism. Again, anthropology provides an excuse. The interaction between the media and the homeless is extremely fascinating and worth further research. There were sometimes hilarious situations in the tunnel, especially when journalists bumped into each other. I could not resist the temptation to mention some of these.

In the end, there were two other journalists apart from myself who, during their long-term projects, had managed to establish very close ties with the tunnel people. We had the privilege of functioning not only in parasitic roles, but also in helpful ones. Namely, we served as liaisons between the tunnel people on the one hand, and the organizations and authorities involved in providing alternative housing on the other. We helped the tunnel people with the paperwork, kept them informed about recent developments, and tried to give them courage and confidence whenever necessary to stay in the housing program. Both Margaret Morton and Marc Singer did great work, and continued to do so long after I had left the tunnel. For some people, it actually made the difference. Their shyly expressed words of thanks were heartwarming.

With other people, however, the best meant endeavors had no results. It was sad to see that some of the tunnel dwellers did not realize that eviction was unavoidable; by refusing to join the housing program, they actively choose the streets.

In a study about a social problem of such magnitude as homelessness, the author is supposed to make policy recommendations. I refrained from making any sweeping statements. As a European, I don't want to tell the Americans what to do. In Europe, the situation of the homeless is completely different and varies even from country to country, so I could not comment on the situation in the Old World. Instead, I gave the stage to other people—case workers, city officials, sociologists, priests, seasoned homeless people—who had intelligent and creative observations and opinions, although I am afraid that some opinions vented by the homeless themselves are not the most politically sensitive ones, In the list of sources, I mention academics of whom I especially want to recommend Christopher Jencks, Peter Rossie, and Martha Burt.

The only intention of my book is to give some insight to the souls of the tunnel people. I hope I have succeeded.

Teun Voeten
Brussels 1996

A SHORT NOTE TO THE
2010 TRANSLATED AND UPDATED EDITION

Tunnelmensen was originally published in the Netherlands in 1996. More than thirteen years have passed since the tunnel people had to leave their underground spaces they called home. I managed to track down most of the former tunnel dwellers. Some have died, some have simply disappeared, but most of them are still in the housing they were offered and are doing remarkably well. The final chapter describes the results of my quest for the former tunnel people thirteen years later.

I have left the theoretical chapter fifteen on "The Homeless Debate" largely as it is, but changed its title to "The Homeless Debate of the '90s," to accentuate that it was a theoretical discussion that took place a decade and a half ago.

Most things discussed in that chapter still make sense today. One of the newer developments, however, is the huge increase in the number of the homeless, especially families. During the ongoing economic crisis that has caused lay-offs and foreclosures on a scale not seen since the Great Depression, large numbers of people have been and continue to be pushed over the edge.

This includes not only the poor, but also thousands of people from the middle classes. Exact numbers and statistics are not yet available, and many victims of the crisis have explored all other possibilities—friends, families, cheap lodgings—before actually hitting the streets. The emergence of tent cities on the outskirts of big cities, the increasing demand for shelter beds, and longer lines for free food are, however, a strong indicator of the seriousness of the current situation.

Not only homelessness, but also the amount written about it, has multiplied. When I finished *Tunnelmensen* in 1996 there were perhaps five books and twenty articles considered to be absolutely essential. Today, I can think of dozens of books, and have stumbled upon hundreds of articles that are extremely interesting. To update my book, I have only briefly gazed over this new body of literature. New and relevant findings and facts were processed in the endnotes. To get a good idea of the current situation of the homeless, I would like to recommend the work of Kim Hopper, Brendan O'Flaherty, Thomas Main, Sam Tsemberis, and Dennis Culhane.

I hope this updated version of *Tunnel People* will shed some more light on the complex problem of homelessness. Much too often, homelessness is discussed in dry, academic studies. Journalistic reports can be superficial, and often tend to either sensationalize or romanticize those homeless living underground. I hope my book will help demystify this group and portray them as the complex, unique individuals they all are. True, in many ways they are very different from us, but in many ways they are just folks like you and me.

Teun Voeten
New York 2010

Autumn

November & December 1994

1. HALLOWEEN

The mouth of the tunnel looms a few hundred feet wide. Broken down railroad tracks wind between a forest of steel and concrete pillars and disappear into the darkness, into the netherworld I am about to enter. Professor Terry Williams leads me inside the tunnel, into the unknown. Slowly, the daylight disappears behind our backs, until we are engulfed by a cold, damp darkness. I shiver. I don't like dark caves with hidden dens, and to make it even worse, today is Halloween. I'm not in the mood for crazy tunnel people popping up out of the darkness with Dracula masks and bloody butcher knives. Quietly I curse at Williams, who thought today would be the perfect day to bring me into the tunnel.

The entrance of the tunnel is under a fly-over from the West Side Highway, where Riverside Park starts at 72nd Street. The park is a narrow green strip that stretches along the Hudson till it reaches the tip of Manhattan. On the east, the park borders posh apartment buildings. Farther up north along the park, the cozy and comfy West Side slowly transforms into the projects of Harlem to finally end in the mean streets of Washington Heights. And right underneath the park winds the tunnel, in a near perfect straight line from south to north, fifty blocks long. In the park people are jogging, yuppies are walking their dogs, young mothers push their strollers, without knowing that right underneath their very feet is a hidden underworld.

At the entrance of the tunnel, people have chained shopping carts with old clothes and empty bottles to a fence. The blades of a discarded fan turn slowly in the chilly November breeze. The hundreds of pillars that support the ceiling are covered in tags and graffiti. Here at the entrance, the ceiling is actually an elegant, late-nineteenth-century cast iron construction. One hundred years ago, this place was a busy terminal for riverboats and freight trains. At the end of the '60s, the terminal became obsolete and slowly deteriorated into a no man's land where only the intrepid or the desperate ventured.

In between the wood of the pillars, I see little shacks. Some are cubicles, constructed quite laboriously from plywood and tin sheeting, other are just sloppy tents flung together with some poles and plastic sheets.

"Some new shacks since I was here last time," Williams says. In the dark, people are warming themselves around a fire that's burning in an empty oil drum. Farther down, a man is sawing a giant piece of wood.

We descend deeper into the tunnel. Some train tracks have dead ends and are covered by garbage. Other tracks merge through rusty switches. In the darkness we stumble over old clothes, broken bottles, empty boxes, wrecked shopping charts. I stumble over a book. With my flashlight I see it is a copy of Lord of the Flies. A nauseating smell of rotting garbage and excrement penetrates my nose. Rats are rummaging through waste but flee when we approach to disappear into holes and cracks beneath the tracks. I'm glad I just had my tetanus, diphtheria, and typhoid shots renewed.

After what seems like half an hour, there is no more daylight left. Now it has become pitch black. With my flashlight I see the tunnel has narrowed with only two train tracks left.

"Watch out for booby traps," warns Williams. "Some people here don't like visitors and have dug deep holes. You'll break your leg if you fall in one of them." Maybe Williams wants to scare me, or maybe he is paranoid. He might also be right, so I just follow his example and proceed by walking on the tracks.

After fifteen minutes of walking, the tunnel bends slightly to the right and we cannot see the entrance any more. Faint daylight falls through grates in the ceiling. The park should be right above us. We hear children playing and yelling. Underneath the grates, the tunnel widens and we enter a space with some concrete bunkers. Williams explains that these bunkers were used by maintenance workers to take their lunch breaks and store their equipment. A deafening barking rings through the tunnel. On top of one of the bunkers is a dirty pack of dogs. An old man appears from behind a moldy carpet that covers the entrance of the bunker. "Joe, everything okay?" calls Williams. The old man grumbles something and returns to his bunker.

"Well, Joe isn't in the mood today." Williams shrugs his shoulders. Joe is a Vietnam vet who has been living in the tunnel for over twenty years, Williams tells me. He lives together with his wife Cathy and their thirty cats. The dogs belong to his neighbor.

We continue. It becomes pitch black again for ten minutes, and with our weak flashlights we stumble through the darkness. Then, there are more grates piercing the roof at regular intervals. A dim light drives the darkness away. After another ten minutes of walking, we come to another widening with six, seven bunkers. "We've arrived," says Williams, "Bernard's camp."

Williams calls his name out loud. Through a grate in the ceiling, filtered daylight illuminates what is Bernard's camp. Boxes with empty bottles and cans are scattered all around. Four identical metal folding chairs are placed against two giant pillars that support the ceiling of the tunnel. A pile of magazines is on one of the chairs: *Sports Illustrated*, *Newsweek*, *The New Yorker*. It looks like a doctor's waiting room.

Behind the pillars lies a huge open space with old cupboards filled with coffee cans, boxes of cereal, and bags of spaghetti. In the middle of the open space, I see some chairs placed around a fire that glows between two large stones. On top of it sits a blackened grill. On the dark wall behind the fireplace I can discern a giant mural. A firing squad is executing several people; one of the victims spreads his arms desperately toward the sky. It is a reproduction of Goya's *Third of May*, Williams explains, made by graffiti artists from the neighborhood.

Williams calls Bernard a second time. Finally, a tall dark man appears from one of the bunkers. "Sorry to keep you waiting, Terry. I just had to finish up something." The two shake hands cordially. "So this is Bernard," says Williams, "New York's most famous homeless man." Bernard smiles and gives me a firm handshake. Rasta curls emerge from under his white baseball cap. He wears a white sweatshirt that has Goofy on a skateboard printed on it. Due to the darkness and his cap, I can hardly see Bernard's features. I only see a row of white teeth shining in a black face.

Williams and Bernard start talking about the latest events. A man was killed yesterday in the park. Bernard knew the victim. It was Walter, a homeless man who slept in a cardboard box under a bridge.

"Slashed by some crazy twenty-one-year-old Dominican kid. Right above us, here on 95th Street." Bernard points up to the gray sky visible through the grate.

"The kid was freaked out. He cut out Walter's eyeball, pulled off his pants," Bernard continues. He seems upset by the murder. "Walter was a good guy. Damn, he never bothered anyone. Can you believe it, Terry? The cops arrested the kid on Broadway while he was waving the knife and the bloodstained pants around." Bernard sighs. "What a world. It can happen to fucking anybody."

He shakes his head and stares at the ground. Williams breaks the silence and introduces me as a Dutch photographer who wants to do an article on the tunnel. Bernard cheers up. In a few minutes, we have worked things out. Bernard will be my guide. We will start after tomorrow. "Just call my name through the intercom," he says. "Then I'll get you up top." He points at the grate. "My mailbox and intercom, it's on the exit of the West Side Highway on 95th Street. You can't miss it."

Bernard apologizes and says he has work obligations. He walks us half a mile farther up north through the darkness. Then there is an opening in the tunnel wall with a stairwell that leads to another gate. We are suddenly bathed in broad daylight again, the gate exits onto a playground in the park. This is the Northern Gate, Bernard explains, another emergency exit from the tunnel.

"Before, we had to crawl through a hole in the ground," he says as he unlocks the chain at the gate. "This way, it's a lot easier." A friendly Amtrak worker gave him the key for the lock. Bernard leaves us at the playground and disappears back into the darkness.

The light and fresh air feel good as we walk back to Broadway. "You can't find a better guide than Bernard," Williams says. Over the years, Bernard had become more than just an object of study; the two became good friends.

"Bernard gets nothing from all these interviews," Williams says. "He knows it too, but he just loves all the attention."

2. THE SIMPLICITY OF BEING

On my way to my meeting with Bernard, I walk down 95th Street towards River Side Park and the Hudson. Under the bridge where Walter must have been killed, yellow police ribbons lie strewn on the ground around the mud and broken bottles. *POLICE LINE. DO NOT CROSS* they say in big bold capitals. A man in the corner sleeps under a blanket. He peeps out from underneath, throws me an ugly glance, then he turns around and crawls back under his covers.

Further down is the entry and exit for the West Side Highway. Dodging speeding cars, I manage to reach a traffic island and see the grates, the tunnel intercom. Bending over, I peer into the darkness below and recognize some of the graffiti and the boxes with empty bottles. As loudly as possible, I scream Bernard's name a few times. Only a few feet behind me, cars are hurling by. I call out a few more times, but no answer.

Sitting on a wall in the park, a black man is waving at me. I had seen him earlier, but somehow he did not register. Now I recognize the Rasta hairdo as Bernard's. "I'm sorry, I had not recognized you without your Goofy shirt," I apologize.

He laughs. "Once in a while, I put on clean clothes."

Bernard wears a Yankees baseball cap and an Adidas sports jacket, clean jeans and fresh white sneakers. Now in broad daylight, I can clearly see him for the first time. Williams had told me that Bernard used to be a photo model. It is believable: Bernard is a handsome man, tall and trim with a straight nose, thin lips and a high forehead. I guess him to be in his mid-thirties. When he smiles, his lips curl in a beautiful curve and reveal impeccable teeth. His lively eyes are scrutinizing me.

We walk through the park to the entry of the tunnel at the playground, the North Gate. Bernard opens up the padlock with his private key. On the stairwell inside, there is hardly room to walk. We squeeze past three supermarket carts that cram the space. Rusty beams above us function as bookshelves. Next to popular magazines and flashy bestsellers there are books with titles like *Handbook Of Dermatology* and *Mathematics Made Easy*. A stone replica of the Acropolis doubles as a bookstand. A plastic pumpkin smiles at me with a stupid, toothless grin.

"All this mess is from Tony," Bernard explains. "The idiot is creating fire hazards. If he goes on like this, we will all be kicked out." He points at the shopping cart. Tony has tied a woman's hat with flowers to it, as well as a Barbie doll, some Christmas decorations and aluminum photo frames. An umbrella and a TV antenna stick out from under a pile of wood. On top, a few empty cans and some porn mags. Tony finds all the junk on the streets and sells it to whoever wants it. Bernard pulls on a few sheets of Formica-covered particle board. "Totally useless as firewood," he grumbles. "The guy doesn't have a clue."

We descend the stairs. Today, it is a sunny, clear day, and the grates allow more daylight in than a few days ago, when the tunnel was dipped in darkness and the surroundings were hard to discern. Bernard points out some graffiti pieces on the tunnel walls. Diffuse light filtering through the grates illuminates the work softly from above, like in a museum. The works are giant portraits, five feet high, which look like photographs because they are spray painted in black and white. I recognize John F. Kennedy, Martin Luther King, and the Mona Lisa. Farther down is a painting of a street kid in a macho leather jacket, striking a cool pose with his hands in his pockets. His head and neck are a phallus-shaped object.

I ask Bernard about the sharply dressed penis. He laughs. "You are the fourth guy asking the same question. You journalists think everything looks like a dick. Don't you see it is a spray can?"

On closer inspection, it does look like a spray can. The pieces are by artist Chris Pape, aka Freedom. The spray can with his hands in his pockets is Pape's self-portrait. When the graffiti rage started, the tunnel became a favorite playground for the graffiti scene. The spray painters entered through emergency exits or the tunnel mouth at 72nd Street. Bernard ran into them and became good friends with many, especially Chris Pape.

Near his camp, Bernard points out the portrait Pape made of him. "It doesn't look like me," he says disappointedly. In fact, the portrait resembles an unshaven American soldier out of the Second World War with a cigarette in his mouth. What looks like a helmet is actually the hood of a sweatshirt, drawn halfway over the eyes.

Next to it is a portrait of an old, wrinkled squint-eyed guy, with a sarcastic grin and a protruding under lip. It is Bob, Bernard's old neighbor who has moved back to the world above.

Bernard takes me to the fireplace, where he offers me a chair and immediately begins to talk. "The world up top thinks we are just drug addicts and alcoholics." Bernard leans back at his ease in an old office chair, his feet resting on the grill of the smoldering fireplace.

"But to survive here, you have to be able to provide for the three basic necessities: water, firewood and food. This is no place for crackheads." He points at the fireplace with the filthy black grate, clogged with chunks of grease and soot. "Our grill. That's where we cook."

Against a wall is a box full of extra thick Sunday *Times*. Next to it sits a pile of pine wood.

"Wood and old papers to start the fire," Bernard explains. "And here," he takes me behind the grill, "unlimited kitchen supplies."

Just below a giant mural, there is a huge collection of pots, pans, kettles and coffeemakers, all covered in a thin layer of dust and soot. On the grill, knives and forks are soaking in a small pan of water. A thin membrane of dirt floats on top of the water.

"Homeless? Here is my home." Bernard continues. "This is the kitchen. Fully equipped with stuff I found on the street. I got a living room of twenty city blocks. Few people up top can say the same. Before I wound up here, I was in a cheap hotel. I could only bear it for two weeks. Ten bucks a night for a place where you could hardly move your ass and where you were surrounded by trash, noise, and chaos. In the tunnels, there is a strange sort of peace. Here I finally found my peace of mind."

Bernard sees me looking at the dark space behind the column, where garbage has been piling up in a big heap. "That's what visitors notice when they come down here. The rats and the trash, empty wine and crack bottles. But hey, you can find that up top as well. And the garbage, well, what the fuck do you want? The Sanitation Department doesn't come down here." Bernard makes himself at ease at the fireplace and continues. "Journalists come here with preconceived opinions," he explains. "They only see the mess, but they fail to see the essence: brotherhood, a sense of community, that's the key thing here. And up till now, no one ever understood that."

I take a note of it. Bernard continues what starts to sound like a lecture. "I've learned more about life here than I ever would do up top. Tunnel life was a spiritual rebirth. And I tell you, if tomorrow my time were to come, I could say at least that I was a free person. Nobody could ever take this experience away from me. And if I could choose, I would do it again."

Bernard is an eloquent speaker, his vocabulary is peppered with sophisticated words like *oblivious, impeccable, elusive,* words I have to look up later in a dictionary. He is orating slowly, so I have enough time to write down every word he says. Later, I will hear him repeat exactly the same monologue to fellow journalists in the tunnel.

Bernard explains that disgust with life up top drove him down into the tunnel. Greed and chaos are keywords in his philosophy. "There is enough for fucking everybody on the planet. Enough living space, enough food, enough water, enough everything. But this world is ruled by greed. Greed destroys everything."

He shows me a colorful graffiti piece on the wall of a bunker to make his point. A brain is squeezed between four mysterious letters that, like Houdini, are tied up by large chains. "The piece is called 'Brains in Chains,'" explains Bernard. "The letters actually form the name SANE, an upside-down mirror image. This was his last work. Made especially for me."

Sane was one of the most promising talents on the graffiti scene. He drowned in Brooklyn harbor. Some say it was an accident while tagging on a bridge; others hold dark conspiracy theories because Sane was an excellent swimmer. On top of the brain in chains is a quote from Bernard: SOCIETY IS GUILTY OF INTELLECTUAL TERRORISM sprayed in aggressive, bold capitals.

"Everybody is always talking about emancipation," says Bernard. "Abraham Lincoln initiated the proclamation of emancipation with the abolition of slavery." Bernard pauses to give me the chance to jot down this complicated sentence in my notebook. "Originally and literally, emancipation meant 'the liberation of hands from manual labor.' But the mind is still chained. Everybody is absorbed by the Dollar Game."

It starts to sound like a philosophy class at some new-age academy. Is Bernard a modern-day Diogenes? Bernard has his answer ready. "A French journalist once tried to impose that role on me. The Gods punished Diogenes because he loathed human beings. He received the most cruel punishment possible: He was sentenced to devote the rest of his life searching for an honest and truthful man. But I don't loathe humans, I only have a problem with them.

"Back in college, I went to my teacher of philosophy. I told him 'Professor, how am I supposed to learn something here with thirty smart-asses in the class who interrupt incessantly with stupid questions?' 'I can see that you are predestined to life as a recluse,' he answered me."

I do some fact-checking later. The story about Lincoln is relatively correct. But with Diogenes, Bernard mixes up Post-Socratic philosophers and Greek mythological figures. It's not that bad, however, because he achieves a creative synthesis and it is clear what he means to say.

Bernard is now unstoppable and continues with an existential variation of the Fall from Grace. "Humanity is living under a curse. People are cursed to think. Humans cannot simply be.

People need chaos. And still they think they are superior and intelligent. But look around you: We have all the technology, but no harmony. Other civilizations on earth do. Like the Lemurians for instance." I look at him puzzled. "Those are the descendants from the old empire of Atlantis," Bernard explains patiently. "They live under the ocean, but refuse to interact with us. Why would they even?"

Bernard lectures on and throws in a pinch of Eastern Mysticism. "An old friend divulged to me the essence of life. Everything is made of three forms of energy: positive energy, negative energy, and the most important—the energy of imbalance. And the last form, the force of no direction, is causing all these problems and chaos."

Bernard tells me he is writing a book titled *The Simplicity of Being*. He is now writing the thirteenth chapter that deals with the Essence of Human Being. "Human Being…" he says sarcastically. "Being human is just a condition mankind imposes on himself. Humanism is an excuse for stupidity. Oh sorry, we're only human." Bernard imitates a childish voice.

"And then you have this amateur, Descartes," he rages on. "*Cogito ergo sum*. What was he thinking? People only think they are able to think. Or this Shakespeare. To be or not to be. How for heaven's sake can someone refuse Being?"

A few harsh whistles interrupt his ontological one-liners. A bright light is appearing in the distance and shines on the pillars.

"That's the one-thirty to Ohio," says Bernard and he gets up. The approaching headlights are from an Amtrak train. Bernard waves, the conductor answers with another thunderous whistle. Like lightning, the silvery train of ten cars hurtles by. A strong wave of air nearly knocks us over.

"It will always be an impressive sight," Bernard says we watch the red taillights disappear around a curve in the distance. Clouds of dust and diesel fumes engulf us. "You get used to it, but it remains dangerous," he warns me. Especially when you're walking under the grates, the noise from outside can drown out the sound of an approaching train.

A few years ago, Amtrak started to use the tunnel again. It looked as though all the tunnel dwellers would be evicted, but after dramatic media coverage, the eviction plans were shelved. Bernard became the *nolens volens* spokesman of the tunnel people and even appeared on CNN with important dignitaries from Amtrak who assured them that everybody could stay as long as they respected some basic rules. The most important were to keep the emergency exits free and clear, and to not make fires. That is why Bernard has a problem with Tony, who makes such a mess.

Ten people used to live in Bernard's camp. Most of them met a sad end. Some developed AIDS and went above ground to die there from tuberculosis, pneumonia, or other diseases. Some perished because of drug abuse. Some were involved in crimes and wound up behind bars. Some are even now roaming the city's mean streets, crazed and high on drugs. Only a few managed to start a new life with the help of welfare, rehab, a shelter or support from family and friends.

The last one to leave was Bob, a speed freak who also had a crack problem. Bob is now in rehab. Tony is the only neighbor left.

"He is a sick pedophile and a rapist," Bernard says. "He spent fifteen years in jail. He tells everybody it was for murder, because it sounds tough. But a cop up top told me that Tony had once raped a minor. And still that pervert is bringing boys down here for blowjobs and dirty tricks. And all the time he drags more junk down here. I would have kicked him out a long time ago, were it not for the fact that sometimes he manages to supply us with water, wood, and food."

Bernard gazes up towards the grate. "Here it was a Heaven of Harmony. It became a Heaven of Headaches," he says dramatically. The sunlight falls down and lightens up his silhouette against the dark tunnel walls. With his high forehead and bald patch, his straight nose, and his powerful chin he looks like a stern prophet from the Old Testament. "But who am I to complain about chaos? Even God has to accept the existence of chaos."

After a turbulent life that took him all over the Americas, Bernard wound up in the tunnels eight years ago. As a young man, he studied journalism and minored in philosophy at the University of Maryland. There he met his first wife. They had a son, but Bernard was not made to settle down as a house-father. After getting his BA, he went to New York where he studied for another six months at the Tisch Film School. In the meantime, he moonlighted as a model for prestigious brands such as Van Gils and Pierre Cardin. Behind the scenes, he met his second wife, a stunning dancer who worked on Broadway when she was not touring with Stevie Wonder.

Later, when I got to know Bernard better, he told me some of steamy details of their first encounter. "After a show, she took me to her apartment. She was dressed in a tiny, tight, red velvet dress. 'Oh Bernie, I think a mosquito has bitten me on my back,' she whispered. 'Could you please take a look?'" Bernard clapped his hands in joy. "Yo! It was a ball…At eleven in the morning we finally went to sleep."

After film school, he started to work as a gaffer for a TV crew from CBS. It was a humiliating job, according to Bernard. The whole time he had to drag floodlights around and tape down cables on the floor, crawling on his hands and knees. If something went wrong—and a lot of things generally went wrong, as Bernard rarely got a good night's sleep because of the hot Broadway dancer—he was scolded and yelled at like some slave boy. It became too much for the proud Bernard, and he quit his job.

"I had to put on a mask all the time, kissing ass and saying yes and please to get my paycheck every week. But when I look in the mirror, I want to see an honest man."

In the meantime, Bernard had a second child with the dancer. Still, he was not ready to settle down. He got a gob as a travel guide in the Caribbean and jetted around between the Bermudas, Venezuela and Jamaica.

Always, Bernard perfected his skills as a ladies' man. He was messing around with an airhostess from Los Angeles and a photographer from Caracas among others. The Broadway dancer got fed up and kicked him out. No big deal for Bernard: he had girl-friends galore and thanks to his hostess girl, he could fly for free wherever he wanted. Whenever it all became too much for him, he'd take the first flight to LA to relax at her place.

At the same time, he had started a lucrative business with some of the other tour guides. They smuggled cocaine from Venezuela and the Bermudas to the States, pounds at a time. It was an easy job. "In the Caribbean, they wanted to stimulate tourism and never bothered us," Bernard says. "In the States, no-body had really heard of cocaine. We could walk right by customs with our suitcases full."

Those were decadent days for Bernard. He became a steady supplier in the amusement business and popped up whenever he wanted at the homes of celebrities like John Belushi, Rick James, and David Geffen. Some weeks, he would spend thousands of dollars without even thinking about it. He threw wild parties at his penthouse on the Upper West Side, ironically not far from his current tunnel dwelling. Bernard loved to flirt with this contrast: "I descended all the way from the top to the lowest point possible," is one of his favorite quotes. And always he adds: "But then again, the question remains: what is High and what is Low? In essence, everything is the same."

During this period, Bernard started to flip out. The flashy life-style became too much. "I never met so many lonely and sad people as in that coke scene," he sighs. The crisis with his second wife, the dancer, and trouble with all his other girlfriends, combined with steady coke abuse made things turn bad quickly. American capitalist society might already be greedy, hypocriti-cal, and money-oriented; in the intense microcosm of the coke dealer and his sycophants, things are even more extreme. The fall of a coke dealer is always fast and deep. Friends turn out to be parasites who are only interested in getting a white nose. No more powder, no more friends. Instead the bill collectors appear on the horizon.

Bernard got his taste of the nasty reality after subletting his penthouse to a friend for a few months while he was cooling down in LA. When he returned, his penthouse was robbed clean. All that his friend had left him was a huge pile of bills on the doormat.

Bernard was broke and could not even return to his ex-wife, who had found a new lover. He moved to a cheap hotel on Times Square and got a job as a cleaner at the Port Authority Bus Station. There, he confronted daily the world of runaway kids and homeless people.

"It was a new world for me," Bernard said. "I was completely broke. I had landed at point zero. But zero is a magical number. Life starts and ends with nothing, with zero. Suddenly, it seemed like my eyes finally opened. It felt like an invisible hand was slowly guiding me to the down side of life. And I knew had to let myself be taken down there without resistance."

Bernard wound up sleeping at Riverside Park where he eventually discovered the tunnel. "And that's when the true challenge of my life began. It was an ordeal, but I endured it."

Bernard never feels any regret that his former luxurious life came to an end. He even feels reinforced by the fact that he had his fair share of limos, champagne, beautiful women, and coke. For only those who have witnessed wealth and richness first-hand can give a true judgment and unmask it in the end as no more than just vanity, according to Bernard. And that is why he is so saddened by people who obsessively chase money but never will be happy.

Although he imposed upon himself the life of a recluse, Bernard did not break his family ties. His mother, a retired nurse, lives with her daughter in Florida. They write each other letters regularly; Bernard receives his mail at the local post office. As a good son, he always sends her flowers for her birthday. "My mother and my sister are my greatest fans," Bernard says. "They always respected my decision to live in a tunnel."

It is with his father, a plumber living in Harlem, that he has problems. "The old man is still telling me how to live my life. Every time he keeps on nagging me that I should leave the tunnel," Bernard says angrily. "Fuck him. Nobody has the right to tell me what to do."

Bernard also has brothers. The youngest is his favorite and is currently studying for his Masters degree in political science at New Jersey State University. Sometimes he surprises Bernard with a visit. His oldest brother is a filmmaker in Atlanta. Bernard will never forget how he was offended by him. Bernard had suggested he make a film about tunnel life. "Your life is not interesting enough," the brother rudely replied. When the first wave of documentaries about the tunnel started, the brother returned on his knees. He even offered a large sum of money. Of course, Bernard indignantly refused.

Bernard's youngest son is a child actor who plays in popular soaps. "That little boy makes more money than his mother," he says proudly. But Bernard hasn't seen him in years because the mother keeps the boy away from him.

His oldest son works for the FBI in Baltimore and is totally used to the fact that his father lives in the tunnel. "I just let him mess around," Bernard says in a fatherly tone. "He makes tons of money, drives a fat BMW and thinks he is happy. Later he will realize it all means nothing."

"Well, we got used to it," the FBI son told me matter-of-factly when I met him over Christmas in the tunnel. He was an impeccably dressed young man, in an expensive long leather coat and an elegant velvet tie. He had come down to the tunnel with Bernard's younger brother, the student from New Jersey. The two of them came to pick up Bernard and take him out clothes shopping and later to a fancy restaurant.

Bernard treated them to some relevant quotes from Ecclesiastes—Everything is Vanity—and then proceeded to warn his son to be careful with all the diseases in the modern world. "I've had my share of pussy, my son," Bernard said. "Just ask your grandma. She got crazy from all those girls on the phone."

3. LORD OF THE TUNNEL

A few days later, walking through Riverside Park on my way back to the tunnel, I see a piece of paper nailed on a tree. "Walter Dorfman died October 27th 1994. GOD BLESS YOU. Loved by friends," it says. It is written with a blue pen in big, sloppy letters. Under the tree someone has put some bouquets of flowers and devotion candles that are now extinguished. So there has to be some truth to the story of Walter's murder. When we had left the tunnel, Williams had told me the tale was an example of tunnel mythology. In his study, Williams is devoting a whole chapter on all the various stories that go around in the tunnel. There are stories about mysterious murders, disappearances, ghosts, and strange animals that crawl, fly, or walk around.

Bernard, as well, has a nearly mythical status. Because of his penchant for philosophical and biblical quotes, Williams calls him Glaucon in his study, the protagonist in Plato's Cave dialogue. Among the underground dwellers, Bernard has the nickname "Lord of the Tunnel."

Bernard shrugs the whole thing off. Once, two guys had posted themselves at the entrance of the tunnel. They were called Hector and Shorty, two bums living in a small shack at the South End of the tunnel. They demanded an entry tax of a few dollars, if you didn't pay, they would beat you up. When the racketeers approached Bernard, he exploded. "Who do you think you are talking to," Bernard exclaimed spontaneously. "I am the goddamn Lord of the Tunnel!"

A few days later, he went to redeem some empty bottles at the supermarket, and was mockingly greeted by other homeless: "Make way, gentlemen. Here is our Royal All Mighty Highness the Lord of the Tunnel." Somehow, the name stuck, and all the homeless on the Upper West Side now used this name to address Bernard. Hector and Shorty didn't stay in the tunnel for long. Together they had raped Sheila, a woman living with her friend in Bernard's camp. Bernard and Bob called the police and pointed the cops to Hector and Shorty. Currently, they are still serving time.[1]

"Whatever, Lord of the Tunnel," smiles Bernard. "I don't mind if the people want to call me that. And maybe they are right. I am the only one who gives the people down here some support."

I am down with Bernard in the tunnel, and he explains his work collecting and redeeming cans and bottles to me. In 1983, New York State introduced a five-cent deposit law. The Bottle Bill, as it became called, was meant to protect the environment, but soon the poor and homeless saw an opportunity to make some money. Most affluent New Yorkers did not find the five cents attractive enough to bring their empty cans back to the store; they just put them out with the garbage instead. Others saved them up and put them in small bags out on the street on purpose, to help the homeless.

Within no time, homeless people carrying huge bags of empty cans started to appear on the streets of Manhattan. People started to call them *can men* or redeemers.

In the mid '80s, when the city introduced mandatory garbage separation with special transparent blue bags for recyclables, it became even easier for can men to earn their daily bread since they no longer had to rummage through the ordinary garbage.

According to Bernard, there are professional can men and losers. The losers roam the streets of the city without a preconceived plan, and go through every garbage can. They even take glass bottles. These are also worth five cents, but because of their weight they are very labor-intensive to handle. A few dollars worth of empty cans weighs hardly a pound, the same amount of bottles adds up to maybe fifty pounds.

Professional can men like Bernard, have a fixed route at apartment buildings where they show up at fixed times every week, when the superintendents put the sorted garbage out on the sidewalk. For can men it is an easy and relatively clean job to go through the bags that contain only glass, plastic, and metal.

The garbage bags are tidily closed after inspection; it is a matter of pride for a serious can man to never to leave a mess.

Bernard also helps the supers putting out all the buildings' garbage, sometimes hundreds of heavy bags. That's why the supers not only tip him ten dollars now and then, but also actively do their best to bag up the recyclables. Bernard's working times are Wednesday afternoon and Thursday morning. "Never skipped one day," he says proudly. "The supers know they can count on us. Last year with the blizzard, it was only me and Bob doing the buildings."

Before his neighbor Bob left the tunnel to enter rehab, he was Bernard's partner in business. It was a smooth cooperation except for a few small glitches. "The idiot spoilt a few of our best business relations. Bob's total lack of long-term thinking and his cheap pettiness were exasperating," says Bernard shaking his head. "Once, we were working and the super asked Bob to get some coffee. He didn't have change so he gave a twenty-dollar bill. Bob left with the cash but disappeared and never returned. He pulled that trick a few times. And I had to explain it all to the supers."

There are a few ways to redeem, or exchange, the empty bottles and cans. With small amounts, the homeless go to the supermarkets. By law, it is mandatory that they accept up to 240 cans per man, twelve dollars' worth. Some supermarkets have a machine you can throw the cans into, but plastic bottles need to be counted separately. That is where the manager has to step in. It is a time-consuming process, not only for the manager, but also for the can man. Sometimes, they have to wait hours before the manager finds or takes the time. Most supermarkets actively discourage the redemption of empties. The storage of huge amounts of empties is a quite costly affair. They feel that scores of unkempt, scruffy, and smelly can men scare off regular customers. Some homeless drink and fight with each other over whose turn it is. The sidewalks are sometimes turned into a pigsty, and in one case, a homeless person threatened and even physically attacked the manager. That's why the managers let the homeless wait for hours, feed them excuses that the machine has broken down, or refuse certain brands.

For a few years there has been an alternative in New York. At WeCan Redemption Center, a special exchange center on West 52nd Street, anyone can come with any brand or quantity of empties. WeCan was established by the idealistic copywriter Guy Polhemus.[2] It has grown into a large organization with two branches redeeming the cans of thousands of poor and homeless. WeCan returns the cans to the soda companies and brewers and gets another extra cent and a half handling fee. WeCan even receives government support since it is registered as a nonprofit working to help the homeless.

Canning gives the homeless an opportunity to generate a small income without resorting to begging. Reliable can men often wind up getting a job offer from WeCan. And of course, recycling makes the streets cleaner and helps reduce the total amount of city garbage by ten percent.

Bernard shows me the big plastic bags WeCan provides custom-made for its clients. A mark at the top indicates one cubic meter, three hundred cans, good for fifteen dollars. He also shows me a list with all the brands, bottles and cans that are accepted, from the most common like Budweiser and Coca Cola to the most obscure.

Another way to redeem cans is through intermediaries, the so called two-for-oners. A two-for-oner buys two cans for the price of one and pays hard cash, no questions asked. Plastic bottles—too big—and glass bottles—too heavy—are normally not accepted. When the two-for-oner has enough empties, he sorts everything out himself and goes to WeCan. People who sell to two-for-oners are normally quite desperate people who want fast cash on the spot. When Bernard has some extra money, he sometimes works as a two-for-oner. Actually, he is currently waiting for some cash for a paint job he did with Manny, another homeless man in the neighborhood. He wants to invest the money in this two-for-one business. Two-for-oneing is very lucrative, especially on hot summer nights, explains Bernard. "Everybody is hanging out on the streets and wants to get high or drunk while the supermarkets and WeCan are closed."

Canning has its success stories. Former homeless man Chris Jeffers rented an empty theater in Manhattan and started a two-for-one business, open 24/7. Jeffers nearly became a millionaire and had to rent trucks and workers to get all his cans to WeCan.[3]

Bernard was one of the first on the Upper West Side to collect cans. "Most homeless were ashamed to go through garbage
looking for cans. Those were the golden days. Bob and me sometimes made four hundred dollars a week. Now there is a lot of
competition. If you are too late, someone else might 'clock' your
building." That is why Bernard is very keen to maintain relations
with all the supers, and makes sure he is right on time to help
them.

Behind us we hear a rustling, and we see a person appear from
out of the darkness. He walks straight up to Bernard and mumbles something incomprehensible. It is a boy, around twenty
years old, so skinny it looks like his jeans will fall down his legs
at any moment. With a mouth filled with rotten teeth, he nervously chews a cigarette and stumbles on his feet. In his hand
he holds a huge bottle of beer. Bernard gives the man a lighter
and he staggers to one of the bunkers.

"That was Jeff," explains Bernard. Jeff is Tony's lover who is
hooked on crack and works as a boy prostitute all over the city.
"Your typical New York inner-city kid. Jeff was already a hus-
tler when he was twelve years old. Boy, I tell you, he won't see
his twenty-fifth birthday. Did you see these purple stains on his
face? Full blown AIDS." Bernard shakes his head. "Guys like Jeff
teach me discipline. They remind me that in the tunnel there
are only two possibilities. To grow, or to perish. And if you perish,
you go deep. Very deep and very fast. Nothing in between.

"AIDS," he ponders, "what a terrible disease ..." He once brought
a tunnel dweller in the terminal stage of AIDS to the hospital. "I
visited him later. He was only seventy pounds. You could slide
donuts over his arms." Bernard claims to lead a celibate lifestyle.
"You have to get your priorities straight down here," he explains.
"Alcohol, drugs, sex, you just cannot permit yourself all these
extracurricular activities."

I make a deal with Bernard to accompany him one morning collecting cans. His working days start at 5:30 AM. Of course I over-
sleep. I have rented a room in Fort Green, Brooklyn, an hour by
train from the tunnel. Half a day too late, I call Bernard's name

through the intercom. No answer. I put a note on the North Gate requesting a new appointment. I come back a few more times, but every time we miss each other. It is another week before I am able to catch him. I feel embarrassed for all the effort Bernard must have been putting in to get the cooperation of other tunnel dwellers.

While having a cup of tea at the grill, I present my problem to Bernard. I have trouble getting up early, and I live an hour away from the tunnel. Wouldn't it be easier if I temporarily move into one of the empty bunkers? I don't mind that there is no water or electricity and it is better for my story if I can taste the tunnel atmosphere. On top of that, I can help Bernard collecting cans.

Bernard is a bit surprised. He has never before met a journalist who wanted to stay over in the tunnels. But then, why not? Bob's bunker is empty and yes, some assistance would make it easier and some companionship would be nice. Bernard misses his old buddy Bob, and has only Tony left to talk to. He does not want new people in his camp. "I don't allow that," he sternly explained to me last time. "New people only create chaos."

A few years ago, the tunnel had become Party Central. There were not only ten people living in his camp, but many people from up top came down to get high or drunk without being harassed by closing times or police raids. "It became wild," Bernard says. "Sometimes we went on for nights in a row."

Bob especially could party hard. "Wild Bob..." Bernard whispers affectionately. Although Bernard lost half of his canning business due to Bob's tricks, his name brings back sweet memories. When you mention Bob to Professor Williams, a soft smile also appears on his face. Bob was a hardcore speed freak. If he could afford it, he preferred coke and crack to the relatively cheap amphetamine. In case none of this was available, he took handfuls of diet pills that he gulped down with pints of coffee. Bob also managed to smoke away half a carton of Camel no-filters, the strongest cigarettes available in the city, on a daily basis. "The guy has the heart of a bull," Bernard laughs with admiration. "Ordinary people would not survive."

Bob originally came from Chicago, but became a drifter at an early age. He went from city to city where he worked as a short-order cook in cheap restaurants. His skills took on mythical proportions: Bob was called the fastest cook between the Mississippi and the East Coast and could fry twenty eggs at a time. To deliver such amazing feats, however, he had to spend most of his wages on coke and speed. Ultimately he wound up in a vicious circle: more fried eggs, more speed and coke, more fried eggs. At some point, Bob broke down and wound up on the streets. In New York, he found a job in a soup kitchen and befriended Bernard. They became friends and Bernard invited him to live down in the tunnel, since Bob hated staying in the shelters.

Bob and Bernard became partners in canning. Bob's addiction to stimulants, however, turned out to be insatiable. Because canning brought in so little money, Bob developed his skills as a con artist and master crook. Bob had something childish and naïve about him, and thanks to his charm, nobody, not even his victims, was able to stay angry with him for long.

Chris Pape once told me how he fell for one of Bob's tricks; it cost him twenty dollars. Bob had played a master game over some rental videotapes, and had tricked even the very streetwise Chris Pape. Bernard was so embarrassed by Bob's behavior that he even offered to pay back Pape little by little.

The first time I saw Bob, I was struck by the likeness of Pape's portrait of him. Bob was a white man with a brash, protruding under-lip. His face was marked by thousands of wrinkles in which shiny eyes twinkled between swollen eyelids. Like a pro-tennis player, he had a white sweatband around his head, keeping together his wild electric hair that still stuck out to all sides.

He was funny, outrageous, and ridiculous. Bob giggled and snickered, unable to utter one sensible word apart from a compliment about my coffee-making capacities. I liked him immediately.

We inspect Bob's bunker. Sometimes, Bob comes down for a weekend to visit Bernard, but on weekdays his place is empty. It is in the middle of a row of bunkers. On a wooden door is a small padlock to which Bernard has the key. With candles and a flashlight we light up the interior. It is a spacious room, nine feet high, twelve feet deep and twenty feet wide. On the left side there is a king-size bed with blankets neatly pulled over it. I smell the blankets: they are a little damp but clean.

An ashtray and a candle stand on a little cupboard near the bed. Next to it is a large table with some chairs and an oil lamp. On the right side of the room there are two lounging chairs, a sofa, and a coffee table filled with empty cigarette packs, crack vials, and molten candle wax. In the opposite corner Bob has an unused, empty fridge.

"Perfect," I say. Just needs a bit of dusting and clean sheets, and it is an excellent accommodation. "Well, well, that Bob," Bernard says, a bit surprised. "He sure had it good together here."

We discuss the house rules. There is no toilet, so to urinate, I have to go outside, preferably as far away as possible. To take a dump, there is a special designated place in a dark spot of the tunnel with a pile of sand. "Just dig a hole and cover it with sand once done, just like a cat," Bernard explains. "I don't want it to smell like at these dirty bums' at the South End." These are the only house rules. I promise to keep everything as tidy as possible, and contribute my fair share in getting food, water, and wood.

My only concern is how to make coffee. Bernard laughs. No problem. Bob also was a hardcore coffee addict. There are a few coffeemakers and three big thermos cans, so there can be hot coffee around the clock.

Bernard is more into herbal tea, he says. He prefers chamomile tea, with a piece of lemon.

It's a done deal. We go up top to make copies of the keys of the North Gate and Bob's bunker. That way, I don't have to call Bernard through the grate and I can come and go when I want. On our way out, Bernard tells me about my interview requests with the other tunnel people. Marcus, who lives down a little farther, wants to talk. But Ramon and Estoban are stubborn. They are Cubans who live at the South End. Williams had already showed me Little Havana—four, five sloppily constructed wooden shacks. "They asked me what's in it for them," Bernard says shaking his head. "Ramon and Estoban live here out of shame. They are not receptive."

It is maybe better if I approach them myself of these days. Halfway to the North Gate, just opposite the Mona Lisa painting, Bernard calls out above him. "Marcus! Are you home?" Behind a small opening in the tunnel wall, a staircase leads to an emergency exit. Next to it is a deep cave between the walls and the ceiling. We hear a rustling coming from the black hole, and someone sticks his head out. He crawls out of his cave and balances over a wall towards the stairs. Bernard introduces me as the reporter from Brussels.

"Ah, *bonjour*," Marcus says. He says he doesn't want to talk to journalists, but proceeds immediately in an unstoppable monologue. Marcus is from Maine but learnt to speak French in nearby Quebec. We discuss Walter's murder. "It would not have happened here in the tunnel," Marcus says. "*Ici, nous sommes des copains.*"

Marcus is an old hippy. His jean jacket is covered in stains and smudges. Long, greasy hair sticks out from under a purple cap; his long beard rests on a purple sweater. Since it is quite chilly, he has also wrapped a purple shawl around himself. Marcus, who wears a chain with a huge yin and yang sign, explains that he is into health food. With winter approaching, he is preparing himself for his annual migration to Florida. He has been living in the tunnel for five years already, but has spent all his winters in Florida. Once there, he will hang around with the Rainbow People, an international movement of vegetarians, dropouts, potheads, and other alternative folks.

Marcus tells Bernard about his new cat. He has only had him a few days, and has tied him to a rope. Once the cat is used to him and no longer jumps out of the cave, Marcus will let him loose so he can catch rats.

When we have left Marcus, Bernard is shocked. "Unbelievable," he says. "Tying a cat on a rope. How the hell can you do that?"

At the end of the day I return to the playground on my bike with my luggage in my back pack. Clean sheets, radio, alarm clock, flashlight and candles, and a pound of coffee. That's all I need to make Bob's space habitable.

With my new key I unlock the padlock and open the rusty, squeaky gate. I look over my shoulder to make sure no one has been following me and quickly enter the tunnel. Next to the tracks is a small path where I can ride my bicycle. The Amtrak police use this for inspection rounds.

A few minutes later I arrive at Bernard's camp. He sits at the grill, stirring pots and pans, and offers me a chair and a tea. We listen to the radio. It is tuned to Bob Grant, presenting his notorious talk show at the evening rush hour. He and Rush Limbaugh are Public Enemies No.1 and No. 2 with politically-correct America.

Grant has been called an anti-Semitic, homophobic, racist, sexist pig. The guests on his talk show always seem to be decent but concerned citizens who deplore the moral disintegration of America.

Bernard loves to listen to the show while cooking his evening meal. "Bob Grant has at least the guts to call bullshit bullshit," Bernard says. "And that has become pretty rare these days."

In his criticism of greedy, capitalist American society, Bernard sometimes has views that might seem left. But at the same time, he can say things that would make Archie Bunker cringe. For one thing, he hates liberals who see every homeless person, thief, or junkie as innocent victims of society.

Once we hear about a murderer who got the electric chair. I did not go so far as to question the death penalty, but suggested that electrocution was pretty cruel and that gallows or guillotines work quicker and more humanely. "Hey man, what that killer did was cruel as well," Bernard commented. "Back then in the biblical times they knew how to handle these cases. Bang, down in the lion's den. No bullshit."

Bernard throws some fresh wood on the fire and adds a few plastic bags and bottles with a metal stick. "Good fuel," he explains. Slowly, the plastic transforms into a dark, boiling paste and catches fire while producing black, sooty fumes. Hot flames scorch the pans while the dark, fat coils of smoke disappear through the grate.

From afar I hear a baby cry. I remember seeing a baby crib close to Bernard's camp and think of the basket in which Moses drifted down the Nile. The crying baby comes closer. "Don't worry," Bernard says. "That is from above us in the park."

Bernard continues peeling onions and throws them with a can of tomato sauce into a big frying pan. Two cats are crawling towards him. "Fuck off, you animal," Bernard screams. The cats fly away. "They are here to catch rats," Bernard continues cooking. "They need to stay hungry. They are just like people. If they are well fed, they become lazy and complacent."

Rats are a problem in the tunnel. Especially in wintertime, when nobody has picnics in the park or feeds the ducks on the river, and food outside becomes scarce. That is when the rats start to invade the tunnels in big numbers. At Bernard's camp, the rats are under control. He keeps his garbage far away from the camp, and keeps his food in closed containers. The cats deal with the rest of the problem. "Only that idiot Tony spoils everything," complains Bernard. "Can you believe it? Last time he brought a fried chicken to feed the cats."

Bernard cooks spaghetti and finishes the tomato sauce with garlic, salt and other spices and herbs he gets out of his kitchen cabinets. From another cupboard, he gets plastic plates, knives and spoons. He tastes the pasta once in a while, and when it is cooked al dente, he drains it, using an old T-shirt as an oven mitt so as not to burn his hands.

"Dinner is ready," he says, serving the pasta and the sauce onto the small greasy plates. It is my first tunnel meal, and carefully I try a little spoonful. "Is the sauce not too spicy?" Bernard asks with concern.

"It's delicious."

"You see, I told you, food is not the problem here," he says proudly.

We go to bed early. Tomorrow is Thursday, the big can day for Bernard. We need to start working at six AM, so we have to get up at five to have a relaxed breakfast.

I retreat into my new tunnel home and light some candles. Soon, Bob's bunker glows in the light of half a dozen flickering lights. The radio plays soft, smooth New York jazz, and I can hear the big city rustle in the background. I hear police sirens wail not too far away, a comforting sound. The world up top is within ears' reach. Commuters stuck in a traffic jam on the West Side Highway honk their horns. I start to read *The Invisible Man* by Ralph Ellison. "The classic study of *the black experience*," blurbs the book. Invisibility is a metaphor for the black protagonist, all but ignored by society.

Just like Bardamu in Céline's *Journey to the End of the Night,* the man is on a journey searching for truth and justice. Needless to say, without much result. Ultimately, he buries himself alive in a dark hole underground. In their publications about tunnel people, Jennifer Toth and Professor Williams love to refer to *The Invisible Man.* At the end of the book, the protagonist has a thousand light bulbs illuminate his cave, while playing jazz from an old record player. Of course, the electricity is tapped illegally from outside sources.

It is impossible to imagine a better environment than Bob's bunker for reading this book. I open a bottle of good wine and light a cigarette. I look around at my new comfy and cozy home. Now I start to understand what Bernard meant when he said "Heaven of Harmony."

After a while, I go to bed and slide between the clean sheets. Bob has a blanket and a sleeping bag as a cover, so it is nice and warm

Up top, the traffic jams have dissolved: now speeding cars are making the concrete plates of the highway create strange sound effects. Through the metal beams of the tunnel, vibrations resonate and start to have a life of their own like the scary sounds from a house of horror or a nineteenth-century jail: rattling chains, clashing metal doors, steps stumbling on metal staircases. A shrill horn indicates the approach of a train.

The bunker vibrates, some chalk is falling from the ceiling. Slowly, the cacophony of sounds puts me to sleep.

4. CANNING 101

Someone is knocking on my door. "Duke, Duke, the coffee is ready!" Bernard tries hard to pronounce my name correctly, but like most Americans he has trouble with typical Dutch vowels and consonants. I offered to let him call me the American version of Teun, which is Anthony, but he keeps on trying names that vary in sound from Duke, Dune, Tut or even Zueg, which always makes me crack up because it is the Dutch word for a female pig. I look at the clock. it is one minute before 5 AM; the alarm can go off any moment.

Outside in the tunnel it is damp and cold. An orange fog has formed, caused by tiny droplets of rain that fall through the grate and reflect the reddish glow of the streetlights in the park and Bernard's fire. Bernard offers me a hot cup of strong coffee and we listen to the radio while he eats a hot bowl of oatmeal. On the morning news there is a big story about a financial scandal involving a policeman, a fireman, and even a rabbi. Bernard laughs cynically. "What's the big deal? This is America. Everybody steals. Why be surprised about a cop and a rabbi?" He tells a story about an agent of the Drug Enforcement Agency who had stolen a million dollars. "The idiot had hidden it in a bag under his bed. And every evening before he went to sleep, he pinched his treasure to make sure it still was there."

He laughs and offers me oatmeal. "Take this, Duke, we need a good breakfast before we go to work."

While I eat my oatmeal, I see an old man approaching in the light of the fire. He is dressed in pajamas and wears woolen slippers. "I can't sleep, B," he says in a whiny voice.

"Come on, Tony, you want some oatmeal?" Bernard serves him a bowl.

This is the first time I meet Tony. He has wild, gray hair on top of his tough looking, unshaven face. From beneath heavy eyebrows, two eyes look softly and sadly into the fire.

"Have you heard it about Walter?" Tony asks me. Walter's murder obviously shook the homeless community. "I tell you, it is fucking dangerous up top." Tony points his head in the direction of the grate. Now I notice his pajamas are decorated with bunnies playing in the grass. Tony starts complaining about his sister; he always goes over there to watch TV, even pays the cable, but never gets offered even a cup of coffee.

"Yes, your sister is quite something," Bernard says with badly faked indignation. Tony has obviously said his thing, and disappears with his bowl of oatmeal in the darkness.

As we leave the tunnel, Bernard explains that every month Tony gets a few hundred dollars worth of welfare and food stamps. During the day, he roams the streets of Manhattan, looking for valuables in the garbage. Late afternoon he visits his sister who lives on the Lower East Side.

Food stamps are a good thing according to Bernard. "They prevent a lot of theft and crime. On the other had, they cause a lot of crime." Many people sell their food stamps to get cash for booze and drugs. Korean groceries and Chinese restaurants are lining up to purchase the stamps for 70 percent, sometimes only 50 percent of their original value.

"But yes," Bernard continues, "this country owes it to us. Our land is built on rape and robbery. They tax the hell out of you. Cigarettes went up another quarter," he complains. "Can you believe it? In New Hampshire they already cost four dollars a pack. If it comes to that here in New York, then I'd rather quit."

Outside in the park, puddles of rainwater reflect the orange glow of the streetlights. Bernard pulls the hood of his sweatshirt over his baseball cap and marches forward, dragging his rattling shopping cart with a leather belt over the bumpy park roads. He is a fast walker with his long legs, and I have trouble keeping up.

It is 5:30 now and the streets are deserted. There is still no traffic on the West Side High Way. The only sign of life is a dark man with fogged glasses, a shiny black leather cap on his head. He is rummaging through some garbage. That's Pier John, Bernard tells me, a successful two-for-oner who rose from living on the street to an apartment dweller. He used to work on the piers of Lower Manhattan, hence his nickname. Although Pier John currently only works as an intermediary, he hasn't forgotten his roots and can't resist going through the garbage every morning.

I want to ask him some questions about the two-for-one business, but he wants one hundred dollars before he starts to talk. Bernard laughs. Pier John makes thousands of dollars a month, and has better things to do than giving interviews to reporters for free. He is past that stage.

Bernard stops by the first pile of garbage bags he sees. "One man's garbage is another man's fortune," he says dramatically. Like a real connoisseur, he looks at the bags, feels them, and lifts one up. "Nothing. Someone was here before us." Bernard continues at his brisk pace, we still have twenty blocks to go. His shopping cart rolls smoothly in a straight track behind him. He gives it a periodical tune up, and even greases the wheels. That's why he gets so mad at Burk, another tunnel dweller, when he uses the cart without asking and loads it full of heavy, empty bottles. "It fucks up the balance of the wheels."

At six o'clock on the dot we arrive at Bernard's block, on 84th Street. We are on time; the garbage has not been put out yet. We lean against a building and wait for the supers who will appear at any moment. This is a posh street with a few apartment buildings, and some nice townhouses and brownstones in-between. A lot of Volvos and big shiny jeeps line the street. Bernard peers through a building gate at the giant heap of garbage bags, and makes an estimate of the expected catch. "It looks good today," he mumbles. The garbage bags come in two colors: black for ordinary waste, and blue for recyclables such as plastic, glass, and metal.

Paper and cardboard need to be tied up separately. We are sitting on a pile of Yellow Pages while Bernard tells me about supers. Some of them crush empties to save space. Super markets, however, do not accept crushed cans. "Ridiculous of course, because they will be crushed anyway during recycling. But some supers are so evil. They get a sadistic pleasure in making our life difficult."

Behind us, a rusty lock screeches and the gate is opened by an old man with a fur coat. Leather flaps cover his ears and he has a sorrowful expression surrounding his toothless mouth. It is Harvey, one of the supers. Bernard had already told me that most of the supers have a thankless job that hardly offers them a decent living. Harvey shows it. As he stumbles around slightly bent, it looks as though he bears all the misery of this planet on his shoulders. Harvey looks like a poor bum; in comparison Bernard seems a healthy, energetic young man. We start to work. The heaviest job is putting the paper out on the sidewalk.

It is a huge pile, about three cubic meters, everything neatly piled and tied up in packets of about 45 pounds. With the three of us working together, it is done in ten minutes.

Harvey pants and breathes heavily, my arms hurt and I have red imprints on my hands, but Bernard walks around like it is an easy and fun job. He even holds the packets with arms outstretched—a good exercise he explains. Then we proceed with all the garbage bags. Although not so heavy, they are hard to handle because they are bulky and slippery with the rain.

In the meantime, Harvey has understood that, with his old age, he is only slowing us down. It makes more sense if he just tells us what to put where. Soon, the thirty huge garbage bags are out on the street and we can open the blue ones to collect the empties.

It is easy work. Because there is no household waste, the contents are not dirty. It just smells a bit of stale beer with a whiff of old Coca Cola. The blue bags are slowly getting smaller, while our WeCan bags grow every minute. The big one-gallon Coke bottles add up especially fast. It is too bad they also bring in only 5 cents, since they take up so much space. Carefully Bernard ties up the garbage bags after inspection. It is a matter of pride to leave everything behind him as clean as possible. In the park, he even puts his cigarette butts in the wastebaskets. Once he scolded me for throwing orange peels in the scrub.

Bernard checks to make sure I don't make any mistakes. To reduce the weight, half-full bottles need to be emptied in the gutter. There are also trouble cans, unknown brands that nobody will accept. Some of them originate in states where there is no deposit. Bernard points me to the small print on top of the can. CT, VT, NH, and NY are okay. If there are no letters, it means they are out-of-state cans, and even WeCan won't take them back. In fifteen minutes, we have sorted out all of Harvey's bags. The result: two full bags, loaded with approximately three hundred cans and bottles. "Not bad," Bernard says, "fifteen bucks for a half hour's work. Better than flipping burgers for three-fifty an hour at McDonalds."

On the other side of the street a gate opens. It is Pedro, another super. He is a good-natured Latino in his mid-thirties. He jokes with Bernard about Bob. "Most probably, he will make it this year to the morgue," Bernard laughs while introducing me as his new intern.

Pedro's building yields the same as Harvey's, and in another half an hour we are finished, resulting in another fifteen dollars worth of empties.

Meanwhile, on the street women on high heels and men in three-piece suits are rushing off to work. Nannies take kids to school and people take their dogs out for the early morning piss. Bernard greets a few passers-by and strokes the dogs he knows by name. One lady spontaneously strikes up a conversation: she lived in Texas for six months, but saw Bernard on local TV in a documentary. Bernard enjoys his national celebrity status and brags about all the documentaries that have been done about him

It is getting cozy. We are sitting on an old cupboard that has been put out on the sidewalk, and Harvey has gotten us fresh coffee. Somehow, the conversation turns to the Kennedys. Every real true-blooded American seems to have his own theory as to who killed JFK. Bernard, Harvey and Pedro are no exceptions.

The three discuss John F., Jackie O., and Marilyn Monroe.

Bernard even brings in the FBI, the Cuban Missile Crisis and the Mafia. Inevitably J. Edgar Hoover enters the picture, the former FBI director and ultimate example of the perverted power-obsessed creep who still fuels people's imagination.

"Oh, man, he was some weird-ass motherfucker! Had steamy tapes of everybody. Can you believe it, that old horny bastard jerking off while watching Martin Luther King's favorite love positions?" Pedro and Harvey crack up laughing.

Bernard is a good storyteller and has warmed up. "That Hoover himself was a first-class faggot. He has been fucked up the ass by Truman Capote himself!" he screams out, while making obscene copulation movements with his hips. True or not, Pedro and Harvey burst out laughing. People walking by with long faces on their way to work, look up with a mixture of amusement and envy at the strange group of people sitting on a discarded cupboard amidst the garbage, sipping coffee and having all fun in the world.

Bernard has now moved on to the topic of Edward Kennedy. "Ted the Swimmer," he says bitingly, referring to the nickname Bob Grant gave him after the Chappaquiddick accident. "People were shocked when he swam away from his drowning girlfriend." Bernard imitates a sweet childish voice. "Oh my God, did Kennedy really do that?"

"I *tell* you," roars Bernard. "Roll back the tapes on them Kennedys! It's rum-smuggling, slave-trading scumbags. And Teddy isn't any better. It's in his blood to be a crook."

End to end, the circle has closed. Everybody agrees that it was the Mafia after all that took out John F. Real crooks never go to jail is the moral of the story.

"They say crime doesn't pay. Hey, my ass! Yes, petty theft is not worth it. But the big guys, I tell you, crime is the oldest and best paid profession in the world."

Two boys with bright colored backpacks come out of the building. These are Pedro's kids, on their way to school. They kiss their father on the cheek and politely shake Bernard's hand. I am surprised they don't call him Uncle Bernie. "Study hard at

school," Bernard tells them. "Otherwise you wind up like me, collecting cans."

It is eight o'clock now, our working day is finished and we go
back to the tunnel. Pedro gives Bernard a ten-dollar tip. In total,
we have collected six huge bags of empties. Some of the bags he
ties to the shopping cart, the others he hangs from broomsticks
that protrude from his cart like antennas. When Bernard pulls
the shopping cart like a mule, he becomes invisible behind the
big bulky bags that are bulging on all sides.

Back in the tunnel, he chains his cart to the fence with a lock
so Burk can't take it. "I have to give that asshole a clear sign that
he has to keep his hands off," he says sternly. We will redeem the
bags later. Today is the day Tony gets his welfare check, and he
owes Bernard some money.

Tony is on the premises of the Broadway Check Cashing Company. It's only nine o'clock in the morning, but the small office
is already filled with people, mostly black and Latino, who are
here to collect and cash their welfare checks. Homeless people
can receive these benefits, as long as they have an address. Even
a P.O. Box will do.

At the door, beggars with paper cups have posted themselves
strategically. They know that everybody coming out has a full
wallet and a good mood. And, as experienced beggars, they also
know that poor blacks give more than the white middle-class.
Around the corner, crack dealers wait for their first clients, while
on the other side of the street, a cop is watching the whole
scene.

Bernard is well known here, and lot of people say hello and ask
him for cigarettes. It is a sad parade before our eyes. A black girl
in a doorway stumbles and produces irregular giggling. All her
teeth have disappeared; rotten stumps remain. "The suck monster," comments Bernard. "Sucks dicks to suck crack pipes."

One man pushes a shopping cart while leaning heavily on it.
It looks like the cart could slide out from under him at any moment, causing him to hit the pavement. A woolen cap has been

drawn over his blank, dull eyes. His gray coat is covered in greasy, black stains and he has no laces in his worn sneakers. He rummages in a garbage can, finds an empty, and throws it in his car next to few other crushed cans. "No discipline. I don't feel sorry for them," Bernard says shaking his head. "They need crack to get the energy to collect cans all night. Once they have enough cash, they get some wine or crack again. Same happened with Burk. Used to be one hell of a big strong motherfucker. One piece of muscle. Look what remains of him now. Crack wore him down pretty quickly."

Tony comes walking out as a slick pimp, whistling and waving a big wad of bills. Without looking and with his nose in the air, he hands one beggar a wrinkled dollar bill. Then he drags us into a tobacco shop and buys us each a pack of Marlboros. Outside, he manages his money. He owes Bernard twenty bucks, but gives him thirty so he has some savings with him. Fifteen dollars is to pay his sister's cable. Ten goes to his little niece. That way, he keeps forty dollars for himself for the next two weeks. Tony leaves. Today, he can take a day off and will hang out on his sister's couch watching TV.

Later we go to the supermarket to return our empties. Once inside, Bernard puts the cans in the machine. I am waiting outside with the bottles. Because we have too much for one person, Bernard introduces me as his new partner who does the plastics. The manager looks at me suspiciously, but there is nothing he can do. In front of the supermarket, a lot more can men have assembled. After an hour's wait, the manager has time and allows me to come in.

A woman who has just exited the supermarket with her shopping curses me when I hit her by accident with my bags. The outside of the bag is covered in a sticky mix of beer, Coke, and 7-Up. I see a dirty stain on her cream-colored suede jacket, but luckily she hasn't noticed it.

The manager doesn't take his eye off me when I count the bottles and throw them into a big box. Inexorably, he refuses

brands from a competing chain. When I make an error, he sternly corrects me. Bernard gloats as he watches me, and puts the
refused bottles into another bag. "My partner is new in the business. He still makes a lot of mistakes," he tells the manager with
a smile.

When we are ready, the manager has a sour look, but still
hands over twelve dollars. I thank him as politely as possible, but he looks at me as though I have tricked him. Outside,
Bernard gives the remaining bottles to another homeless person
with a grand gesture; he nearly falls on his knees extolling his
thanks. Bernard says he has some errands to do, and I return to
the tunnel.

Tired from all the work, I take a nap on Bob's bed. After an hour,
I hear Bernard return and I go to knock on his door. I know
Bernard appreciates his privacy, but I am just very curious about
how he lives.

"Please enter, Duke," he says with a friendly voice. He pushes aside a brick and slides away the plywood sheet that is his
door.

"I was just relaxing a bit." His home is a cubicle eight feet high,
deep, and wide. The walls are pitch black with soot; once, a tunnel dweller went berserk and set fire to Bernard's place.

Against the back wall is a mattress with a pile of blankets. His
radio and alarm clock stand on a crate that doubles as a night
table. I see a big trunk and more boxes, suitcases, and clothes
piled up high against the other walls. It is hard to distinguish
them; the only available light, a few burning candles on the table, is sucked up by the darkness.

Bernard's table is a square sheet of wood on a big box, scattered with empty crack vials, small plastic bags, disposable light-
ers, mirrors and small knives. Dirty brown crack pipes and metal
sticks rest in a small flower vase. It looks like an average junkie's
den, with all helpful paraphernalia within arms reach.

"Hope you don't mind," Bernard says as he picks up a few pieces of crack. They look like hail stones. He carves them up with
a knife into small pieces and wriggles them into a glass pipe.

The flame of the lighter is at its highest possible setting as he lights his pipe. Bernard sits on a big, bamboo chair; with its huge round back it looks like a throne, giving him a regal aura. I watch him from below, sitting down on a small folding chair. The crack starts to glow red and sears with a crackling sound when he sucks his pipe. That is why they call it crack. Bernard keeps the smoke inside for half a minute, before finally exhaling in one big puff. "The chemicals make me nervous. It is garbage these days," he says in a soft voice. "There is just too much chaos involved in the whole process. They smuggle it in vaginas, they transplant it under the skin, they swallow it and shit it out. Overall chaos." With a lighter, he heats up a few more crumbs of crack. To burn the chemicals, he explains. A faint smell of acetone permeates the air. "Drugs cause complete satisfaction or complete frustration. There is no middle way," he says cryptically.

With a metal scraper, he cleans the glass pipes and mixes these remains with a few crumbs of fresh crack. The last hit for today. "A master blaster," he explains. Bernard inhales deep and puts his hand in front of his eyes. "Wow, un-fucking-real..." he screeches in a weird, high pitch. "Wow, check this out..." With his arm stretched out he flashes his lighter above the piles of clothes behind him. "Un-fucking-real. Really..." he whispers a few more times. After a few minutes, he returns to speaking in his normal voice.

"Government sabotage...Everything that has to do with expanding consciousness is discouraged. Chemical sabotage. They try to conform you to the Dollar Game. If they don't succeed, they dispose of you like a piece of trash. That is the true evil of this society. Who refuses to conform himself becomes a dropout."

5. SOUTHERN NEIGHBORS

I am feeling a bit bored and am playing with candle wax in Bob's bunker. The radio broke down, and I am looking at the bottles of piss that are standing between the bed and the bookshelves. Obviously, Bob never went outside to take a leak and developed the habit of urinating in bottles. I can understand that; maybe Bob didn't have night slippers and he did not want to walk out in the tunnel in the middle of the night in his bare feet on ground littered with broken glass and other junk. Or maybe he was just lazy. But the problem is that Bob never emptied his bottles, and now I am stuck with about ten gallons of his urine. How long have they already been here? Dirty foam floats on the dark yellow fluid. Sooner or later I will have to clean it, before they tumble over. I decide to postpone that operation until the following week.

Kant's *Critique of Pure Reason* stands out among all the books. They are from Larry, a former roommate of Bob's, Bernard has told me. "Larry is too semantic," he had added. I am not in a semantic mood tonight and leave Kant where he is. Outside there are sounds of dogs barking, and voices coming closer.

A few blocks south, a lighter is flashing. A fat, dirty dog appears and starts to sniff me. "Lady Bug, come back, damn it!" booms a deep voice from the darkness. Using my flashlight, I see two people approaching. Intermittently, I shine the light at myself and at the ground in front of the two guys. In the tunnel, you never blind people with a flashlight. That can cause unpredictable reactions. Better to light yourself, signaling you are decent person who has nothing to hide.

When they get closer, I see they are two skinheads, one short and stocky, the other thin and tall. They carry a baseball bat and a big hammer. I introduce myself politely and ask who they are and what they are doing in the tunnel. "We live a bit farther down the tunnel," the fat one says. "We came to pay Bernard a visit."

Bernard is not home, and I invite the two into my place and offer them chairs. "Frankie is my name," the fat one says. "And this here is my buddy Ment. And Lady Bug, my dog." Bob's bunker is being penetrated by the filthy smell of the dog. Lady Bug sniffs at the piss bottles and wags her tail.

"We live on top of Joe," Frankie says. He brings his Marlboro carefully to the ashtray, an empty beer can, but the ashes fall on the carpet. Frankie apologizes and picks up the ashes with wetted fingers. "I'm sorry. I tried to keep it clean as well at my place."

It is only now that I realize these are the kids from the South End. I had seen the fat one a few times on the roof of Joe's place, amongst a pack of mean-looking dogs who barked ferociously at every passer-by. But since it was so dark over there and he'd had the hood of his sweatshirt pulled up, his face had been invisible.

Ment is an old friend of Frankie's. In fact he is the son of Joe and Kathy, he tells me. He is a graffiti artist by profession. Ment is his artist name; his real name is not important. He had left the tunnel for a year and a half. Today, he came back from a big journey upstate.

I try to imagine it. Trekking and hiking and sleeping at youth hostels? Ment answers vaguely and changes the subject to electricity. It's a nice space, he says, but I would really need to have electricity. It's easy: just get a cable down from the park. All that hassle with candles doesn't make sense. And what will I do later, when it gets really cold? I really need an electric heater they suggest. Frankie has two cables at his home. Electricity all around the clock. "Come over later for a coffee, and then you will see."

Later on that evening, I jump on my bike and ride down to Joe's place. After fifteen blocks, the tunnel gets very wide, and in that expansion is a row of bunkers. The first is inhabited by Joe and Kathy and their thirty cats.

In the next bunkers live Leon and Ozzy. Leon was once saved by Bernard from freezing to death. On a cold winter night, Leon had drunk too much and had passed out on a bench in the park close to the North Gate. Bernard dragged the nearly-frozen Leon back into the tunnel and brought him back to life at the fire. Ozzy is a shy, reclusive man. According to Bernard, he used to work with computers.

The last bunker in the row is empty. This used to be the place belonging to John Kovacs and his dog Mama. Kovacs had transformed his bunker with Christmas decorations into what looked like a temple. After the *New York Times* wrote an article about him, he was offered a place in a live-and-work community upstate. A movie producer offered him big money to make a film about his life. With some trial and error, Kovacs left the tunnel. The movie deal fell through and he could only stand it a few weeks in the upstate community, but Kovacs was at least left with a pretty woman. After reading the *Times* article, a woman wrote Kovacs a letter and the two began a correspondence. She fell in love with him, and they are now living together in her apartment.

Frankie has constructed his home on top of Joe and Kathy's. It is a wooden shack, wrapped with ropes around white plastic sheets like an installation of the artist Christo. A hundred meters before I arrive at Frankie's, the dogs are already barking.

A light outside goes on and Ment shows up. "Fuck off," he yells at the dogs. After screaming a few more curses, the dogs finally become silent. Ment jumps down from the roof and opens the gate, a plywood sheet that closes off the narrow way between Joe's bunker and the tunnel wall. A suffocating stench of dog shit and ammonia nearly knocks me down. "Around the corner is a ladder," says Ment, while he himself climbs up a rope in three quick movements. Trying to be tough, I also try to climb up using the wet and moldy rope. My shoes slip on the slimy outer wall and I have to work my way up with my elbows.

Ment drags me onto the roof. My clothes are soiled with a smelly muck. "Next time, just take the ladder," Ment says. "This is in fact the emergency exit." He lets me in and closes the door with a chain. A Persian carpet keeps out the draft.

Inside, it is like a student dorm—a bit messy and frugal, but overall nice and comfy. The only things lacking are windows and plants. Lady Bug is snoring in front of an electrical heater. Frankie is sitting on the couch watching TV. A mustached man sitting next to him introduces himself as Buddy.

While Buddy keeps on watching TV, Frankie makes coffee in the small kitchen corner. A six-piece pan set hangs on the wall next to the baseball bat and the claw hammer kept within arms-reach. The interior of their home has been neatly painted in a pastel blue color. The construction of the corners and the attachment of the plywood to the supporting beams show the craftsmanship of an experienced carpenter.

"My domain," Frankie says proudly. "Of this whole goddamn planet, I decided to call this small space, this spot of ten by fourteen feet, mine. Nobody will take it away from me. You can't take it over. If you enter the space of me and my man.... You see that big-ass hammer over there? It is not hanging there so I will bump my head into it. It is over there for other people to bump their head into. It's simple," threatens Frankie. "You trespass against the rules of the tunnels? You will die by the rules of the tunnels."

While Frankie talks, he pumps up his chest. He barks simple sentences as if they were orders and commands. He puts a focus on every word and spits them out like machine gun fire. His steely blue eyes are staring at me, but not making contact. His eyes are focused on a spot behind me.

In the meantime, Ment is busy leafing through the *High Times* magazine I brought with me as my credentials. The magazine contains an eyewitness report I wrote about the Rwanda genocide, but Ment is more interested in the centerfold, a close-up of the bud of a marijuana plant with shiny droplets of resin.

The coffee is ready and Frankie fills up the mugs. "I'm sorry," he says. "We are out of sugar and it's too late to borrow some from Joe and Kathy."

Frankie gulps down his coffee. "They call us homeless," he starts. "But what is this?" He makes a wide gesture with his arms. "Okay, I admit, it's not totally luxurious. But here comes the catch: no rent. See that TV? Thirty channels. Free. Electricity? We got two lines. Never saw a bill. Piece of pie with your coffee?" Frankie gets an apple pie out of the fridge and cuts big slices with a Rambo survival knife.

"If the people up top lost their fucking jobs, I swear to God, 95 percent wouldn't know how to survive. Summers are okay, but in the winter, I tell you, it is a lotta hard work to carry big-ass jerry cans of water at ten degrees."

Frankie looks at the floor. "Sometimes it is not easy. In the summer, when the mothers let their children play in the park. You walk past them with your shopping cart and they look at you like you are some filthy animal. It looks like they are ashamed of us. While in fact, they should be ashamed of themselves for being embarrassed with us."

Buddy hardly opens his mouth but nods with every word Frankie says. His breath smells of cheap beer. "My man Buddy," Frankie says and hits him on the shoulder. "He used to live in a hotel around the corner. We always went there to take a shower. Didn't even have to knock on his door, we just came in and walked into the shower. Then Buddy got problems. Last week I saw him sleeping in a cardboard box in the park. I said: 'Buddy, this is no good. Come live with us.' Buddy helped us, now we help him. It's simple. On the other hand, if someone fucks me over, I get back to him. Always. Even if I have to wait for fifteen years around the corner. Vendetta, that's what life is all about."

Frankie is originally from North Carolina. That's where he got his heavy Southern accent. At sixteen, he was kicked out of high school and started a wandering existence all over the East Coast. Sometimes he had a job, other times he robbed truck drivers or broke into restaurants. He saw the inside of half a dozen penal institutions and youth correction centers.

In the end, he wound up in New York. With a few friends—"me and my crew"—they rented a small apartment on the Lower East Side. They discovered the tunnels on graffiti expeditions. When the crew broke up and lost their apartment, they hit the streets. Frankie went into the tunnels and put up a tent close to the entrance at the South End. Later on he moved half a mile deeper in the tunnel and build his shack on top of Joe's roof.

Frankie also makes his money canning. Like Bernard, he has a steady route with supers he has befriended. In a good month, he makes a thousand dollars. "Not bad, considering that for that money I don't have to rob anyone nor do I have to steal. Enough food for me and the dogs, some beer and smokies and once in a while a puff of Buddha."

Ment shows Frankie the *High Times*. They get sentimental. Back then, in the correctional facilities and jails, they had to read the magazine in secret, and sold it to each other. They take the centerfold carefully out of the magazine and glue it to the wall with toothpaste. An old trick learned in jail, Ment says. They never had adhesive tape there.

"They should legalize that stuff," Frankie says. "Would really make a big difference with all that bullshit we have now with crackheads. Never heard of a pot smoker who sold his shoes to score some weed in the middle of winter with two feet of snow."

Frankie works three, four days a week. "The best is, you are self-employed. No boss telling you what, where, how, and when to do. Some people don't see it as work. Hell, I swear to you, we are not going through the garbage for fun."

"Especially not if you hit a diaper full of shit," Ment adds dryly. He is playing tricks with a razor blade in his mouth. Sometimes he sticks his tongue out with the blade, then he closes his mouth and blows up his cheeks. After a few chewing movements, he sticks out an empty tongue. Then he winks and takes the blade, now sticking to his palate, out of his mouth.

"This is to give someone the one buck fifty," Ment says swankily. I look at them puzzled. Frankie and Ment snigger over my ignorance. "They also call it the Kool-Aid Smile," clarifies Frankie, referring to Kool-Aid's logo of a carafe with an enormously wide grin. "You just go slash! From one ear to the other." Frankie makes a gesture of cutting someone's throat. "You say, here's one fifty. Keep the change. The guy needs at least a hundred and fifty stitches."

Frankie fills up the mugs and talks about his work. "I don't beg from nobody. Actually, a beggar says: 'Please, feel sorry for me.' Not me. I'm a man, I got my pride. I never begged. It was never even necessary. Back then, before the tunnel, I had my spot in an emergency exit of the subway at Columbus Circle. Me and Lady Bug, we were sleeping in a card-board box. Lady Bug was always on my feet. And I can tell you, New Yorkers have a heart for dogs. Every evening a lady came to bring us a big-ass fucking sandwich and a can of dog food. And a twenty-dollar bill. Each evening. I tell you. Had I been there without a dog, nobody be givin' me no shit."

Frankie strokes Lady Bug. "Yeah, me and my dog…Always together. Sometimes we walked twenty miles in a day. When we were still living on the streets, Lady Bug never slept. She was laying flat, but kept one ear open. If she heard a strange noise, she put up that ear. And was there really something wrong? Snap! There she went. One guy once threw a rotten egg at us. Snap! Lady Bug chased that guy for twenty blocks."

Buddy is dozing off at the couch, but when we talk about dogs, he wakes up. He used to have a dog himself. It was a purple-tongued chow-chow. The dog was run over by a car and left for dead. Buddy fixed up the dog and called her Samantha. Street name, Mookie.

"Boy, everybody on the West Side loved Mookie," tells Buddy. "When I was living in the Hotel, Mookie was always laying in the sun on the fire escape. Her own private balcony. And when Frankie and Ment stopped by, she recognized their footsteps from far away. Scratched on the door to welcome them. Boy, Mookie could really talk to you."

One day Mookie disappeared. Buddy thinks she was kidnapped. "She is still walking around on the West Side. A few people have spotted her. And last week a cop told me he had seen Mookie."

When Buddy is finished talking, he falls back asleep. Frankie starts to talk again. "Me and my man Ment, we are as close as brothers. If I make a mess, Ment's mother comes here to raise hell." Ment nods and smiles mysteriously. He pulls a book from the shelf. It is a tag book, filled with tags—the signatures—of friend and colleague graffiti artists. Some of Ment's old friends are no more. Killed in accidents, shot dead, died from AIDS. Others are behind bars. "Me and my crew, there are not many left anymore," he says in a soft voice.

"A crew is a group of friends that have decided to do something together and who will push that," explains Frankie. "It can be spraying graffiti or, ahem," he says cryptically, "something deeper."

It is nearly midnight. I go back to Bernard's camp. "Watch out," advises Frankie as I unlock my bike. "At night it's dangerous in the tunnel. Especially over the weekends you have a lot of strange people hanging around. Remember, always carry a baseball bat. If you run into a stranger, hit first. Then ask questions."

In the morning, I join Bernard at the grill and tell him about my visit to Frankie and Ment.

He gets angry. "They are bullshitters. Especially that Frankie, he is a loudmouth. If you're a lotta talk, you ain't but shit! Damn, I can handle that guy. He is just like ... just like ..." Bernard thinks and stirs up the fire. "He is just like most people on this planet. Just another asshole."

I tell him the son of Joe and Kathy seemed like a nice guy. "Hmm, strange," Bernard says, "I didn't know Ment was their son. But yes, why not. But what did he say? A year and a half traveling in upstate New York?" Bernard laughs. "He was in jail all that time. Armed robbery on a clothes shop. He was boasting that they got fifty grand. At the most, it was a few thousand."

"And of course a lot of cursing about crackheads?" Bernard continues. "Frankie is always telling negative bullshit about crackheads. But he himself smokes the stuff just as hard. Most people here never mention drugs when the crews come down. They are afraid they won't get paid because they would buy crack."

Bernard talks about the camera crews that come underground regularly to make documentaries about the tunnel. Most of the time, Bernard is the contact person, guide, fixer, and assistant, all at the same time. He is not only the most reliable and eloquent tunnel dweller, but has some film experience as well. His day rate is one hundred dollars. Other tunnel people get twenty dollars to tell their story in front of the camera. The difference in salary causes envy and anger.

"They are cowards and hypocrites, most of the people here," continues Bernard. "Manny asked me last time if you knew I smoked crack. Of course, I said. And I don't give a damn. If I have to justify myself to anyone else but myself, it is about time to leave this planet. Period! I mean, one day I saw Marcus with some chick in his cave. They were smoking crack like a bunch of old sailors. Next day I come with a journalist. She asked if he did any drugs. Man, I tell you, you should have seen the script he had ready. The slime had a three-foot-long sermon: 'Oh no, I never touch drugs anymore since that fatal day my brother died in front of me after an overdose.' Fuck it. But me? I am always the bad guy, because I smoke crack and don't keep it a secret."

6. DAILY ROUTINE

"Jesus Was Homeless Too" says a flier from the Colorado Bible Society. Tony has picked up a few of them and has put them in the hooded hair dryer that has been in his cart for more than a week but for which he has not been able to find a buyer. The laces of the Timberland shoes have gone. Tony tried to sell me the shoes several times, although I told him clearly that they were two sizes too small. Maybe Burk stole the shoelaces, although I can imagine Tony managing to sell just the laces to someone on the streets. I push his cart aside and wriggle myself between his other junk to go down the stairs. It is 6 PM and the tunnel is pitch-dark.

Bernard sits at the fire complaining about the park police. Normally, they keep themselves busy with sawing off old branches, raking fallen leaves and showing off in fancy four wheel drives. They know that people live in the tunnel but never made a big deal of it. Now suddenly they do.

"The idiots put a new lock on the gate," he grumbles. "I immediately cut through it. Who do they think they are?"

Bernard soaks his clothes in a few buckets. It is getting cold, so it is time to get his winter clothes out. Tomorrow is laundry day, but because everything is so dirty from the soot and dirt, pre-washing is needed.

Linda, a fat black cat, jumps on his lap. Bernard strokes her neck softly. "Poor Linda," he says to the purring cat. "All these horny cats who are chasing you. But yes, even you have to pay your dues to society. And thanks to you we don't have any rats here anymore."

The poor cat has already given birth five times, Bernard tells me. Now she is pregnant again. Linda is one of Bernard's favorite cats. She is a ruthless killing machine, chewing up every rat, even ones that are bigger than she is. Sometimes in the night I hear blood-curdling screams. Then Linda is off, chasing one of her victims for blocks.

Once, Bernard locked up Linda for three days without food because he wanted to deal with a particular rat that had been bothering him for nights. "She was sitting at the trunk looking mean at me," Bernard tells me. "I wanted to pet her, and *Rang!* She slashed me with her claws as sharp as knives. Pure energy! The blood was dripping from my hands." The cat looks around proudly. She feels we are discussing her.

"Well Linda, maybe you are just a spy sent from up top, " Bernard pats the cat on its back. "Just hanging around here to create chaos."

We go outside to get some beers. Bernard is a modest drinker, but loves an imported brew as a nightcap. Our little evening stroll up top has become a daily routine, during which we discuss the things of the day.

This evening, Bernard is in a melancholic mood and ponders the meaning of existence. "Suffering…" he whispers, "Life consists of suffering. Nobody is happy. How can mankind be happy anyway, with all the misery around him? And this country, most people don't realize how good they have it. But the wrath of God will soon descend upon us. The signs are all over. Hurricanes, tornadoes, earthquakes. From one moment to the next, you lose everything."

We are walking through the park and see the traffic jam on the West Side Highway slowly creeping ahead like a giant caterpillar. The air is filled with horns and sirens and alarms. On the other side of the Hudson is the skyline of New Jersey. Office buildings and commuter homes bake in an orange glow. In between, we see white and red lights slowly moving around. "Wait a minute. Look at the madness over there. Where are they all going, these robots? It's madness. Just to keep the dollar going. Cars, gasoline, parking lots, garages, bridges, toll lanes, tunnels. Every year they introduce a new model car, while the latest one hasn't sold out. And listen to the fire trucks: all cars that are on fire. It's only plastic and electronics now. If they get stuck in a traffic jam, they heat up and combust spontaneously." Bernard shakes his head.

Bernard is a beer connoisseur and he has trouble choosing between Beck's, Guinness, Carlsberg, and Tuborg. He would never touch bum brands like Country Club or Ballantine's Ale, or even worse, White Deer, malt liquors very popular among the homeless. Bernard finally settles for a Guinness. On the way back, we walk past the garbage bags at the high school on 96th Street. "My greatest source of food," Bernard says while checking the contents. "A good harvest," he mumbles when he finds half full bags of pretzels and chips, and a tray full of drumsticks that spoilt school children did not eat.

On a wall in the park, we drink our beers while munching damp chips and tough pretzels. Bernard is telling about the early tunnel days. The first year he was on his own. "It was a paradise of quiet and peace." One by one, more people settled in his camp till finally there were about ten people. As the only responsible man who also managed to control his drinking and drug habits, Bernard soon became a surrogate father for a bunch of unruly and ungrateful children. Chaos had entered the tunnels. Now, after eight years, Bernard is getting tired of tunnel life. "It is no longer a challenge. It's routine. I mastered this existence." Bernard has passed forty and feels the cold and dampness is taking a toll on his body. "It's time for a change. This spring I want to move out."

Bernard says he might have an interesting deal. A production company in Hollywood wants to make a dramatic rendition of his tunnel life, and is willing to pay a few hundred thousand for the movie rights. I have heard Bernard brag about it before to the supers Harvey and Pedro, but it is hard to check how serious the story is. In earlier documentaries about the tunnel, I read that Bernard said he wanted to move out of the tunnel as early as 1990. The Hollywood story has been going for years as well. Chris Pape, the graffiti artist, was also approached by Hollywood. He sent his archive with tunnel videotapes, but never heard back. Now Pape is using a bailiff to get his unique tapes back. "You can't trust those rats from Hollywood," Pape told me.

With a mouthful of chips, Bernard inspects the drumsticks and nods appreciatively. "Everybody that walks around hungry in New York is a complete idiot." Bernard used to help clean a few restaurants in the neighborhood. He could take home all the leftovers: cheeseburgers, big steaks, and trays full of corn. "I could hardly drag it back into the tunnel."

Now that the number of homeless has multiplied, good food is getting harder to come by. There are restaurants that throw bleach on their garbage to prevent people from rummaging through it. It hasn't happened yet, but restaurant owners defend their behavior by saying any homeless suffering from food poisoning could then sue them for putting out spoiled food on the public road. Bernard has another theory: "The assholes just can't stand that we sometimes eat lobster and crab for free."

Other restaurants, however, donate their leftovers to organizations such as Meals on Wheels, who distribute it to the homeless or give it to the soup kitchens sprouting up all over Manhattan.

All in all, according to Bernard, no homeless person has the right to complain about food. "Food's not the problem. It's pride," he concludes. "Even on our level, we have an excellent life…I have my little extra things, sometimes a modest splurge…I even have the luxury to deal with society when I want."

Bernard takes a sip of beer and watches the New Yorkers who walk their dogs in the park. "Hello, mastiff," he calls when a cream-colored dog walks toward us and sniffs at the chicken legs.

The owner is surprised a homeless person knows the breed of his dog and starts to chat with us. Bernard scratches the dog's neck. "We have some magnificent dogs here on the West Side," Bernard says, like he is one of the people owning an expensive breed. He tells us about the lady who had a Shar-Pei, a Chinese wrinkle dog. "Could you believe it? Only in food bills, the dog cost two hundred dollars a week. Six grand she had paid for the pup. I said 'Lady, I am not out here to offend you, but this dog better do more than just bark. Can he do the dishes and vacuum as well?'" The owner of the mastiff has to laugh.

"People can't give love to their fellow humans," Bernard thinks aloud while we walk back. "They give it to dogs. Nothing wrong to love dogs, but still … So much wealth in this country, but also so much loneliness …"

The lottery jackpot is now seventy million dollars and New York is grabbed by lotto mania. If Bernard wins, he will buy an island in the Pacific Ocean. "Or a big-ass estate of a thousand acres. Then I wanna be left the fuck alone. Bottom line!"

Back home in the tunnel, Bernard prepares supper. Again spaghetti with tomato sauce, but this time with chicken. "Last winter, with the blizzard, we couldn't get rid of the food. On the streets, people spontaneously gave us hamburgers and pizzas. The Jews in the neighborhood were hanging sausages in the trees. All in all, there are still a lot of good people. Not everybody is corrupted by greed and progress."

Tony joins us, now dressed in a light T-shirt and shorts kept up with enormous red suspenders. Shivering from the cold, he keeps on throwing plastic bottles and Styrofoam cups on the fire. Bernard stirs the pan and lifts the lid to let me smell. I bend over, but nearly suffocate in the sooty, sharp, and poisonous fumes. Tony has just thrown a piece of laminated OSB board on the fire.

He hacks up a loogie, lights a cigarette, and gives some chicken legs to the cats who are crawling around him.

"Stop feeding these dirty cats," Bernard says irritated. "The animals are here to catch rats."

"Sorry, B," mumbles Tony absently. Linda jumps on his lap. The two like each other's company at the warm fireplace. Tony pets the purring cat while humming *I can see clearly now, the rain is gone …*

Bernard starts to rant and rave now about the inconsiderate behavior of the Kool-Aid Kid. The Kool-Aid Kid is a black itinerant kid who now and then shows up at Bernard's camp. In fact, he's named Junio, but they call him after his favorite drink.

"Unbelievable. The little prick again dirtied all my spoons with mayonnaise. And watch this." Bernard gets a couple of coffee cups and shows me the sticky, green residue inside. It's mint-flavored Kool-Aid. "All over he leaves his trademark."

"You are right B," adds Tony. And then to me, "Anthony, if you run into him, just tell him to see me."

"The kid is no good," Bernard continues. "He steals my food, he finishes the water and wood. Never will he bring something himself. He burns my kettles and fucks up my pans." Bernard drains the spaghetti, but burns his hands. "And goddamnit, now I even lost my kitchen gloves! They were here lying on this chair." Bernard gets up to look for them, but stumbles over a cat nibbling on a drumstick. "Dirty cat, fuck off!" he screams, and kicks the animal, who runs away with a loud howl.

Bernard's irritation is understandable. After years of tunnel life, he has totally streamlined his household. He's arranged the kitchen so that from his chair he can grab anything blindfolded. And it is an unwritten tunnel rule that everybody contributes to the daily wood, water, and food. Tony, and sometimes even Burk who lives half a mile away but who sits now and then at the fireplace, make an occasional contribution. It is Bernard, however, who is responsible for the supplies in the end. Water, especially, is a heavy job. In the summer, Bernard uses the fountains in the park. But in the wintertime, he has to fill up the jerry cans in a gas station more than a mile away.

The water is then transported in a shopping cart to the Northern Gate. In the tunnel, you have to drag the heavy jerry cans for nearly half a mile.

Bernard is frugal with water. He seldom washes himself in the tunnel; most of the time, he showers at a friend's place in a residential hotel. He even recycles his dish-washing water; after rinsing his coffee cups, he throws the water in the little pan where his silverware is always soaking. But the Kool-Aid Kid wastes water. Sometimes he uses five gallons of water, nearly a jerry can full, just to wash himself. One night I saw him do it. Four kettles of water were boiling on the fire, and the kid had a ball splashing and washing himself with steamy hot water.

Bernard fills our plates and goes on about the Kid. "It's fucking unbelievable. I have never seen this in all the time I am down here. What do you think, Tony, shall we poison him? Should be an easy job. We just have to put some rat poison in his Kool-Aid."

Bernard is gnawing on a drumstick, and throws the bones over his shoulder. A few cats jump on it. "On the other hand, do we want to have that on our conscience?'

Tony ignores the murder plans. "The Kid is afraid of something," he says understandingly. "Just a hunted-down animal. Goes from place to place. Never sleeps in the same spot."

Nobody knows where the Kid comes from. He is the silent type and hardly speaks English. Tony spoke with him a few times in Spanish, but hardly learnt anything new. A few weeks ago, he suddenly turned up. Since then, he comes at irregular intervals, sometimes walking from the south, sometimes from the north. Somehow, he has chosen Bernard's place as base camp.

Tony leaves for his shack with his plate of food. "I tell you, the guy is really sick," Bernard gossips. "I think he got the virus. That's what you get if you do tricks with kids that let themselves be fucked up their ass for a few crumbs of crack and then proceed to spread the virus all over town." Bernard is getting tired of his problem-child Tony. He receives welfare but blows his money the same day betting on horses. "Sometimes he wins, but then he continues till he has lost everything," Bernard shakes his head. "You're better off doing crack. At least you see your money go up in smoke in front of your eyes."

Tony's dream is to become a millionaire by winning on the horses, Bernard tells me with a sigh. Then he will rent a nice apartment, send his lover Jeff to rehab, and live long and happy with him forever.

Bernard suspects that Tony has AIDS, or the first symptoms of Alzheimer's. He is suffering from amnesia and hears the strangest things. He's totally convinced that the weird whizzing sound we sometimes hear is an enormous bat flying through the tunnel with the speed of sound. And not just a normal bat, but a bat with leather wings. The eerie sound is actually caused when cars with wet tires drive at high speed over road marks on the West Side Highway. Add the resonations from the steel columns and beams in the tunnel, a few echoes, maybe a bit of Doppler effect, and you have a ZOOVE! sound that even scares the cats.

Professor Williams had explained that audiovisual hallucinations are completely normal in the tunnel, like *fata morganas* in the desert. They are caused by physical, psychological, and chemical factors. First, the strange architectonic construction of the tunnel causes extraordinary acoustic and visual effects. In addition, a lot of tunnel people are mentally unstable and are haunted by panic attacks, visions, delusions, and flashbacks. Alcohol and drug abuse on top of that cause the proverbial pink elephants to appear.

Still, some unexplainable things are happening in the tunnel. Bernard and Bob once saw a ghost. "We were sitting one night at the fire," Bernard tells me. "From the corner of my eye I saw near *The Third of May* trails of fog that slowly transformed into a person. I said, 'Bob, do you see what I see, or am I getting goddamn crazy.' Bob was sitting petrified on his chair. 'Bernard,' he trembled, 'I just wanted to ask you the same thing.'"

The next morning, Bernard is serving grits with salmon burgers, an old family recipe Bernard learnt from his mother in the Deep South. They are amazing, and Bernard is proud when I jot down the recipe. Contrary to habit, Tony doesn't show up. "He told me he is not feeling well. You see, it's the virus. The idiot is crazy. No way will I serve him breakfast in bed."

Today is Bernard's big laundry day. He's saved everything up and now has more than four garbage bags full.

Outside on the playground, the park police are driving around. "There are those assholes again," Bernard says agitated. "Bunch of losers, thinking they're big shots 'cause they cruise around in big cars, picking their noses while making fifty grand a year."

They approach us and open their window. A fat guy with a mustache asks what happened to the new lock they installed. Bernard tells them politely he has cut through the chain, but that he has kept the lock and can even return it if they want.

"You don't have the right to lock our gates," he says confidently. "Amtrak is okay that we live down here. The whole world has seen it prime time on CNN."

The fat guy is not impressed. "Sorry, guys, but I have my orders," he replies. "We get complaints about the mess." The ranger is not just mentioning all the stuff in the emergency exits, but all the crack vials, empty cans, old blankets, and cardboard boxes that are scattered around the park. The corner near the Northern Gate is a favorite spot for crackheads and there are always street people sleeping on the playground benches in the evening. Bernard remains polite and explains that the mess outside is not from the tunnel people, but that he will make sure the exits are kept clean.

The fat ranger is not convinced. "I'm sorry, guys. It is really getting out of hand. I'm gonna put an elephant lock on the gate. Impossible to cut through. Only with a diamond saw."

Bernard is tired of the discussion and leaves with his dirty laundry. The ranger shrugs his shoulders. "I don't know why you guys are down there," he says. "We can bring you to a shelter, free food, medical care, everything you need." I thank the ranger for his thoughtfulness and say it is pretty okay down there. He shakes his head and drives away.

Bernard is mad as hell. "Goddammit, that mess is not my responsibility," he raves. "And I told everybody to keep it clean inside. Fuck the guys. I have been their spokesman for too long. Now you see what happens. And fuck that diamond saw. We can break any lock. Worst case with nitro or dynamite. Holy shit! The idiot really should not think he can kick us out that easily. We'll just get some TV-crews here and gonna make a big show."

Bernard is not exaggerating. He learnt a few things the last time the tunnel people were threatened with eviction. He has the phone numbers of Professor Williams, Chris Pape, and Margaret, a conceptual photographer who has been working for years on a project about the tunnel people. He's also kept all the business cards from the CNN, ABC, NBC, and CBS crews that have ever visited the tunnel. If necessary, he can mobilize the New York media with a couple of phone calls. The networks would love a juicy story like tunnel dwellers being evicted from their under-ground homes.

Bernard takes his laundry very seriously and it takes a few hours. He meticulously sorts out everything into white, colored, and delicate laundry. He applies Ring Around the Collar on the deepest stains. He fills up five machines and doesn't even forget to add perfumed fabric softener on the last wash.

Outside, we meet Manny. He is a small sleaze-ball with shiny, ratty eyes and a nasty boil on his cheek that changes with the weather from deep purple to a yellowish green. Sometimes I see Manny at the Northern Gate as he enters the tunnel through Marcus' rabbit hole. This is a little tunnel dug by Marcus to an exit in the park, and named after Alice in Wonderland. But usu-ally Manny doesn't want to dirty his clothes and waits at the gate till Bernard or I open it. Most of the time, it is to smoke some crack with Bernard. I noticed that he only shows up on days he knows Bernard has money.

Last time, the creep wanted to know how much I paid Ber-nard. I told Manny I just got groceries instead of giving money that might be spent on drugs. Later Bernard asked me indig-nantly if I really had told Manny that he was a junkie. The little scumbag had twisted my words around.

Manny shows us a golden ring with a diamond he is off to sell. Found honestly on the streets. I don't believe it. "Everything is possible," Bernard says. "The greatest treasures are lying amidst the garbage." Manny promised to give Bernard a share. Later on we see him again, telling us he only got five dollars for the ring. Too bad, nothing for Bernard, he says, walking away with a smooth pace.

"Fuck that guy," Bernard fumes, "he is a dirty snake."

For the umpteenth time I knock on the door of the little shack belonging to Ramon and Estoban in Little Havana. It has become routine for me to show up here several times a week trying to establish contact. I did speak to Estoban a few times. He is an emaciated Cuban with a long unkempt beard and hands where the dirt seems to be tattooed. With his narrow eyes squeezed half-closed, he looks like Ho Chi Minh. It is difficult to talk with the shy Estoban. He hardly speaks English, and speaks Spanish in a heavy Cuban accent.

He's also cagey about giving information. He arrived in the States fifteen years ago and found work as a carpenter. The company went broke and Estoban found himself unemployed and on the street. Since his English was so bad, it was hard to get a new job. On top of that, all his documents were stolen. He started to sleep in Riverside Park and eventually Bernard, who had seen him working around when he still had his job, invited him into the tunnel.

Bernard told me that the guy to talk to is Ramon. He speaks English well and is open to journalists. But I never catch him at home. This time, I see light burning from his wooden shack and his door is ajar. I peep inside and see a figure under the blankets. "Excuse me, Ramon?" I call softly. From under the blankets a man with a woolen cap appears. "I heard you came a couple of times to see me," Ramon says. "Take a seat."

I sit down on a milk crate in the corner of his place. Ramon has a frugally decorated home. Besides the bed, there is a little table with some candles and a statue of the Madonna. In the corner are a couple of old radios that he's repairing to sell on the streets. A bare bulb on the ceiling lights the room. Cardboard boxes nailed to the inside walls provide an extra layer of insulation against the cold.

Ramon doesn't like interviews. "What are we getting out of it? The only one getting better is Bernard. He makes thousands of dollars." I manage to convince Ramon to talk with me and we make a deal. Next time, I will bring him half a carton of cigarettes and a tasty sandwich.

"Everybody here in Little Havana is a Marielito," Ramon explains and gives me a small lesson in contemporary history. It was 1980. A group of people who wanted asylum had fled to the Peruvian embassy in Havana. The world was surprised that Castro let the group leave and announced that everybody who wished was free to leave the country and come to the U.S.

The smart Castro then gave criminals and other antisocial elements the choice between leaving or staying to rot in jail. The enormous stream out of the port of Mariel became known as the Mariel boatlift.

"Latinos say all Marielitos were criminals," Ramon continues. "But they are just envious because Cubans are very successful in the U.S. When I hit bottom, I didn't get any support from the Latino community. They were snickering with *schadenfreude*."

In Cuba, Ramon taught philosophy. "I didn't want to teach Marxism-Leninism the rest of my life for nearly nothing," he says. "So I grabbed the chance to start all over in the U.S." Ramon wound up in Union City, a city just across the Hudson, the biggest community of Cuban expats after Miami. He started a business in car parts, and soon had a few men working for him.

"But then the problems began. I started doing coke. And lost everything I had." Ramon says it without regret, as though he has accepted his fate. "I don't blame society. I had all the chances I could ever dream of. I could have been a millionaire, but now I live in a tunnel between rats."

He lights up a cigarette and pulls the blanket over himself. "Every homeless person only has himself to blame," he says as if he were a New Republican. "I tell everybody: Don't do drugs. You wind up in the street."

Ramon says he wants to write poetry. "I am waiting for inspiration. But I will never get that here. Watch my lips: Before the winter I want to be out of here."

When I return some time later to bring him the promised cigarettes, I see him outside in the park, taking a stroll with Estoban. "I don't live no more in the tunnel," Ramon says proudly. He went to a temporary shelter and is undergoing rehab.

At the end of the day, Bernard is smoking crack at his place and he invites me in. "I just made you a thermos of coffee," he says hospitably. His bad temper has disappeared and he is a friendly as can be. He gives me a big bottle of white wine he has found near the high school, maybe a left over from a party. "Saves you a couple of bucks when you want to have your nightcap." Bernard is getting his pipe ready for another hit of crack. I want to take a photo, but Bernard protests.

"You journalists always focus on our crack abuse. So vicious… Without mentioning the context in which it happens. The media are spreading the idea that crack and coke are the keys to the homeless problem."

It is difficult to tell just how addicted Bernard is to crack. He denies he is an addict, but every day he smokes at least a bit, most of the time before going to bed. He calls it euphemistically "my nightcap." He prefers to refer to himself as a recreational crack user, who lights up a pipe after a hard day's work.

There were times it was different. Bernard started to neglect his primary needs, "but down here you notice pretty quickly when you have gone too far. When you wake up without money, water and you know it's time to slow down."

Because he is relatively in control of his crack habit, he's a harsh judge of the heavy users. "Not the stem, but greed and gluttony brought her down," he says about the suck monster we always see hanging around on Broadway. "Evil comes from all abuse."

"Do you want to try it?" Bernard asks amicably. He sees me doubting.

"No, you don't get hooked after the first time," he laughs. My curiosity takes the upper hand.

After breathing a few times in and out, I take a hit from the glass pipe that Bernard has prepared for me. I suck the sharp smoke deep inside my lungs and hold my breath as long as possible. After a few seconds I already feel the effect: a strange lucidity that lasts a very short time before it transforms into a laconic melancholy, mixed with a very pleasant dizziness. A few minutes later, these effects are gone, changed into a strong desire for another hit. This is what crack smokers call thirst.

With greedy eyes, I see Bernard pulling another vial out of his pocket. We smoke a few more pipes. Later, when all of it is gone, we start the pathetic part of the crack ritual. With metal sticks, we scrape the residue from the glass stems and wriggle the last crumbs out of the vials with a tooth pick to make a last hit. I keep the lighter so long at the stem it burns red. I nearly burn my lungs with the hot smoke.

It is a very modest high, caused more by a lack of oxygen to the brain because I have held my breath for nearly ninety seconds. It is time for a decision. Are we going to get a few extra hits up top or are we going to sleep? "Bedtime," says Bernard.

7. THE SECRET LIFE OF PLANTS

After a long journey that started in the Netherlands city of Leiden, the *Mayflower* hit shore in 1620 on what is currently a popular gay holiday destination, Cape Cod. On board were religious refugees, the Pilgrim Fathers. It was a tough winter for the boat people. Hunger and disease killed half of the new asylum seekers. It would have been worse, were it not for friendly Indians who brought food to the Pilgrims and introduced them to new agricultural techniques in the unknown land. For instance, the Indians taught the newcomers to wrap a herring around corn seeds before planting. The rotting fish would provide the corn with all the necessary nutrients. Thus it happened; the next autumn, the Pilgrims had an incredibly rich harvest.

To give thanks for their help, the Pilgrims threw a big harvest party, the first Thanksgiving dinner. The Indians were royally treated to turkeys, corn bread, fried fish, and freshly fermented wine.

Every decent American family, except those irreversibly disintegrated by divorce, incest, or inheritance issues, still celebrates Thanksgiving by coming together on the fourth Thursday in November every year. With the excuse of giving thanks to the kind natives and honoring their ancestors, they gulp down big quantities of turkey, pumpkin pie, and cranberry sauce. Originally meant as a sacred celebration, the festive day has passed through a profane intermediate stage to end up eventually as a rather vulgar event. Many people just call it Turkey Day. The pharmaceutical industry anticipates the intestinal complaints

by advertising for laxatives and other medicines that prevent
gas, constipation and bloating weeks ahead of the holiday.

On these special days, just like Christmas, it's not just loneliness that hits home hard but charity as well. All the soup kitchens in the city organize special Thanksgiving dinners for the less
fortunate. Philanthropists venture into crime-ridden neighborhoods to hand out turkeys to the poor and needy.

The *New York Times* writes about Franciscan Father Benedictus
who drove a van loaded with ham and turkey to the South Bronx
to perform his good deeds. The article mentions a Puerto Rican
mother on welfare who is so overwhelmed by this that she
helps the Father out by pointing out all the bad guys who were
scheming to exchange their turkey around the corner for crack
or smack.

"Every year the same bullshit with the holidays. Everybody
gets the guilties," Bernard sneers over the sudden outburst of
generosity. We are sitting around the fire with Tony and the Kool-
Aid Kid, eating the minestrone soup that Bernard had made the
day before.

The radio plays easy-listening music and the DJ mentions
the holiday after every song. "Fuck Thanksgiving!" says Bernard.
"All Indians exterminated. That's a nice way to say thank you."
Bernard doesn't have any special plans for the day. He actually
hates holidays. When he had his forty-first birthday a week ago,
he announced he was going to do "nothing fucking special: just
breathe and thank God I made it through another year."

I wasn't there, but Bernard told me that it had been a nice day
after all; Professor Williams had paid a surprise visit and had
given him some money. Bob had also come by with a couple of
vials of crack as a birthday gift.

Tony is getting ready to eat turkey at his sister's place. Bernard
leaves for his bunker to "relax," his euphemism for smoking crack. The Kool-Aid Kid doesn't seem to have a clue about
Thanksgiving, but has understood that his previous behavior
was unacceptable. Maybe Tony taught him a lesson. Now he
cleans every plate he uses, he even rinses the cup from which
he just drank his lemonade Kool-Aid.

The Kid throws a few more newspapers on the fire and is getting wood, but he stumbles and with a crash the wood falls out
of his hands. Bernard storms out of his bunker. "Goddammit,"
he screams. "I only try to relax and that is already an impossible
challenge. I just have to light my lighter, and it is just like an
alarm that goes off! And that fire, by the way, is only for cooking, not for letting it burn for hours for nothing. And don't let
those empty pots burn on the grill." We see the flames licking
the handles of the pan. A smell of burned Bakelite hangs around
the fireplace. "And by the way, there are still fifty gallons of water
at the exit." Bernard disappears into his place grumbling, and
the Kid tries to wash the frying pan and the coffeemaker. The
metal filter of the coffeemaker now falls in the dust and dirt on
the ground, along with the lid of the frying pan. The Kid puts
everything back together; it's dirtier than it was before. He looks
helplessly at me and leaves.

I have an appointment with Marcus. We've gotten to know
each other pretty well, especially since I gave him a copy of the
key to the Northern Gate, so he doesn't have to get in through
the rabbit hole. Every time he hears me passing on my bike, he
calls out: "Antoine, ça va?" from his cave and we have a little chat
in French.

Last time we discussed the healing properties of carrot and
beet juice. Marcus advised me to drink at least two pints daily
as a heavy smoker and coffee user. Before that, we talked about
neo-realism in cinema. He mentioned illustrious names such
as Margaretha von Trotta, Werner Herzog, and Andrej Tarkovski.
In better days, he studied biochemistry and anthropology at
Columbia University and took a course in modern film. It's a
shame that talks with Marcus consist of his confused mono-
logues in which he jumps from one subject to the other and
can't seem to focus on anything.

To enter Marcus' well-hidden cave, you have to go up the stairs
of the emergency exit and then balance along a dangerously narrow wall. His place is triangular, bounded by the slanting tunnel
wall and another six-foot wall that is on the side of the tracks.

His cave consists of three interconnected spaces. Marcus gives me a little tour. The back space is basically storage space for firewood. Every day, he drags a few broken branches from the park into his cave so he will never run out of fuel. The middle space is a library. Piles of books and newspapers are stacked and orderly. In the corner is a sculpture of bicycle wrecks and old vacuum cleaners, a critique on the wasteful Western culture of discarding and disposal. The front room is his living room. A little daylight penetrates this space since it is the closest to the exit.

Marcus grabs a few plastic bags with newspaper clippings and magazines. "My portable archive." He smiles. "I am hooked on information."

Marcus shows me an article he is studying at the moment, a long piece from the *New York Times* Science supplement about the Space Lab. According to Marcus, the Space Lab needs serious improvements and he is planning to write NASA with some suggestions. Every important word in the article is underlined; in the sidelines are unreadable notes and exclamation marks. When I look closer, I notice actually that every verb, noun, and adjective has been underlined.

After Marcus puts his huge backpack on his shoulders, we are ready to go. I would like to talk about his time in college, but Marcus has already started an unstoppable monologue on the situation in the world. Every time he finishes a sentence and I want to change the subject, he has already launched into the next stream of associations. In fifteen minutes he covers: Chomsky's conspiracy theories and his thoughts on U.S. imperialism; the eviction of a squat on the Lower East Side; international solidarity between the squatters of Berlin and Zürich; capitalist abuses of the Swiss pharmaceutical multinational Ciba-Geigy; the growing rate of genetic defects and cancer cases among yuppies on Long Island; the repression of the student protests on Tiananmen Square compared with Gorbachev's handling of the unrest in Estonia, Lithuania and Latvia; the Mafia in Little Italy versus the Triads in Chinatown; and the disturbed ecological balance on this planet that he illustrates with illegal logging on Borneo and the dwindling salmon population in Northwest Canada.

Marcus' factual knowledge is astonishing. When he is finished, I have a headache. I realized many things were wrong in this world, but I have never heard such a condensed critique of modern society. Marcus now rummages in a garbage can in the park, and carefully gets out a plastic transparent bag with a big clod of toilet paper. These are poopy bags for dogs, he explains. Since the city heavily fines dog excrement, there is a new market for special bags with disposable gloves. The glove is made from paper tissue and once the poop has been picked up, can be turned inside out in the bag. Marcus collects these bags, because a copy of the *Village Voice* fits into it exactly.

While Marcus is checking every garbage can for the useful stuff, he greets fellow homeless people who are cruising the streets with their shopping carts. He points them to the West Side Community Center as the place that serves the best Thanksgiving meal in the hood.

Marcus is in a jolly mood. He greets strangers with "Happy Thanksgiving!" and makes lewd comments to "hot West-Side babes," who look back at him in disgust. Marcus unzips his pants and urinates against a tree on the curb of the street. He doesn't care the West-Side girls seem to ignore him: soon he will be in Florida and there all the chicks are just crazy about him.

At the West Side Community Center dozens of shopping carts full of junk have been parked near the entrance. At the coat check, they also accept garbage bags with personal belongings. I want to tell them I am just a reporter, not a poor and hungry citizen, but they have already handed me a meal ticket and pushed me together with Marcus into the dining room. Fluorescent lights shine brightly on long rows of plastic tables. Two very old ladies with blissful expressions on their very wrinkled faces play "Alle Menschen Werden Brüder" on piano and violin.

Indeed, there is brotherhood galore among the motley crew of guests who let themselves be served by an army of volunteers who are just as shabbily dressed. Only by their badges can the volunteers be distinguished from the needy and the poor.

I recognize a few black men I have seen at the can deposit machine at the supermarket. Suck Monster is also present. The Vietnam Vet without legs I often see begging with a big straw hat in front of the bike shop on Broadway is there, as is the white girl with a disgruntled face: I always see her with a paper cup at the exit of the Chemical Bank. She and her boyfriend once tried to sell me a brand new Krups coffee grinder for only three bucks, the price of a capsule of crack, Bernard explained. Bernard knew all about the downfall of the two white kids, who were actually from a very wealthy background.

There are also a lot of lonely old women who make me wonder how they can survive in expensive, dirty, and dangerous Manhattan. They remind me of old flappers out of the roaring twenties, when Manhattan must still have been livable. I once saw one of the old ladies slumping over a shopping basket with twenty cans of cat food and a few bananas. Was the cat food for her pets, or did she eat it herself? Sometimes you read stories like that in the paper, but I did not want to ask her.

A lady with a pink-brownish cotton candy hairdo smiles at me; it nearly cracks the heavy layer of makeup that gives her the expression of a waxen statue. We see each other quite often at the diner where we both are treated as pariahs, because we only spend fifty cents, consuming one cup of coffee in an hour. I read the *Times* there, while she smokes half a pack of menthols, powders her nose, and paints her lips. She even has the nerve to always ask for a free refill. On top of that, she leaves sticky lipstick traces on the coffee cups and even the ashtrays.

Marcus and I have barely found a chair before our Thanksgiving dinner is dumped on our plates. It is turkey with a greasy gravy, a dry stuffing of spiced breadcrumbs, and a rubbery piece of cranberry gelatin.

A lady with an overly concerned face asks if we need silverware. She returns with plastic knives and forks. "Happy Thanksgiving and enjoy your meal," she says routinely before she is off to the next homeless person without silverware. As I try to eat the tasteless stuff with my plastic fork, I wonder why all these do-gooders just annoy the hell out of me.

Maybe it is all those happy interviews on TV post Turkey Day, where volunteers with radiant smiles declare how good they felt and how great it was that the Good Old Lord gave them a chance to help the homeless. I guess they would have been just as happy handing out saucers of milk to scabby stray cats or doing something swell for clubbed baby seals.

On the wall are depressing decorations: a creepy overachieving Mickey Mouse dressed up as a cute Pilgrim Father who empties a cornucopia, dumping pumpkins and dead partridges in front of that bitchy Minnie Mouse. I try to ignore the environment and do my best to enjoy my meal. Also, I am touched by a blonde schoolgirl serving a couple of hardcore winos. Marcus is spicing up his meal with Tabasco, soy sauce, and a yellow sauce he has stocked in his backpack. Loudly smacking, he empties his plate and orders another serving, for "on the road." From his backpack, he pulls out aluminum foil to cover his plate. Gravy is dripping on his clothes as he stuffs the hot meal in between his portable archives. He is not the only one asking for a second helping. Most guests have small plastic buckets that on request are filled up with turkey and gravy.

Marcus has now been living in the tunnel for nearly five years. His problems started at college. He was a heavy heroin user and started to do strange things. At a Vietnam protest, he doused himself in gasoline and lit himself on fire. He was admitted into hospital with third degree burns.

Later, he wound up in mental institutions. Once he got out, he started doing drugs again and got a girlfriend pregnant. She was also a junkie and got a spontaneous abortion. When his girlfriend left him, Marcus started to wander. At the moment, he is in a rehab program downtown, but he prefers his cave in the tunnel not only for reasons of privacy, but because, as a "new-age traveler," he prefers to be closer to nature and the elements.

At rehab, Marcus can follow courses. At the moment he is busy with computers, because he would love to scan all his archives and put them onto just a few floppy disks. His biggest dream, however, is to become an acupuncturist.

Marcus is constantly updating his knowledge of his favorite subjects. Out of a small poopy bag, he shows me the *The Secret Life of the Plants*, an anthroposophist treatise on the spiritual life of the flora, by Peter Tompkins who earlier surprised the world with his works *Secrets of the Soil* and *The Mystery of the Cheops Pyramids*.

Marcus also carries a few glossy magazines: *Longevity*, filled with ads for vitamins, smart cocktails, and pills that bind free radicals and so prevent aging. The magazine has big photos of Paul Newman, Tina Turner, and Paul McCartney, people in their early sixties who still look pretty young.

Marcus also looks young for his age. He must be well over forty, but still he has not one crowfoot or wrinkle on his baby face with its red cheeks. Maybe it is all that carrot and beet juice; maybe it is because Marcus is not a man to worry and stress a lot.

On free afternoons, he goes to the music library to listen to the classic composers or to the public library to read popular science magazines. In the *Village Voice* he finds cafes with free concerts, and if there is a jam session, he brings his flute along.

It is getting to be evening, and the dining room empties. Marcus is going downtown for his rehab. In a garbage can he finds a used bus ticket that with a little luck will still be accepted by a distracted bus driver. I stay out a bit longer, and return to the tunnel later that night. To do Bernard a favor, I carry two jerry cans of water back. Each is about fifty pounds and I arrive at the camp half numb from back pain. Bernard is not even there to pat me on the back. I light the fire to warm me, and then hear rustling behind me. I only see two shiny eyes and a pack of newspaper that floats in the darkness. It is the Kool-Aid Kid, almost invisible since he is dressed in black. He is also trying to make his contribution to the household.

8. TONY THE TOMATO PLANT

In the middle of the night, someone starts knocking on my door. It is twelve-thirty. I put on my shoes and get my flashlight.

"Anthony, it's me!" someone calls. I open the door and see that creepy Jeff. The light shines at his face from below and, accentuating his hollow eyes, gives him an even spookier appearance. He can hardly keep his head straight, it is wobbling on his neck as though it might fall off at any moment and roll over onto the ground. Liquid is dripping from his mouth, and he mumbles something like "lighter" and "candles." Obviously he has scored some crack, but cannot light his stem with damp matches.

I don't have a lighter, but I give him a few candles. Jeff hands me a Marlboro to thank me and staggers away, back to Tony's bunker.

I go back to bed and put the baseball bat I found in Bob's place under my pillow. If there is one guy I don't trust, it is Tony's crack-addicted hooker lover. In the middle of the night I wake up again. It is four-thirty. Someone is yelling through the intercom. It goes on for half an hour

"It was that idiot Manny," Bernard tells me next morning. "Yelling in the middle of the night through the intercom. The guy really doesn't know where to stop. Does he really think I'll get out of my warm bed just for a few crumbs of lousy crack?"

I'm having breakfast with Bernard at the grill. This morning, oatmeal and chicken franks are on the menu. Bernard is up early, because at nine o'clock he expects a French film crew. He already showed them around yesterday, and brought them to Frankie and Ment's. With Joe and Kathy, they had some problems.

"Kathy was whining that Joe deserves more money because he has been in the tunnel the longest. Always bullshit with the two of them," Bernard grumbles. "Difficult people. They are not receptive to others."

In the morning, the crew will shoot at the grill. In the afternoon, Bernard will bring the crew to see Marcus.

Tony enters. He rubs his sleepy eyes and bums a cigarette; we listen to the morning news. Riker's Island is about to explode. Prisoners have started to mutiny in several sections. Tony shrugs it off. "Riker's Island? Come on, that's just like the YMCA. *I tell you*, when I was doing time, I saw the boys cry like little kids when they heard they would be transferred upstate to Sing Sing or Attica."

Tony starts again about the notorious Attica prison revolt in 1971, where thirty-nine people died. "They sent in the guards. They were shooting at us like we were sitting ducks. I saved the life of two guards," he brags. "One I hid under my bed. The other one I threw from the stairs." I look at him puzzled. "You don't get it, do you?" he says impatiently. "The second one got a broken arm and a concussion and lay unconscious under the stairs. Other prisoners thought he was dead. That saved his life."

People scream through the intercom. "That must be the French crew, right on time," Bernard says and leaves to pick them up at the Northern Gate.

Fifteen minutes later, the French crew arrives with all their equipment. Since Bernard doesn't have electricity, they have to drag tons of batteries and lights. Bernard puts extra chairs around the fire and treats them to his tunnel hospitality. "Coffee? I can also make chamomile tea if you prefer."

Sabine, the reporter, is a cute French girl in her late twenties. She has been living for a few years in New York, and soon all of us are having a lively conversation at the fireplace.

Her sound and camera men are older guys, and hardly speak English. They give a dirty look at the dishwater Bernard used to rinse the coffee cups. Bernard pours the coffee and apologizes that it is so strong. "This one here loves diesel," he laughs, pointing at me. "Milk and sugar?"

Bernard is soaking beans in a big pot while Sabine watches his tunnel household, fascinated. He is exaggerating a bit, "I got here excellent Mexican beans, and delicious wild swamp rice. Tonight we make a stew. Duke, can you do the groceries?" I get my notebook and jot down the list. "Let me see," Bernard thinks. "We need a big onion, a few carrots, celery, and maybe some garlic. And of course a pound of smoked turkey wings. You see, Sabine, I don't eat pork. That clogs up your veins."

Bernard is a ladies' man with a weak spot for pretty reporters. Last week, there was a beautiful Japanese documentary maker in the tunnel with Chris Pape. Bernard blew all the dust from her chair and even brought her a pillow from out of his shack. Once Bernard told me he had had a short but steamy affair with a Dutch filmmaker.

"We are all prisoners of this existence," Bernard opens eloquently. "Might as well finish our sentence down here." With this catchy quote he immediately grabs Sabine's attention. The other crewmembers are starting to set up lights. They stumble over pots and pans and curse that they will never have enough light for the dark space. Bernard interrupts his monologue to suggest that they put a mirror in front of the fireplace so the reflection will light him up.

"You see, Sabine," Bernard continues, "Last time, I was in a CBS documentary and did a stand-up at the Northern Gate. I told them I was grateful to God for this experience, that I had become a stronger man, but that one thing made me really sad—in the tunnels I never encountered a real human that accepted his fate. Most people here allow their past to haunt them." Sabine listens attentively.

"And CBS just cut out this piece. It was too threatening. Someone who has opted out of society, but still has all his mental capacities together."

Bernard throws more wood on the fire. Big flames, reflected by the mirror, light up his face. The cameraman nods approvingly.

"But you see, Sabine, it is sad. I never saw here any spiritual growth. I saw people becoming rancorous against society, I saw them flee in alcohol and drugs and ultimately I saw them go down."

The hooting of a train interrupts him. Fascinated, the crew watches it rush by. Between the pillars hangs a little plane, cut out of a Budweiser beer can, its propeller blowing in the squall caused by the train. "We need that shot of the plane," Sabine tells the cameraman. "How often are trains coming by?" Bernard is still caught in his sophisticated philosophical vocabulary. "On the weekends, the schedules tend to encounter unpredictable fluctuations," he says.

Bernard assists the cameraman with some test shots around the fire, and I talk to Sabine. She has already been dragging her crew into tunnels for a week. They shot extensive footage in the tunnel labyrinth under Grand Central. "Compared with there, this is the Fifth Avenue of the Tunnels," she says. Her cameraman is getting tired, she confides to me. "Every evening he is looking forward to a good restaurant, but we have to work low budget. Most of our money I give to the tunnel people."

The crew starts to work. "Dinner at seven," Bernard says as I am about to leave with Tony. "Will that work? By the way, would it not be easier if I buy the groceries? Six, seven dollars should do." I give Bernard some money. "Food is not the problem. It's pride," I hear Bernard start his tunnel talk again as I walk with Tony to the Northern Gate.

"What kind of work you actually do?" he asks. I have already explained to him four times that I am a reporter, and he saw me taking a lot of photos, but he seems to forget it every time. I repeat it again and tell him I want to do an interview with him. Tony thinks. "You just can't do that for nothing. It's gonna cost money. A lotta money…" He explains that it would take at least three weeks to write down his life story. "Then you will hear everything. Everything about the revolt in Attica. And I have seen things nobody else has seen…"

Actually, Tony is looking for a ghostwriter to write his life story. If I do a good job, I can easily make a million. That's why an advance of a hundred thousand seems to Tony a reasonable amount. I will think about it, I say, when we split at the Northern Gate. Tony is going to watch TV at his sister's. His voice turns secretive. "Remember, I know things…I helped a few guys escape from a maximum-security prison. But I am sorry, I can't tell you. I would endanger my own life."

Early in the evening I return to the tunnel. I put a couple of branches I found in the park near the fireplace. The pans are empty; the grill is cold. No stew in sight. Bernard is scraping crack pipes in his shack. That was the money for the groceries.

"Tomorrow we will cook that stew," Bernard says bluntly. "To-day I didn't feel like it. Are you hungry? I will make something else."

I have already made a fire when Bernard joins me. He is in a foul mood and looks haughtily at the branches under the grill. "How often do I have to say it? The wood from the park is worth-less. Way too damp. We are not camping out."

He looks disapprovingly at the huge crackling fire. "You will never make boy scouts. Look, this is the way to do it." Bernard grabs a few plastic bags and bottles from behind him and push-es them with a poker onto the burning wood. First an enormous acrid plume of smoke develops, then five-foot flames light up the tunnel.

He gets a can from behind him, and throws its contents along with some water into a pot. Once it boils, he adds some salt and pepper. "We need a new grill," he says. In the middle, the bars are burnt through and the coffee pot nearly falls through the opening.

Bernard serves dinner on orange plastic plates. With my flash-light I can see a gray, crumby substance. "Dehydrated potato slices, Marcus gave me a huge can this afternoon." I take a bite. It tastes like wet cardboard. "You want ketchup?" Bernard grabs a few small, dirty plastic bags. I wipe off the dust and ashes with my napkin and see it's indeed little bags of McDonald's tomato ketchup. Drenched in ketchup, the food is just eatable.

"Marcus played some flute for the crew," Bernard tells me. "He performed a special composition that he called the 'Carrot Juice Symphony.'" Bernard takes another serving; I kindly refuse, and go up top to eat a Cheese Burger Deluxe.

Later in the evening I come back. The streetlights in the park are off, so the tunnel is now completely dark. I will never feel at ease in the tunnel. Walking the five blocks underground to Ber-nard's camp is just scary. Especially since tonight I am not on my rattling bike, so I can hear all the strange sounds that resonate through the darkness. Car lights shine now and then through the emergency exits, creating weird patterns and shades of light on the tunnel walls. It even looks like the Mona Lisa opposite

Marcus' place smiles differently at me. I once asked Bernard if he was ever afraid of the tunnels. "Why?" he had asked surprised. "It is safer here than up top."

But I always feel like a very muggable person with all my expensive cameras under my coat. On the other hand, no tunnel dweller I know will harass me. I trust everybody, except Jeff who is actually pretty harmless. Still, I always expect some bogeyman with a big bat to jump out of the darkness behind the row of pillars halfway to Bernard's camp.

My flashlight is shining on the ground. My heart jumps a beat when I nearly step on a rat. I look closer, it is dead, nearly mummified, and with its tail in an elegant curl. The flat rat must have been here for some time, but I never noticed him.

At the camp there is a big fire. It is the Kool-Aid Kid, burning up all the wood I brought today from the park. It was not that damp after all. The kid has three pans on the fire. Pretty gutsy to cook a three-course meal with our wood.

I try to talk with him. No results in English, a combination of French and Spanish works better. I gather from incoherent sentences that he works in a clothing store in Harlem. Strange story.

"Yummy, yummy, good food," I say, rubbing my stomach and pointing at the pans. The Kool-Aid Kid smiles and lifts the lids. Franks are frying in one pan, in another pot the Kid is cooking bananas. He offers me a cup of the hot chocolate that is simmering in the third pot. I kindly decline and go to bed. Tomorrow is the big day, when I will interview Tony. He has finally agreed, and we only have to negotiate a price.

The next day, Tony is having trouble getting up and I bring a cup of coffee and cigarettes to him in bed. His bunker is right between mine and Bernard's, but a little behind us in a small alley, between piles of garbage and boxes that I can hardly squeeze myself through.

Inside, I nearly get lost in the enormous quantity of sweaters, coats and shirts hanging on coat hangers from the ceiling. On the floor are clean-picked chicken bones and saucers with milk and cat food. When my eyes get adjusted to the darkness, I see

Tony lying on a mattress on the floor, two cats snoring next to him on the pillow.

A little late, when we all have breakfast at the grill, we discuss the cats. Blacky, Tony's favorite cat, disappeared a few days ago. "He is hanging a block down against the wall," Bernard says with a mouth full of oatmeal. "Splashed and flattened. Must have been hit by a train."

Tony pours himself some more coffee. "Jezus, how the fuck could that happen?" he mumbles. "I mean, the cats are fucking scared of the trains." Bernard shrugs his shoulders. "Who knows? Maybe it was chasing a rat."

On our way out, Tony and I negotiate over the price of the interview. I carefully explain to him that unfortunately I don't have the time to write a bestseller about him. My story is about the tunnel in general, where he is not the main character, but still a very prominent one. A hundred-thousand-dollar advance is too much, I tell him. How about I treat him to a big breakfast up top? And, of course, a pack of Marlboros and ten dollars as compensation for his valuable time.

Tony is disappointed, but as we leave the Northern Gate, he agrees. "Okay, I am making an exception for you because you are also living down here."

It is a beautiful December day. In the park, squirrels are jumping all around and people are jogging with chests bare. Mothers with strollers send frightened looks at Tony as he pushes his rattling shopping cart full of junk over the park tracks. They hold extra tight to their children.

Tony nods amicably at them, and tells me that he is on probation for life. One misdemeanor, however small, and he goes straight back to jail. That's why, for years, he hasn't even jumped a turnstile and always gets a token for the subway. His probation officer is not supposed to know he lives in a tunnel. From a legal point of view, all tunnel people are breaking the law while they are trespassing on Amtrak's private property.

Officially, Tony lives with his sister on the Lower East Side. That is also why I can't photograph him recognizably. Once he got in trouble when they saw him in a TV documentary on the tunnels; he managed to talk his way out of it by telling the probation officer that the man in the movie was just one of the many body doubles he has in New York.

I want to take Tony to a fancy place on Broadway where they serve a big brunch. But Tony takes me to his favorite spot, a no-smoking fast food joint with Formica tables where they serve breakfast at the counter on plastic plates.

He parks his cart in the middle of the sidewalk in front of the big windows. "Chain your bike to my cart," he says. "Safer is not possible." Tony enters the place and orders two breakfasts in Spanish with grand gestures.

We take a table at the window and Tony points at his cart blocking the sidewalk. Pedestrians nearly bump into it, and their coats get caught in the aluminum picture frames that are sticking out. "Nobody dares to touch my cart," Tony says proudly. "They all know me here on Broadway."

Tony starts to tell me how he wound up in the tunnels. As an ex-convict who served his time, he has the right to get housing through a program called Section 8. But Tony has been on the waiting list for a few years. "I wound up in the shelter. Crazy dangerous. You get killed there faster than on the streets. You can't sleep in peace, there are always some guys sneaking around you. They steal your pants from your ass. I heard about the tunnel and built a little shack on the South End. But when the trains started to run, I had to leave there. Bernard offered me a spot in his camp. It is okay there. But a real house would be nice. Just returning home at the eve and putting your key in the door..."

As a young man, Tony lived on Staten Island with his stepfather. He worked as a bus boy and a dishwasher. Then he started a mattresses business with a friend. During the week, they roamed the streets of Manhattan, looking for mattresses put out with the garbage. On the weekends, they rented a truck and sold their harvest at a market at the Bronx.

"Good business," Tony says. "Sometimes we made a thousand dollars in a weekend. But then I got ambition." Tony becomes silent for a moment and lights a cigarette. The waitress yells that smoking is not allowed. Tony tells her to stop whining and offers me a Marlboro.

"You know what ambition is?" he asks. "Over there, that's ambition." He points at a big chocolate glazed donut with colored sprinkles in the window. It looks awfully delicious, and I nod at him that I get it.

"Okay," Tony continues. "I got ambitious and got greedy. I started to deal drugs. A few times I got caught by the police. But I was lucky. Every time, I was released on bail, paid by my step-parents. But the real trouble started in 1961. I started to use drugs myself. And you know, you need money to maintain an addiction. A lotta money."

Tony looks down at the floor as though he regrets his past. "We started to rob people. All in all I robbed a few hundred people. Sometimes I did two on the same day. And no bullshit with nine millimeters. These days, every kid walks around with a gun. In our time we did it bare handed. You see, I was very strong at that time. Everybody was afraid of me."

I look at Tony. He must be over fifty, but he still looks pretty tough. "And one time it went wrong. I had kicked a guy unconscious. The victim was brought to the hospital. The cops arrested me and I was thrown in a cell. After a few hours, a cop came in. 'You just killed a guy,' he said. 'How do you feel?' I was shocked and told him I did not feel anything because I did not believe I had killed a person. But it was true. The victim had died in the ambulance. I went before the judge, but I hardly understood anything. My English was not so good at that time. It was a kangaroo trial."

I look at him puzzled. "A kangaroo trial is when you don't understand anything that goes on. They tell you one thing, they do another. The attorney said I had to plead guilty to manslaughter. Then I would get a light sentence, seven to fifteen years. I told him I would go for the deal. At the trial, the judge asked if I knew why I was there. Yes, your honor, I said. Do you take the trial or the plea, he asked. I told him I take the plea. Are you ready for the sentence? Yes, your honor. Twenty years to life, was the sentence. I felt knocked to the ground. I just could not believe it. My step-parents comforted me. We will visit you, we will send you packages. But okay, there I was."

Tony goes further back to his past. Originally he is from Puerto Rico. When he was fourteen, he came to the U.S. "They call it adoption now," he says bitterly. "But I was just sold." His mother died young and left eight children. His father couldn't take care of them all.

The deal was closed in a cafe, remembers Tony. "I saw my father put a big wad of bills in his pocket."

"My step-parents were good people," he continues. "They had a nice wooden house on Staten Island and bought me a puppy. They flew over my sister because I missed her." Tony's stepmother died a few years ago. He doesn't talk to his stepfather anymore, not since the day he deeply offended Tony.

"I visited him last year for the holidays," Tony says. "He told me straight in my face in the presence of my sister; 'What's the matter. Is there no food in New York that you have to visit me?'"

Tony is silent for a moment, and then goes on about his prison experience. "Attica was terrible," he says. "Twenty-three hours a day you were in your cell. One hour a day they let you out. I can still dream the dimensions of my cell. After the riots, things changed. We got a TV in our cell, we got more recreation, they made a baseball court, we could work. I got a job as a maintenance painter. But fifteen years is a long time. Do you know what I mean? You don't think Monday, Tuesday, et cetera. You start to forget there are days and weeks and even months, you start to count in years. You gotta change your state of mind. They have your body, but they don't have your mind."

He pauses and lights up another cigarette. Arrogantly, he blows big circles towards the ceiling. The waitress has understood that we will just ignore the non-smoking policy, and she is not bothering us anymore. After confessing his past, it's like a large load has come off his shoulders and Tony is in a good mood. Confidently, he talks about his future plans.

"Actually, I am a designer. In prison I already made glass paintings. Now I got a brilliant design for a T-shirt." Tony unzips his fanny pack and takes out a carefully folded piece of paper. With great pomp and circumstance he unfolds it at the table, drawing everybody's attention. His design is a busy drawing of some serrated and fingered leaves, halfway between marijuana leaves and ferns. In the middle he has painted some orchid-like flowers. It looks like a psychedelic record cover from the sixties. Tony apologizes that the design is in black and white. "The original is in color but is at my sister's. Too valuable to keep in the tunnel. People might steal it."

Tony carefully puts his design back. "I am gonna print T-shirts of this. Three hundred pieces. I know the vendors on the Lower East Side, on Canal Street who will sell it for me. Twenty dollars apiece."

Tony grabs my pen and makes a calculation on a greasy napkin. "Three hundred times a fifteen dollar profit. You see, that is 4,500 dollars!" Tony hands me the napkin as proof of how much money he can make, as if he is looking for serious investors. He goes on enthusiastically. "Boy, you have to see it in color. Fantastic. Makes your head spin. The tourists at Rockefeller, they see me, they will run at me and ask me 'Where'd you get that design?' No hesitation!"

Tony jokes with the waitress and lets her refill our cups. "The people, they laugh at me when they see me with my cart walking the streets. Just let them laugh. I have more money in the bank than they."

Tony mentions a big inheritance that is waiting for him. For some reason, the money is blocked, maybe because he is on probation. It is a vague story I have heard before. True or not, it keeps him going. "I am in no rush. I know the money is coming," he says confidently.

Tony goes on about his plans. "I got ideas. I am working on creations and inventions. Not one, but ten at the same time. At least. I'll tell you three of them. I know how to stop a cab on the street. Do you know what I mean? You hold up your hand, but every cab whizzes you by. I invented a machine for that. Something else. I know how to stop a bank robbery in progress. I know. But I can't tell you."

With a face triumphant as though he just threw four aces

down on the table, he looks at me expecting me to faint with amazement and admiration. That does not happen, so he goes on. "Liquid earrings. I have a design ready. I am the only one who has it, it's here, in my mind. The ladies see it, they go wild! They'll all wanna have it…."

Overconfident, Tony starts to talk really loud now. People turn around with annoyed expressions. Tony loves the attention and elaborates on his invention to stop bank robberies. "I have the phone numbers of the top guys in banking," he says. "I just have to call them. And one other call, and all the TV networks are here. But only with my permission. If not, I'm gonna sue 'em!"

Again, he gets that triumphant look in his eyes. "But I can't tell you," he whispers secretively.

Tony rummages through his fanny pack and pulls out a business card from the office manager of the Chase Manhattan Bank. "Look, this is their headquarters at Fifth Avenue. They kept me waiting for goddamn fifteen minutes before giving me the card."

"You know," he goes on, "they come at the bank with a big truck to load and unload the money. You don't need no goddamn nine millimeter. Just a hand grenade." Tony gets up and gives a demonstration. I don't understand if he is showing his invention against bank robberies, or if he is showing me how to disarm a punk with a gun. He walks a circle in the coffee place, and sneaks up stealthily towards me. Then he pulls out his fist and holds it near my cheek.

"You keep the grenade at his face and you say: 'You wanna shoot me? I blow away yer face!'" The whole coffee shop is now looking at us. "I tell you, when they enter the bank with a big case and a bomb and they say 'Fill up the case, or we blow up the bank!' Yes, I know how to stop that! I am the tomato plant. I have creations like ripe tomatoes!"

Tony sits back down at the table and goes on in a secretive voice. "You know, tomatoes are very expensive in New York. It is not a vegetable but a fruit. A tomato plant grows in the earth and needs water…And…and…uh…" Tony is getting lost in his analogy of a tomato plant and realizes it is time to go.

Outside, we say goodbye. "You saw that man with that big notebook behind us?" Tony asks. "That was a writer. I saw he was eavesdropping on us. I bet he will approach me sooner or later to write about me."

9. BIG-ASS BEAMS

On a Saturday night, I hop on my bike and ride the twenty blocks southwards through the tunnel to Frankie and Ment's. I've started to like the two, and I bring a six-pack of Coors, their favorite brand. Coors is a politically incorrect beer because the owner is said to have close ties to the KKK. Frankie and Ment don't mind. I had a friend in New York who didn't know, and once threw a party where he bought a few dozen six-packs of Coors. All his liberal friends left in disgust.

"Doggies, doggies, keep quiet," I try to calm their barking dogs. They go more berserk, until the outside light goes on. Ment jumps outside and screams at the dogs till they stop.

Inside, Frankie and Buddy sit on the couch. They all have a serious hangover. Yesterday it was Frankie's birthday, his twenty-sixth, and the old crew came to visit. It became a wild night in "the club house," as they call their place. The whole night, they drank, smoked pot, and sprayed the walls with graffiti. The *High Times* centerfold is now filled with Ment's tags and taped to the speakers of their sound system. Frankie shows me their new electric heater, found on the streets. The other one was kicked to pieces during a wild party moment. They also have a new coffeemaker. This one is a computer-controlled machine, Frankie proudly explains, so you can program the number of cups and the temperature. A lady from the neighborhood who was moving out gave it to him.

Ment and Buddy have both moved in, and the space is getting small. That's why Frankie has decided to make an extra room. Maybe even another story. One of the walls will be broken down and they're going to make a "small-ass hallway" that can double as cloakroom and guest room. Double boarded, insulated of course, and possibly even with a drainage system.

Tonight they're going to get material from a building construction site at the South End. Ment did some exploration at the viaduct under construction and discovered a lot of big beams and twenty-seven sheets of plywood, each several square meters wide. More than enough material for Frankie's planned extension.

Ment opens the beers and plays a cassette of the hardcore rap group Onyx, his favorite band. It is the newest trend in rap, a crossover between heavy metal, punk, and hip hop.

With spastic movements, Ment mimes the words. Frankie, in the meantime, talks like a connoisseur about the evolution of rap music. The rock riffs that later became so predominant in Run DMC were already present in old school rappers like the Sugar Hill Gang and Grandmaster Flash. To prove his point, Frankie plays a song from the Sugar Hill Gang with heavy guitar riffs. Frankie doesn't like the notorious West Coast rapper Tupac Shakur, just accused of rape. "He's full of shit. He raps against violence against women, but he is just as bad."

The loud music brings back sweet memories for Frankie. For his fourteenth birthday, his father gave him a red Ford Mustang with the condition he wouldn't drive it until he was sixteen. Of course, Frankie couldn't have cared less.

"Blasting on the highway, no driver's license, no insurance, no fucking nothing!" Frankie reminisces. "This bad-ass sucker would go one sixty..." Frankie means miles an hour, not kilometers. He had installed a state-of-the-art sound system in his Mustang. "I tell you, a power blaster, a PA-system and on the back seat big stage speakers with, check this out, four big-ass woofers!"

After this wave of enthusiasm, he grows silent and stares at the floor. Maybe he thinks about his parents. Frankie had told me last visit more about them: His father was in the military. Most of the time, the family lived in and around bases. That's why Frankie has this military manner. His parents died in a car accident when he was sixteen. The spoilt brat suddenly became an orphan.

Frankie pulls himself together. "In fact, that's what I regret the most. That I don't have a car anymore." He finishes his racist beer and gets dressed for the night job.

It has to be a stealthy operation, so Frankie and Ment put on dark sweatshirts. With hoods up their white, bald heads are covered and invisible in the darkness. They check my clothes and approve, only my white scarf needs to be tugged under my dark coat.

Buddy's filthy, gray-brownish outfit is acceptable.

Outside, Ment and Frankie unlock two carts, releasing them from heavy chains. These are small but heavy carts, of the kind used on construction sites to transport cement and bricks. We have to push and pull them over the bumpy tunnel ground, over holes, stones, and railroad ties. They make an awful rattling noise that echoes through the whole tunnel. After some time, we see an orange glow in the distance, the South End.

Stumbling, we work our way slowly through the darkness, towards the light. Ment tells us about one time he discovered a huge pile of wood at the South End. It was too big and heavy to drag by hand in the tunnel. He stole a truck from the building site, and entered the tunnel driving over the path next to the tracks. He had gone all the way to Bernard's, honked his horn, said hello to a shocked Bernard, and then turned around. At Frankie's, he had unloaded the wood and honestly returned the truck.

After half an hour, we are only halfway there. We come to a dead end track with a bigger car on it, a contraption with small metal wheels that roll exactly on the tracks. We leave the two small carts and take the big car. On the front there is a big handle to push or pull it. The ingenious construction is the work of Joe and Kathy. To prevent the car from sliding off the tracks, they have even placed small beams on the side to keep the wheels in position.

Frankie and Ment pull the car and it slides smoothly over the tracks. With their hoods on their heads, they look like malicious smurfs. Buddy is lagging behind. It is obvious he doesn't like the trip, and would have preferred to stay home drinking beer and watching TV.

The moon and the park's orange streetlights illuminate the wood of the pillars at the tunnel entrance. Beams of light penetrate the darkness and throw spooky shadows on the walls.

Frankie shows me graffiti high on the pillars and metal beams of the ceiling. Ment and his crew made them. They must have performed neck-breaking acrobatics to get there, but that is exactly how graffiti artists earn respect.

Ment has suddenly disappeared. Using an emergency ladder, he has climbed onto the viaduct that's under construction, and is walking around looking for the loot he will throw down. After fifteen minutes, giant sheets come falling down from the five-story-high overpass.

"Stay clear," Frankie warns, "this will cut you right in two." Then a few sheets of plastic and insulation float down. We wait for more stuff, and Frankie points at the apartment buildings on the other side. One of them is the hotel where Buddy used to live. Top floor, all the way to the right was his room. "God, I wish I was back there...." Buddy sighs, shivering from the cold.

Buddy used to be a night watchman, but he lost his job due to drinking in particular, and being unreliable in general. He couldn't afford the hotel anymore and wound up on the streets.

Ment has come down and reports his findings. Too bad: the stack of sheets is gone. Maybe the construction workers used them to make casings.

We walk around the building site hoping to find other useful material. It is a poor harvest, just some beams and a few small plywood sheets.

Ment looks temptedly at a bulldozer. He wants to climb in and start it up. "So I can push out all the garbage in front of our house," he says. "It has become a lot dirtier since I left." Compared with Bernard's, it is indeed a filthy mess at Frankie's. In front of their home is a big stinking pile of household garbage mixed with dog shit. Rats rummage through it. Their toilet is only ten meters from the bunkers, but contrary to Bernard's hole that he keeps covered with sand like a cat, they leave their shit outside and the ground is strewn with soiled toilet paper.

Ment decides to leave the bulldozer; in the distance we see the lighted shack of the night watch. We carry the wood to Joe's cart and make a last round. On the bank of the Hudson is a strange metal construction between decaying and sinking piers. It is a high bridge, to load and unload barges. Like a tourist guide, Frankie shows me around the old desolate harbor that must be a paradise for industrial archeologists.

"This was the biggest commodity terminal of New York State," he says solemnly. "Warehouses, railways, cranes, it was a coming and going of trucks, barges and trains. We're talking the 1900s now," he adds, to complete the picture of the turn of the century. I can imagine the chaotic and busy ant heap of carriers, porters, and dock-workers, of horse carts, sailing boats, and big black smoking locomotives.

Ment invites me to climb the loading dock and together we scale the narrow staircase with its rusting and rotting steps, holding onto a shaky banister.

"Hello, anybody home?" Ment screams a few times when we are nearly to the top. Sometimes a homeless man sleeps in the engine room, and we don't want to startle him. He might kick us off the stairs. Nobody answers and we enter the engine room. It has a leaking tin roof, the floor consists of rusting beams and a heavy pulley. In the middle there is nothing, just a gaping black hole. On a couple of planks balancing on the rusty beams is a mattress and a few bags of clothes, a little saucer with milk—for a cat maybe—and a pair of rollerblades.

As on a tight rope, we carefully walk over the rusty beams. If the man gets out on the wrong side of bed, he will tumble down three stories of rusty beams, protruding nails, and pieces of wire mesh into the cold river. Maybe that has already happened. In the corner there is a bucket used as a toilet. Not really necessary, since there is not even a floor.

Ment takes me across some narrow beams and shows me the outside, where he has sprayed his tag. To make the piece, Ment had to balance on a one-inch ridge while another crewmember held onto his other hand.

We watch the skyline of the city. The Empire State Building towers majestically above all the others, and is bathed in green and red, the traditional Christmas lighting. Huge new apartment buildings are slowly popping up along the West Side Highway. It is a new project of Trump to revitalize the downtrodden West Side. The loading bridge we are in now will probably be demolished sooner or later to make room for a building with a generic name like "Hudson View."

Ment stares dreamily at the skyline and admits he told me some little white lies. In fact, he was in jail for a year and a half. But because they moved him to different institutions, in a way his story of a long trip in upstate New York was true. And don't tell anybody, but he's actually a wanted man now. He was allowed a weekend out of jail for good behavior, but he never went back. And by the way, Kathy and Joe are not his real parents. That was meant purely as a metaphor. His real father died a long time ago. His mother, who works on the West Side as a secretary, kicked him out because he was such a nuisance. Sometimes they still meet.

Back down on the ground, we drag the collected wood to the car. Buddy says he has to take a piss and he disappears behind some trees. He doesn't come back. "The asshole," Frankie swears while dragging the heavy beams. "Gone again." Ment in the meantime has found a huge wooden box that would make a great dining table.

Together, we put the box on Ment's shoulders, who staggers like an Atlas inside the tunnel. He groans under the heavy weight and finally throws the box on the cart. He bends over from the backache, an old stab wound starts hurting again

Frankie also suffers: "Fucking big-ass splinter. I'll kill that Buddy!" With a flashlight, we remove an inch-long splinter from Frankie's thumb.

A black man walks towards us. It's Clarence, who lives near the tunnel entrance behind a few sheets of plywood. Clarence is nearly crying and hugs Frankie. "Just heard I got the Monster..." he sobs. "I can kiss my black ass goodbye... Must have happened with that blood transfusion a few years ago..."

"We call it The Monster," explains Frankie, "because we are all scared as hell of it. And fuckin' easy to catch...Like the bogey man or Dracula when we were kids. But AIDS is real. My God, I've lost so many friends to The Monster..." Clarence introduces himself and gives me a firm handshake.

"Don't worry. You can't get it from shaking hands," he says, spreading a heavy smell of alcohol. After hearing the bad news, he must have seriously hit the bottle. Frankie gives the wobbling man advice. "Better get welfare and get the hell outta here before the winter starts. If it gets really cold, you won't survive here. One bout of pneumonia and you are gone." Clarence mumbles something incomprehensible and pulls two giant bullets out of his coat pocket, anti-aircraft caliber.

"They are live," he says shaking the bullets. We can hear the gun powder move inside the cartridge. Clarence wants to throw one against the wall.

"Don't play with this shit, man!" Ment says, frightened. "It's a felony carrying one of those," Frankie adds. Clarence says that he threw one yesterday against a metal pillar. "It went BAM!" he laughs. "The bullet ricocheted to all sides." It is impossible to have a reasonable talk with Clarence, and we take off.

It is difficult to push the car back over the tracks, since now it is loaded with a few hundred pounds of wood, plastic sheeting and insulation piled on top. Every time we push the car forward, something falls off or the little wheels derail. Instead of making a lighter load and doing two trips, Frankie and Ment stubbornly try to pile up the wood different ways. When the handle breaks, Frankie swears at Buddy.

"The filthy asshole always pulls these kinda tricks. Dirty-ass snitch. That's what we say in prison. Snitches get stitches. There is a reason he's missing his front teeth. Someone kicked them out because he talks too much." We unload Joe's big car and drag the wood a few blocks up to Frankie's small carts. Sweating and cursing, we manage finally to get everything home. Upstairs, the light is on. "You are disgusting!" screams Frankie even before he enters. Inside is Buddy in his dirty socks, watching TV.

"I swear to God, I lost you guys," Buddy cowers.

"Cheap bullshit excuses! You goddammit could have waited at the car," Frankie thunders.

"How should I have known?" Buddy answers desperately. And then, in a slimy voice: "Can I still help?"

"Fuck off," Frankie screams. "It's too late. Just stay inside."

Buddy must have snuck in through the park police's parking garage. Halfway to the South End, a small door gives access to the garage. "The last time he pulls something like that," Frankie says in a threatening voice while we pile up all the stolen wood. When we are ready and come back inside, Buddy is smoking nervously and shaking like a leaf.

"Stop shaking!" Frankie barks. "I still have a bottle of Jack Daniels, but you get nothing. Goddammit, if our man the journalist would not have been here," Frankie slaps me on the back, "he has been carrying big-ass fucking beams all night." Frankie slouches down on the couch and opens a can of beer.

Ment pulls off his dirty T-shirt to show me the scars from his stab wound. In sloppy capitals, CRIMINAL MIND is tattooed on his back. The scar must be right below the L, but I can't distinguish anything. He is disappointed and pulls down his sock to show me a scar on his ankle. "Some guy freaked out in jail and stabbed me with a screwdriver," he says coolly. Frankie in the meantime has come up with a good punishment for Buddy "You make sure there is money on the table tomorrow, goddammit," he yells. "Five, six dollars, some food, and dog food as well. Just walk my route and do all the plastics and cans. And don't even try to come back without money. Or your clothes will be packed up in a box outside on the dog cage."

Buddy is whining like a small kid. Frankie and Ment walk me out when I leave. They thank me again for my help. "No problem," I say modestly.

At breakfast I tell Bernard about the evening. He gets angry. "That Frankie! The guy is not even twenty-five, but he's already seen every prison from the inside. Crooks and thieves, that's what they are. They got criminal minds." Bernard probably never saw Ment's tattoo and doesn't realize how right he is.

"One time they came walking up the tunnel and I asked them what they were doing here. 'Oh, just taking a stroll to Harlem,' they told me. Bullshit! No way two white boys can hang out there safely. Later it turned out that Tony was missing a pile of books and a TV. I tell you, Dune, this guy Ment is gonna bring trouble in the tunnel."

Chris Pape also made the connection between Ment, Frankie and problems. "The two of them together..." he once sighed. "Looks like they have an irresistible attraction for problems. Trouble magnets, that's what they are." Kathy also shared her concerns about Ment. "Seems like his middle name is trouble," she once told me.

Bernard's scolding of Frankie and Ment merges seamlessly into a sermon about the Kool-Aid Kid. "This idiot. A whole dozen eggs disappeared. Had not one myself. And then this fool Tony trying to calm me down: 'C'mon B., can't be that bad...' Why in hell does Tony play public defender for the Kid? This has never happened before! The other day I told the Kid that he was driving me to a point where I was gonna crash his skull with a crowbar and bury him right behind the garbage pile. Fuck it! I'm gonna poison him. Goddammit, this time I'm gonna do it for real."

This is the third time that Bernard has said he's going to kill the Kid. Still, when the Kid sits with us at the fireplace, Bernard is always very friendly and hospitable. Bernard pours tea and farts loudly. "Hey, a good sign. That fruit basket is working. I feel my guts turning again." Yesterday I'd given him a few pounds of grapes, oranges, and bananas because he'd been feeling weak for a few days. It was the flu season, and a night of crack smoking with Manny did not help.

Joe and Kathy also felt unwell, and cancelled their appointment for the umpteenth time. I'd been to their door a few dozen times, but every time they had a different excuse. Joe has to go out and work, or Kathy has to see a doctor. Other times they just don't answer, even though I know they are inside. Bernard can't mediate, because it is clear that the folks at the South End don't like him too much.

Bernard withdraws to discharge himself, and comes back clearly feeling relieved. He continues cursing Frankie. "I told Frankie last time: 'Man, I don't have a problem with you, just got too much burial space.'" Bernard lights a cigarette.

"And then there is something else with that guy." He is silent for a moment. "I don't know if I should tell you…" he pours another cup of tea and looks at the fire…I am overwhelmed by curiosity. Finally Bernard tells the story.

"It is about Donny and Ricky. They were lovers and lived together in a wooden shack at the Southern End. Donny died last year of AIDS. Frankie visited Ricky once and they had a fight. Thing went out of control…" Tony has joined us at the fire and listens attentively. "Ricky is buried somewhere here in the tunnel," Bernard concludes. Tony nods and confirms the story. "The point is, they're not mean, but stupid," he says.

Bernard gets up and leaves. "If someone is asking for me, tell them I moved to fucking Sarajevo!"

Later that evening I knock at Bernard's door. Amicably, he invites me to enter. The crack pipes are finished and put away, and he pours me a cup of orange juice.

Agitated, Bernard tells me he was approached by a social worker. He was parked with a big four-wheel-drive at the playground by the Northern Gate. "The guy was giving me this sweet-talk like 'We are here to help you, we can get you an apartment' and all that bullshit. Fuck it, an apartment! Some rat hole, he meant. And then he dares to tell me: 'You got a problem? We can put you in rehab.' Really, Duke, what a fucking insult! You should have seen his eyes. This guy was obviously high himself!"

The social worker didn't know that drugs and addiction are sensitive subjects for Bernard. "I was just going to the store to cash three bags of cans," Bernard continues, "Do I look like I got a problem? If I was a real junkie, I would have shaken him of that fancy leather coat he was wearing. And then he said he was from Brooklyn. The fact that he is from there tells you the whole thing is bullshit. Don't they have any problems down there?"

I recognize Do-Gooder Galindez from Bernard's description, a social worker working for the community center a few blocks down the road. I had bumped into Galindez a few weeks ago while I was trying to enter the Northern Gate. "Poor souls," he spoke softly while pulling out a baloney sandwich from his coat pocket. "It's no life down there. Are you hungry?"

I told him I did not like baloney, but Galindez had already jumped out of his car. He had a small hunchback; his two frog eyes stared at me through heavy glasses. He asked me about life down in the tunnels. I broke out laughing and had to confess I was just a reporter living there. Suddenly his attitude changed. His well-meaning but condescending demeanor changed into something conspiratorial. From victim I had turned into partner. Four times he had tried to approach the tunnel people without much luck. He did not dare to go down himself. I suspected access to the tunnel people had become an object of prestige at his work. A few days later, I visited Galindez at his office.

I wanted to know more about his work, and thought maybe I could give him some good advice on what the tunnel people really needed. I had been living for three days in the tunnel, and I was dirty and smelly. In the waiting room, I bummed a cigarette from a homeless person. When Galindez took me to his office, he complimented me on how perfectly undercover and discreet I was. I did not get it. But a week later I made the mistake of calling the center and telling the operator that I was the tunnel reporter that had stopped by earlier. Galindez came raging onto the line: I had spoiled everything by exposing my real identity. Since then I'd left the do-gooder to his secret agenda.

Bernard has to laugh when I tell him the story. He shows me a pair of expensive gloves, a present from Galindez. "They were laying on the dashboard," Bernard says. "I told him, if you really want to help me, gimme the gloves, keep the sermon, and fuck off! And if you want to do some good deeds, whatever, do your deeds, but leave us alone. God has it on tape. They don't care about the people," Bernard continues. "Really, they don't give a shit. They care about themselves and their jobs. All those flim-flam artists, they give me nothing but a big-ass headache!"

Bernard has heated up: "Everybody wants to give you all of this. Man, I have been living here for eight years. I know how to do it. We are not homeless; we got shelter here. And a lot of folks are envious. We don't have to punch in that time clock every morning."

10. A RAT CALLED MOUSE

"I was lying on the couch watching TV when I saw this rat walk-ing on this beam against the wall," Frankie tells me.

"And then I grabbed my big-ass sledgehammer and smashed the small-ass motherfucker," I think he is going to say. But Frankie has recently developed a tolerant attitude towards the nasty ro-dents. "This crazy-ass rat, he looked me straight in the eyes, he said *peep,* and went his own way. You see, if you don't bother the rats, they won't bother you."

I'm having coffee over at Frankie's place. Kathy has just walked in and she is chain-smoking menthols. The TV is tuned to Oprah Winfrey, but all we see are hazy orange and green streaks. Some-times we vaguely discern Oprah's purple head. Now and then, Frankie slams his fist on the TV set, Oprah changes the color of her skin, and general reception remains lousy. It is also impos-sible to hear what she is saying, so we wind up discussing rats.

The night before, rats visited me for the first time, so I also had something to say about the subject. The rats started to crawl in one corner of my bunker, but soon they were under the bed, and occasionally even ventured across the blankets and my pil-low. Chasing them away didn't do much good, and I was in for a night of horror.

"Take Linda with you one night," Bernard advised me the next morning when I complained about my sleepless night over breakfast. "She will take care of it. And I don't wanna say it over and over again," Bernard chided me as a small child, "never leave food in your room." Upon inspection, I found the rats had eaten a bag of stale cookies I had thrown under the bed. A tiny piece of plastic wrapping paper was all that was left.

Tony once told me he was having problems with rats in his bunker. Out of necessity, he befriended one of them and started calling his new pet Mouse. The rat slept on Tony's pillow and soon learned all kinds of tricks. He could jump up on two feet and grab a piece of chicken that Tony would hold in the air. "Boy, Mouse could raise hell if I didn't feed him on time," Tony says softly. "When he was hungry at night, he would crawl over my face and start pulling my sideburns. Then I would have to get up and give him a saucer of milk." Poor sweet Mouse didn't live to see a happy ending. The ferocious Linda devoured him.

"You gotta keep friends with the rats," Frankie continues. Once in a while, he puts bowls with bread soaked in scrambled eggs outside. "It's damn simple," Frankie explains with his irrefutable logic. "If they can't find food outside, they will come inside to get it."

Kathy and Joe are never troubled by rats, because they keep thirty cats in their bunker. But unlike Frankie, Joe sees the rats as an enemy to be annihilated. Every once in a while, he baits the area with rat poison, which he mixes into meatballs. Joe uses extra strong rat poison, not the weak stuff used by the park police up top.

"Most rats have grown resistant to that stuff," Kathy says. "They eat it just like M&M's. It only kills the baby rats." She whispers it, as if she feels really sorry the war on rats is also taking innocent lives. Silently she extinguishes another menthol in the ashtray.

Kathy was an afterthought in a family of six. All her brothers and sisters somehow wound up as decent hardworking citizens all across the nation. With Kathy, things took a different turn. After one year in college, she dropped out and took a job as a secretary in midtown. But she suffered a nervous breakdown, and eventually couldn't afford her downtown apartment anymore. She moved into a tiny place on the West Side with her disabled mother. While walking her mother in her wheelchair, she met Joe who was selling books at Broadway. The two started meeting every day, and their chats became longer and friendlier. Eventually, they fell in love and got married, and Kathy moved in with Joe. The two of them are hard to talk to. Kathy is shy and suspicious of strangers who approach her; Joe is both reticent and grumpy. It is only here, at Frankie's place, that Kathy feels at ease and opens up to me.

I'm wondering what happened to Buddy. "As a matter of fact, I kicked him out," Frankie explains. "Couldn't stand the sucker no
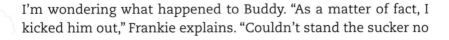

more. No respect for the rules. He's sleeping now in a cardboard box in the park."

There are few rules in the tunnel, but those that do exist are simple and self-evident. Nobody can violate them without being excommunicated or worse, being first beaten up and then kicked out. Simple rules. Respect each other's privacy. Help each other a little bit whenever necessary and/or possible. Do not steal each other's property. Show at least some form of consideration. "If you don't live by the rules of the tunnel…It's simple. You gonna die by the rules of the tunnel," Frankie had explained to me once in a deep voice. Buddy had indeed violated all the rules. He never went out to get water, never brought money back home, or even food for that matter. He was just gulping down beers, hanging out in front of the TV, and generally being an unreliable person and a rude loudmouth.

"It happened a week ago when we were all down with the flu," Frankie explains. "I was lying on the bed, feeling weak and sick. I asked him, 'Buddy, can you take a turn to get water?' Now, this drunk asshole started to create a scene. I told him to shut the fuck up and get water. Goddamn, the most natural thing to do. When I'm getting water, I always take some jerry cans for Joe along. Joe is getting old. You can't expect him to carry those ten-gallon containers all the way down."

"That's right," says Kathy and she lights up another cigarette. "Soon Joe will be fifty-four years old. Nineteen years he spent in the tunnel."

Frankie goes on: "Buddy went ballistic. Started to scream. It was just too much. I grabbed the motherfucker and kicked him outta the door. If it wasn't for Ment who cooled me down I would have thrown him off the roof. And all his clothes, I just tossed them behind his dirty ass."

"No good, the idiot. One night, Joe came in to borrow the ball cutter. He had lost his keys and wanted to cut through his lock." Frankie shows me the ball cutter. It's a gigantic pair of pliers with a sharp cutting edge of titanium. With this machine, Frankie can always cut through the chains the park police put on the gates.

"They got the locks, we got the cutters," Frankie proudly smiles.

"But all right. This is the deal: when I need something and I ain't got it, and Joe he's got it, he gives it to me. And of course the other way around. But Buddy freaked out. He started to yell at Joe. And you just don't do that to Joe."

"It's simple," says Frankie. "We're all living in the same shit. Might as well be nice to each other. When me and Ment were doing some construction work on the house last week, we first waited a few days till Joe and Kathy were all right again. They also had the flu and kept a few days in bed."

"That's right," confirms Kathy. "We all try to be nice."

Frankie goes on cooking chicken and tells another story to illustrate Buddy's unacceptable behavior. The two of them had managed to get tickets for Ricki Lake who had a special talk show on youth and crime. Frankie especially was looking forward to it, and all the smart things he was going to say from his firsthand experience. But Buddy was drunk and started a fight with one of the doormen. "It's sad," Frankie says. "I'm the kinda guy like *You sing together, you dance together*. Even before the show started, we were kicked out."

Yesterday, Frankie was also approached by an outreach worker. He holds the same kind of grudge as Bernard towards the do-gooders that try to intervene in his life. This time it was a friendly man who gave him a baloney sandwich and offered him a place to stay, that is to say, a city-operated shelter. Of course, Frankie was deeply offended.

"What the fuck do they think they're talking about?" Frankie says angrily. "A shelter and a lousy sandwich! I told the guy, 'Come to my place, I'll make coffee and cook burgers and we gonna watch the ballgame on TV.' But this asshole, he didn't dare to come down." It sounds like it was Do-Gooder Galindez again. "Something wrong with the system," Frankie ponders, "when you got those guys making thirty grand a year driving fancy cars and handing out baloney sandwiches."

When Frankie first arrived, homeless, in New York, he spent a few nights in the shelter. "You lie in this dormitory trying to sleep and the guy next to you on the left and another guy on the right, both of them are sucking on their crack pipes. At night, you'd better have kept on your shoes, else they were gone when you woke up."

"As a matter of fact," Frankie continues, "I just went to this shelter 'cause word was on the street that after three days they'd give you new sneakers." So Frankie waited for three days and finally got them. "It was a pair of real cool Converse All Stars. I tell you, brand new, straight outta the box. I tried them on and they fitted me perfectly. I said 'Thank you guys, but gotta go right now.' And right in front of their eyes I ripped up my shelter ID. And I was gone."

"It was just like jail," Frankie remembers. "You had to be in by 11 PM, and at 7 in the morning they kicked you out. When you entered, they body searched you for guns and drugs. And then there was this soda machine that didn't give cans, but plastic cups, you know, the same model they have in the prisons. The food was no good. Small portions, like a kindergarten lunch. In the morning just a small-ass box of cereal. No food for a grown up."

In another shelter a man tried to break into Frankie's locker. "Those were all my possessions I had left and this guy was going to steal it," Frankie says. "I got so mad at him, I smashed his face against the locker." After the man was rushed to the hospital with serious head injuries, Frankie was kicked out of the shelter. It was his last experience with the shelter system.

Kathy shares the same distrust of homeless agencies. "Us, they don't wanna help," she says bitterly, "because we are white and we don't do no drugs. If you're a black crackhead they give you everything for free. Honest people like us, they're left outside in the cold."

"Damn right you are, Kathy," Frankie interrupts. "When I just got homeless, I tried to apply for public assistance. They kicked me out of the welfare office. 'You're white, young, and healthy. Go out and get yourself a job.' That's what they told me. And every black or Puerto Rican who came in, they all left smiling and waving with a big check."

"But, I may sound like one," Frankie says moderating his earlier remarks, "but I'm not really a racist."

In a way it's true. Frankie and Ment might look like extremist skinheads, but most of their buddies hanging out with them in the tunnel are black or Latino. They all address each other as *yo, my nigger.* Taking into account also the rap music they love to listen to, the style of clothes they wear, the ghetto slang they talk, the trouble with the law they run into and all the graffiti pieces they do, Frankie and Ment have a lot more in common with kids from the black urban culture.

Frankie continues. "I tell you again, I'm not a real racist, but there's just one race I despise. And every time I cross 'em on the streets I still spit in their face. And that's the goddamn gooks. 'Cause of what they did to my father and what they did to Joe."

The Vietnam War is still not over in the tunnel. Frankie explains what happened to his father. "He was caught and kept POW. Fucking gooks tortured him for eighteen months before he saw a chance to escape. He never got over it again." Frankie bites his upper lip and stares at the floor.

"Joe did four tours of duty. He can survive a whole week just on a piece of bread and a pot of coffee," Kathy says proudly. But sometimes, Joe is plagued by flashbacks. "I'm afraid of him when he has drunk too much," Kathy admits. "Then he starts to scream strange things in his sleep." One of those nights, Joe went crazy and chased Frankie with a big jungle knife. Frankie had to lock himself up in his own place and wait till Joe calmed down.

"Can happen," Frankie shrugs his shoulders "We didn't make a big deal out of it. Next morning Joe came to apologize. He had had those dreams again."

"The Mayor thinks he has been here the longest, but I came twelve years earlier," says Joe. Kathy and Joe sarcastically call Bernard "The Mayor." "Not that anybody ever chose him," Kathy normally adds, full of venom. It is another few days before I finally get Joe ready to talk to me. This time he keeps his promise, so I am not knocking for nothing holding a six-pack of beers and a box of cat food like countless times before.

"I had to get away from my flashbacks," says Joe, "That's why I came to the tunnels. Here nobody is bothering me." A curious cat is sticking its head out of the door of Joe's bunker. Joe strokes the animal's neck. A few other cats come out and soon Joe is surrounded by a dozen meowing animals.

When Joe came to the tunnel twenty years ago, the premises were still being used as a terminal for trucks and freight trains. At first, he lived under a weight bridge at the entrance to the tunnel. "For years I was there without anybody even knowing," Joe says. "They thought I just was a railway worker. Later Jimmy the Juice came here. And Black Mike, a big negro. Good guy. We fought together in Nam." Jimmy and Mike left years ago. "Jimmy couldn't stop coughing, and Mike started to see weird things." Joe doesn't know where they went. "And Kovacs, he was also from that time," Joe continues. Kovacs was promised a movie deal after the *New York Times* article about him, but instead he just wound up with a nice wife.

In 1957, Joe joined the army. He never expected that seven years later he would be in a C-130 on his way to Vietnam, where he spent a total of four years. "We had three hundred kids in our division. Fifty is all that's left. Many died after they got home. Too much exposure to Agent Orange." Joe is eligible for veteran's benefits, but he's refused it. "I tried once. They wanted to give me only 10 percent of what I'm actually entitled to. Told 'em to go to hell. Never tried again. Don't feel like waiting in line."

He looks at the ground. "Four times wounded. Bullets, shrapnel, all this weird shit. I got a couple of metal bolts in my bones. And I tell you, it's not like in Westerns. You hardly know you are wounded, that's how fast it goes. Only when you look down, you realize what happened. And then you start to scream." Joe opens a beer and gulps down a Bud. "Any more questions?"

11. SUICIDE ON CHRISTMAS EVE

It is the day before Christmas. Not a White Christmas. It is dreary, windy, gray weather in the city. Santa Clauses roam around on Broadway. They wave big bells and try to sell the last Christmas trees for special prices. Bernard and I are sitting at the fireplace, listening to the radio. Instead of good rock and Bob Grant's right-wing talk show, his favorite station W1010 is now broadcasting non-stop Christmas carols.

"Fuck this Frosty the Fucking Snowman," Bernard grumbles. It's a funny American song about a merry snowman who, in fact, dies a horrible thawing death. Frosty accepts his fate courageously, actually quite cheerfully, but in a completely naïve way. We hear the song at least three times every hour. It drives us crazy. Bernard decides to go back to bed, I go to the South End to deliver my Christmas wishes.

It is not that cold, but a chilling wind blows through the wood pillars at the South End. Icicles are dripping from the ceiling. Last winter it was worse, Bernard told me. At that time there was a curtain of icicles, some up to fifteen feet long. One nearly killed him when it broke off.

At Clarence's, a fire is burning in an empty oil drum, but there is no one in sight. Little Havana is deserted. I don't even see any rats. Even they must have decided to stay in today. Deeper in the tunnel, a group of kids are coming towards me. Hoodlums that don't belong in the tunnel. As they come closer, I see Ment among them. We chat a bit, but Ment is aloof. The boys look uneasily at me.

One of the guys, a Latino with a wild expression in his eyes, scratches his back and as he pushes his sweater up, I see a shiny gun next to his beeper. I don't know if the kid showed it accidentally or as a veiled threat. I politely say goodbye and stop at Joe's; he is sorting out cans outside. We watch the group of kids. "Friends of Ment," Joe says indifferently. "Sometimes he hangs out with strange people." I wish him a happy Christmas. "Fuck Christmas," he says bitterly. "And you're also some kinda asshole to leave your wife alone back home at the holidays and hang around here in the tunnel."

Joe fakes indignation, and has a grin on his face for a moment. But soon he returns to his usual sad expression, the look he normally has. Joe told me last visit about his five daughters. Two were born dead. Two died as toddlers. It had to do with Agent Orange, according to Joe.

The devastating effects of the defoliation agent on human

genetic material were not yet known during the Vietnam era. His oldest daughter died when she was sixteen. Joe heard too late to go to her funeral; he had already been on the streets for a few years.

Christmas night. I am having a cup of wine at Bob's bunker and feeling sad. Every year I curse the holiday and family obligations, but Christmas underground is no fun either. Doing something with Bernard is not an option, as he remains incommunicado in his bunker.

I decide to offer Joe and Kathy the bottle of champagne a friend gave to me. The bitter way Joe said *Fuck Christmas* still rings in my ears. He could sure use a little present for the holidays. Also, I feel it is fitting to show the tunnel elders my respect. While I pack up my backpack, I hear a long train whistle, louder and longer than normal. Maybe the train conductor is blowing his whistle as a Christmas greeting to the tunnel people. I jump on my bike and ride with my flashlight to the South End.

After five blocks, it becomes clear something is wrong. In the slow bend of the tunnel, I can see the bright headlight of the train. It has stopped and blue flashing police lights flash along the walls. As I get closer to the 83rd Street exit, I see people walking around with powerful lanterns. I am blinded by one of their lights and stop my bike right in front of a police officer.

"Excuse me, officer," I ask as politely as possible. "Could you please tell me what happened?" The cop is flabbergasted.

"Who the fuck are you and what the fuck are you doing in this fucking tunnel?" I show my NYPD press card and explain I am working on a story about the tunnel. The press card is like a red flag to a bull.

"Git yer fuckin' ass outta here," he barks.

"But officer," I try again. "TO CROSS ALL POLICE AND FIRE LINES" is printed in big bold capitals on the press card.

"Now don't get fuckin' smart with me…" he screams. When cops start to talk like that, you know it's time to go. Quietly, I slip through the emergency exit. Outside is an ambulance and a few police cars. I try again with another cop. He threatens to billy club me with his enormous Maglite, handcuff me and throw me in jail. The message is clear. I leave the scene. Over the park roads, I bike to the entrance of the parking garage. There Frankie and Ment are nervously smoking cigarettes.

"What's up, Ant," Frankie greets me. "Did you hear what happened?" They have also been kicked out of the tunnel, but Frankie saw everything.

"Lady Bug started to bark so I took a look to see what was happening. Outside some idiot is stumbling on the tracks. I yelled at him not to walk on the goddamn tracks and went inside. That must have been the last words someone told him." Frankie leaves a significant silence.

"Those words obviously brought him little luck," Ment tries a joke.

"Shut up, asshole," Frankie says angrily. He is shocked by the accident and is smoking one cigarette after the other.

"A few minutes later I hear horns, whistles, hooting, screeching brakes. I knew immediately what time it was. I tell you: it was not an accident. It was goddamn suicide."

Frankie has seen the body. Tangled beyond recognition. P.O.—police officer—Anderson from the 20th precinct was there first, Frankie says. They know each other from the hood. "P.O. Anderson shone her flashlight on the man and asked if I knew him. I could only see he was black. Otherwise, he was ground meat. When I saw his brains dripping out of his head, I had to throw up." Frankie puts his hands over his eyes. "P.O. Anderson told me to go home and get a drink. The other cops that arrived after kicked us out."

We wait in the park for half an hour. Frankie tells us more about Anderson. "She's a cool cop. She often talks with us and sometimes we get a beer. Unlike most cops who are just out to fuck you." Ment now and then glances through the gate in the tunnel to check if the coast is clear.

Frankie and Ment have known Anderson for a few years. At one point, it started to smell terribly in the tunnel. Everybody thought it was a dead cat or rotting garbage. But Joe as a war veteran knew that it was the smell of a dead body. Ment called the police and they went on an inspection. Together they found the man somewhere hidden deep in a crevice. The body was partially eaten by animals. A rat came out of his eye socket.

"We couldn't find any traces of violence," Anderson said, when I interviewed her later at the precinct. "His hands were under his belly as if he were asleep. Probably he had crept into the cave to die in peace." About Frankie and Ment, she said, motherly, "They are not bad guys." Once she was harassed by a drunk guy from the neighborhood. Frankie and Ment had offered to "take care" of the guy. Anderson refused. "I fight my own battles. But it was a nice gesture. It was their way of saying 'P.O., we think you are cool and we like you.'"

Ment calls when the police have gone. "It's no good," Frankie says once we are back in their place. "This kinda bullshit only brings trouble in the tunnel. Why this stupid nigger had to kill himself of all places in front of my home? Soon, we all will be kicked out for good."

Ment is not interested, and plays with his beeper. That's how he stays in touch with the outside world: if someone beeps him, the nearest pay phone is two minutes away in the parking garage. I ask about his friends who I met in the morning. "Oh, nothing," Ment says, "just my crew."

Frankie wants to turn on the radio when we hear a loud bang, followed by a dog barking and whining. "Something goes wrong," Ment says dryly. He gets up, grabs the baseball bat, and jumps outside. Frankie follows him, his shoes not even tied. As I am about to follow them, they have already returned with Lady Bug in their arms.

"Oh my God," sighs Frankie. The dog groans and cries. The poor animal fell off the roof and was slashed by a protruding nail. Across her lower abdomen stretches a nasty cut, blood dripping from it. We put Lady Bug on the couch and use a flashlight to inspect the wound. It is nearly four inches long. "Fuck this tunnel," curses Frankie and he grabs his head. "And fuck this Christmas."

We discuss what to do. Going to a vet is out of the question. Most of them are not working on Christmas Eve, and it would take an hour of walking to get to the nearest one. And there's no way a cab would take us with the bleeding Lady Bug. On top of everything, a vet would cost a few hundred dollars. Without a cash advance, they wouldn't do anything.

The only thing remaining is to perform the operation ourselves. In my backpack I carry a sewing set, and my father was a vet. I used to look over his shoulder when he set broken sheep legs or delivered calves. I also remembered seeing in a Rambo movie how he pulled a bullet out of his shoulder with a knife, and afterwards sewed up the wound himself. Frankie and Ment have seen the movie, too, and are comforted. It can't be that difficult.

We need hot water and soap to shave the skin and wash the wound. Frankie heats the water in the coffeemaker and goes looking for soap. The only thing he can find is toilet disinfectant and detergent. The latter should do. While Ment and Frankie hold on to the dog, I clean the wound. Now we can see how deep it actually is. Frankie puts his hands in front of his eyes. "I can't see blood," he moans.

There is no razor, and so we try to cut away the hairs around the wound with blunt scissors. It is not easy. Surgery is much more difficult than we had imagined. The other dogs start to bark. The neighbors are coming home. "Let's get Joe," Ment suggests. "He got experience sewing up people in Vietnam." Ment returns with a bottle of aspirin drips. "Kathy told me first give this to the dog to sedate her."

We open Lady Bug's mouth and administer drops of the painkiller. The poor dog looks at us with frightened and fearful eyes. Now I notice how skinny and dirty she is. She smells awful, and leaves smudges and smears on my coat. A moment later, Joe enters with his sleeves rolled up. "What a night," Frankie says. "First this guy that needed to throw himself under a train in front of my house and now this with Lady Bug." Joe remains calm, lights up a cigarette and looks at the wound. "It's gonna be a difficult job," he mumbles.

Meanwhile, Kathy has also come up, and she strokes the moaning dog's head. "I told you so, Frankie, you need to make a fence," she says sternly. "This is already the third time a dog has fallen off."

"I know, I know," Frankie says impatiently. Joe goes to work. But the sewing set is clearly meant to fix buttons, not to sew dogs. It takes all our force to restrain the writhing Lady Bug while Joe grumbles and curses the needle and thread that keep slipping out of his thick fingers. The wound is big, and the skin as tough as the sole of a shoe. After half an hour, we give up. According to Joe, the only thing we can do is put a bandage around the dog and hope for a miraculous healing.

With duct tape and an old T-shirt, we bandage the dog. She now looks like a walking sausage and Kathy bursts out laughing. Lady Bug starts to feel better and wags her tail. Frankie's mood also improves when the dog licks his face.

It's late. I say goodbye and bike back to Bob's bunker. On my way home, I realize the champagne is still in my backpack.

Next morning at the grill, I tell Bernard about the suicide. He has already heard the news on the radio. "A train takes no prisoners," he comments simply. Actually, the news is now dominated by a new tragedy: A cop shot himself through the head just before midnight in Times Square.

Bernard pours a glass of white wine and steals nibbles from a piece of Emmenthal cheese. The delicacies are from a Christmas package that Sabine, the reporter from the French TV, gave him. Satisfied, he leans back at the warm fireplace and takes a sip of wine.

"What the fuck are they whining about?" he says. "If someone wants to leave from this earth, goddammit, he has the fullest right to do so." Bernard stares at the glowing embers. "Fuck it. We are still down here with our daily trouble. At least these two guys managed to escape."

Summer

June, July, August & September 1995

12. BACK IN THE TUNNEL

I return in the summer. I have been kept a little up to date by Margaret, a photographer who has been working for the past three years on a conceptual photo project in the tunnel. Every Sunday at 12 o'clock sharp, she calls through the intercom and goes around with Bernard for a few hours. He introduces her to other tunnel people, carries her tripod, and doubles as a bodyguard.

I met her last autumn for the first time in the tunnel. A spark of mutual antipathy sprang up between us. I can't help it; I just hate non-smoking vegetarians who always dress in black. Margaret questioned me extensively about my work methods and potential publication possibilities, even wanted to know the size of my notebooks. She herself was very stingy with giving info.

But somehow, we stayed in touch. We are sitting at a sidewalk cafe in the East Village, close to the prestigious Cooper Union School of Arts where she works as a professor. "That's one fifty for you," prof Margaret says as she puts a paper cup of espresso in front of me. We discuss the tunnel situation. Amtrak has resumed its efforts to evict all the tunnel people. Every year, they try the same thing, but this time it looks like they are serious. The Amtrak police have been to the tunnel a few times, and have told everybody they needed to leave in a few weeks. A British documentary maker, Marc Singer, was nearly arrested. Singer was shooting a black-and-white 16 mm documentary last winter and spring. A few weeks ago, he ran into the arms of Captain Combs, the feared chief of the Amtrak police.

Captain Combs is a black woman, a difficult combination for someone working in a white, macho, male police culture. That's maybe why Captains Combs opts for a ruthless Law and Order policy. The captain pointed out to Singer that he was trespassing on Amtrak property. Next time, she would arrest him and confiscate his equipment. *No kidding!*

I shiver. The captain seems like a woman I should try to avoid. Or maybe visit and start a charm offensive.

Margaret tells me the latest. The Coalition for the Homeless, one of the biggest advocacy organizations, is trying to find alternative housing. But things go slowly.

"Looks like the people down there don't want to be helped," she sighs. "And all these poor cats, what should happen to them?" She has already contacted an asylum where all the animals can be sheltered in an emergency.

Reluctantly, Margaret gives me the name of Mary Brosnahan, director of the Coalition. She pronounces the name a few times so fast I can't understand it. Only after I explicitly ask how to spell it does she write down the name on a stained napkin. She doesn't know how to reach Singer. And Captain Combs is somewhere in Penn Station. Where exactly, she can't tell.

I call the Dutch Consulate. Is it true I can be arrested when I enter the tunnel, even if I am an accredited journalist?

"Yes," is the reply.

In that case, what can the consulate do for me?

"Not much," is the answer.

So what do they advise?

"Don't go to the tunnel," they say.

I thank them for their help.

It is not possible to reach Captain Combs by phone, so I go look for her at Penn Station. It is a huge station. Eight subway lines stop here; it is also the terminal for the Long Island Railroad, New Jersey Transit and the Amtrak line to upstate New York, the train that runs through our tunnel.

Finally, I manage to find the office of the Amtrak Police. It is a tiny place in a corner near the toilets. Captain Combs is not there, and a friendly black lady receives me. Officer Samaliya is her name.

"What a nice name," I say. On her well-rounded hips, she carries a Glock, the new service weapon of the police. Because of its enormous firepower, the weapon is controversial. Officer Samaliya sees me staring and smiles shyly. I decide to be straight with her, and tell her that last autumn I lived down in the tunnel.

"In between the rats and those creeps?" she asks in disbelief. She doesn't mention the fact that I was trespassing.

"It was not too bad," I say. "Hardly a rat and I met a lot of nice people. Actually, I had a good time." Samaliya giggles softly.

I carefully ask whether she has also heard the rumor that Amtrak wants to kick out the tunnel people. "For everybody's safety, of course, we want to have the tunnel empty sooner or later," she says decisively. "But of course we will not kick people out. We will look for a humane solution." Her deep brown eyes look deeply into mine. I can do nothing but believe her.

At the Coalition for the Homeless, the new computerized phone system is not only annoying and time-consuming but expensive as well. It eats up all my quarters at a pay phone. It seems much faster and cheaper to stop by their offices.

A bored receptionist is reading *Vanity Fair*. She hardly looks up when she tells me in a rude and uninterested voice that Mary Brosnahan is on holiday. After a lot of pleading, I manage to talk to her replacement, Bob Kelty. Kelty chews on a pencil and knows little. Yes, there seems to be some federal program to provide housing for the tunnel people. Who, where, what and when is unknown to Kelly. Mary has all the information, come back in two weeks, Kelly says.

The sun is straight above me as I lie flat on the grate at 95th Street and call out Bernard's name. The tracks are bathed in sunlight. The rest of the tunnel is pitch dark. A few minutes later Bernard answers. He recognizes me. "The gate at 91st Street," he screams. I remember there was an exit there, but we never used it since we had the keys to the Northern Gate. I find the gate hidden behind bushes at a pedestrian tunnel under the West Side Highway. One bar has been sawed through and I manage to squeeze myself through the opening. Down the stairs, Tony has obviously created a new storage space: piles of empty bottles, sneakers, books, and a few old teddy bears. Down on the tracks, Bernard is walking towards me. We embrace each other as old friends. "Welcome back, Duke!" he says happily. "I had expected you earlier."

Bernard is dressed in his summer clothes, shorts, bare chest, and light sneakers. Compared with the sticky heat outside, the tunnel is nice and cool. Bright rays of sun have managed to penetrate the tunnel though the grates and have driven away the dampness and deep darkness of last autumn.

We lounge in chairs in the sunlight, and Bernard reports on current and past events. "Oh, Dune, it's terrible. Disorder and chaos all around!" He lost the keys of the gates. "This bitch Combs…" he growls. From a confused story, I understand that Captain Combs entered the tunnel with a crew of officers. At first, she had started a friendly chat with Bernard, who as usual, had told her all about tunnel life and the philosophy behind it. The good Bernard also let slip that he had the keys to the gates.

"That is interesting," the captain has answered slyly. "Can I see them?" It was like the fable of the Raven and the Fox. Bernard had shown her the keys in his outstretched hand. The captain had immediately snatched the keys, leaving a furious Bernard powerless against a crew of armed cops. Bernard is considering steps. Which, he doesn't know.

There has also been a fire in Tony's place. Sleazy Jeff was to blame, Bernard says. Jeff was smoking crack when a few candles tripped over. He was "high as a motherfucking cake" and had run away in panic. Tony stores a lot of inflammable materials, and soon his place was engulfed in flames. Black clouds of smoke rose through the grate. Bernard was taking a nap and woke up to the sirens of the Fire Department. They stuck their fire hoses through a hole in the grate. Not only the trains, but also the traffic at the West Side Highway came to a standstill. Firemen entered through the emergency exits and put out the fire.

"They also took care of your place," Bernard says. The firemen wanted to take a look to see if there was any danger in Bob's bunker. Bernard had offered to open the lock, but they had already smashed the plywood sheets at the windows. "They were only out to destroy everything," Bernard says angrily. Jeff has disappeared in the meantime. He is in rehab upstate.

Tony hasn't changed a bit. Still full of great and genial ideas to get filthy rich in one masterstroke. Shaking his head, Bernard tells me his latest plan. Together they would dig a tunnel to Broadway. There they would tunnel upwards to enter a jeweler's store. Broadway is parallel to the tunnel, only half a mile to the East. According to Tony, they could not miss. He had just not realized that you need sophisticated drilling equipment to cut through the solid granite rock that New York is built on.

He still has his gambling addiction. "The idiot won seven hundred bucks last time. I told him. 'Tony, lend me a hundred so I can do some two-for-oneing, and use the remaining six hundred to go finally print your T-shirts.' 'Let me think,' Tony said. And what happened next morning at breakfast? He is bumming a cigarette from me. The idiot had lost all his money the same day on the horses."

Bernard updates the tunnel news about Burk, the black man from ten blocks up north. Burk is slowly sliding away into his madness. Not very surprising. Last autumn, he already made an impression of complete incoherence, and could only mumble vaguely when asked something. The latest news is that he is starting to harass others and has developed aggressive tendencies. "Last week I was up top to cop a couple of bottles," tells Bernard in an agitated staccato voice, "a few for me, a few for Burk."

This is the usual way business is done. Bernard knows the reliable dealers up top and never gets fooled or tricked. Since he also knows how to evade the cops and is very discreet, he normally gets the stuff for Burk, Bob, Manny, or other guests. For his efforts, he gets one or two bottles.

Burk paid for his crack with a bag of empty cans. "One hour later, Burk came and demanded his cans back. I told him to keep his hands off. The idiot started to rave and rant and told me it was theft. He threatened to call the police. I said: 'Go ahead, asshole. Up top is the fucking phone.'" Burk left but later returned with a big metal bar. Bernard only barely ducked the attack. "I tell you, Duke, with a little less luck, I would not have been here," he says shaking his head. "I chased that idiot all the way to the South End with a big wooden stick." A few days later Burk returned. For the moment, the two are on speaking terms, insofar as Burk utters anything sensible.

"Frankie, still the same little prick. Big mouth, small heart." Frankie came a few weeks ago knocking on Bernard's door. After too much drinking, Joe got his flashbacks again and thought Frankie was Vietcong. He had threatened Frankie with a baseball bat. "Our macho comes running here for twenty blocks and cries and begs me for help, Bernard says sarcastically. Bernard and Kathy managed to calm Joe down.

Frankie's buddy Ment was hauled back to jail. On a nice sunny day, he was hanging out in the park with some friends and having a beer. Some cops in a patrol car drove by, they rolled down their window, just to ask about a fugitive who had been spotted in the park. Ment panicked and ran away. In a few minutes, the cops got him and found out he was on the run as well.

How about Marcus? "Still as crazy as the Mad Hatter," Bernard replies. "The idiot gets five hundred bucks of welfare every month, but never got the idea to get a new lock for the gate. That's up to me to take care of. And every month the same thing. When he gets his money, he is gone for three, four days. Partying."

Bernard also has had to deal with vandalism, a new plague from up top. During school holidays, adventurous school kids venture into the tunnel with spray cans. Among graffiti artists, it is a code of honor not to spray on someone else's work, but a few pieces by Chris Pape have been defaced with sloppy tags. "The kids of today," he grumbles. "No respect for anything." Bernard plays the bogeyman now and tells the kids that the tunnel is inhabited by murderous crackheads and sadistic pedophiles. "You should see them run," he laughs.

The coffee is ready and he pours me a steaming cup. Dramatically he raises his hands above him towards the grate. "Oh my God. Why are you sending me all these morons who only disturb my peace of mind?" Then he turns around and tells me: "I am completely fed up being the only responsible guy between a bunch of infantile imbeciles. And this time I am goddamn fucking serious."

Bernard tells me his plans to leave the tunnel are becoming concrete. The first step is to get all his papers together and get onto welfare. Maybe he can go to a cheap hotel, maybe the coalition can arrange something.

Bernard is already participating in the newest coalition experiment: a few hundred homeless people have been given voice-mail numbers. The experiment has been successful: homeless people can escape from their isolation; some of them have even found jobs.

We take a look at Bob's bunker and assess the damage. We have to board up the windows again. No big deal, Bernard has a hammer and plenty of nails. Inside, not much has changed: the piss bottles are still there, only their contents have thickened a bit. A new layer of ashes and dust, fallen from the ceiling, has formed on my worktable. The small whiskey bottles I used as candleholders have not moved a millimeter. Bob has been back a few times, but he only sits on the couch using the little coffee table that is again filled with drug paraphernalia. And I see to my surprise that Bob has taken over my habit of folding the blanket neatly in a square. I say goodbye to Bernard. A few days later I will return to repair the bunker and settle in again.

I am trying to reach Mary from the Coalition. I start to understand their phone system and manage to reach an operator. Mary just stepped out, I am told, Mary is in a meeting, Mary will be back in a moment. Mary this, Mary that. After half a dozen calls, I start to count. I have already written her a polite letter explaining that I have spent some months living in the tunnel, and that I am now doing research on organizations that help the homeless.

After calling for the forty-seventh time, I am fed up. I show up at the office. The operator is now doing crossword puzzles. She has the same bored look on her face; it turns a bit dirty when I explain to her that it seemed easier to stop by in person after making forty-seven phone calls in vain.

When I tell her I am from Brussels, she gives me a puzzled look. I have to explain to her that Denmark is not the capital of Brussels, but that I am from the Kingdom of Belgium, which happens to be in Europe. "You know," I add. "That continent on the other side of the ocean."

Behind the annoyed operator is the employee schedule, a big whiteboard with the initials of all staff members. White magnetic disks provide the reason for absenteeism. I see four discs with "sick," two "holiday" discs, one "to the bank" disc, two "in a meeting" discs, one "jury duty" disc, three "lunch" discs, two "out in the field" discs. Mary B. is not absent. Actually, in a few minutes she will be up front, I am told.

The few minutes have turned into an hour before Mary Brosnahan appears. She has decided to give me only ninety seconds. She doesn't have a press kit, just a carelessly designed flier about the Coalition. She confirms that there is a program to find alternative housing for the tunnel people. The program has been initiated by some secretary for housing. The secretary has appointed ten organizations to execute the pilot program. Which organizations, Mary doesn't know. Someone in the HPD, the New York City Department of Housing, Preservation, and Development has the list. Who exactly, she can't tell me. She does know the name of the secretary, but just like Margaret, she has the annoying habit of pronouncing the name too fast to be intelligible. She sloppily jots it down with manifest reluctance.

"Do you want to go down?" Mary asks. She has not understood that I have already lived "down" there for a few months, and that I don't need an introduction. Her face brightens up when I explain this to her. She tells me she is getting tired of journalists who approach the coalition to be introduced to the mole people.

"We are having a lot of problems," she confides. "It takes us a long time to gain the confidence of a tunnel dweller, and suddenly a slick journalist enters the tunnel and pretends he works for us or has spoken to me. 'I'm cool, I spoke with Mary.' And there goes the confidence that we worked so carefully on."

A *New York Times* article explains a lot. It is November 1994, and Henry Cisneros, secretary of the Department of Housing and

Urban Development, descends into the dark caves of the subway tunnels. He steps on used needles and human excrement. A rat nearly crawls up his pants. The secretary shivers, and nearly falls on the third rail with its lethal six hundred volts.

Secretary Cisneros is not on his own. Charles King and Keith Cylar, directors of Housing Works, an organization that caters to HIV-positive homeless, are guiding him around. A lot of their clients originate from down in the tunnels.

Cisneros is shocked. He asks a tunnel person how he could help him. He gets a simple answer: "Do you have a room for me?"

"We all ought to be ashamed that there are Americans that have no better place to live than with filth and 100-year-old dust," Cisneros declares the next day in the *Times*.

Cisneros throws in nine million dollars and 250 Section 8 vouchers. Section 8 is a federal program that provides subsidized or free housing for a very small percentage of the poor, as well as for emergency cases, helping victims of natural disasters or wounded war veterans.

Of the few dozen organizations in New York that cater to the homeless, the Secretary has chosen seven that will distribute the vouchers. They have been selected on the basis of their experience with the underground homeless. Among those appointed to take care of the Amtrak tunnel are Housing Works, the Bowery Residents Committee, whose outspoken director Eric Roth I would meet later, and Project Renewal.

The Coalition is not among them; they specialize in lobbying for the legal interests of the homeless. They have a tough reputation on this: in 1993, the Coalition sued the city when they wanted to make it illegal to panhandle in the subway. The Coalition said the prohibition went against the Fifth Amendment. The city won the case. In a new case, the coalition is suing the Amtrak police for using excessive force to kick homeless people out of Penn Station.[4]

Mary Brosnahan is also mentioned in the *Times* article. In the media, she is a well-known homeless expert who regularly gives her radical opinion. Not surprisingly, Mary is very critical.

She calls Cisneros' program ineffective in the direct quote from the *Times*: "If the same secretary who's trying this bold move is willing to give us a hundred- or a thousandfold this number of Section 8 vouchers, that will make a difference. But this demonstration program will not."

It's a piece of cake to make an appointment with the directors of Housing Works, and within a few hours of my first phone call I am already sitting—with a big press kit—at a table with the helpful vice director Keith Cylar. While Cylar only has a few meetings a month with the housing secretary, they know each other very well. "After Cisneros read a few articles about tunnel people, he asked me for a tour," explains Cylar, an unusual step for the secretary. "Up until now, only a few tunnel people have taken advantage of the special offer. The problem is that a lot of the homeless can't just go move into an apartment. We have to offer them a complete package of mental help, health care, and rehab. It takes time to make the people housing ready. Cisneros overlooked this in his enthusiasm."

Cylar tells me that for many people who wind up at Housing Works it is already too late. "Only when they get the first symptoms of AIDS and are getting really sick, they come up. Housing then can't help them anymore."

The budget cuts in social programs are another big problem. On all levels of government, conservative Republicans are in power: George Pataki as senator of New York State; Rudy Giuliani as mayor of New York; and the Republican majority in congress headed by the right winger Newt Gingrich. All have little patience with expensive programs that don't result in immediate economic profit. "A cold wind blows over this country," concludes Cylar somberly.

13. LITTLE HAVANA

"This crazy-ass bitch Combs…She fucked me with no grease…" Bernard is still raving mad at the Captain and curses her to hell while we try to saw through the chain at Marcus' fence. Drop of sweat form on his forehead while I try to hold the chain that keeps slipping away under the saw. Up top we have bought the best saw and the heaviest lock. We intend to put our lock on the chain while we leave the Amtrak lock there as well so everybody will be happy: they can enter with their key, we with ours.

Sitting on the stairs, Marcus watches our work with great interest. Last winter it did not work out for him to go to Florida. Now Marcus wants to go to New Mexico. In a few weeks the annual meeting of the Rainbow People is happening there. Do I have a car and am I planning by any chance to go that way? I have to disappoint him.

Marcus jumps from one subject to another, and now starts to talk about the South African photojournalist Kevin Carter who won the Pulitzer Prize, and Primo Levi with his Nobel Prize. Both committed suicide. "I don't understand," Marcus says. "These people had fame and money and still were not happy." From one of his archival poopy bags he pulls out an article from the Village Voice about the tragic end of the photographer. Carter achieved world fame with his image of the starving African child and the vulture. "Gimme chicks and beer, I'm happy…" ponders Marcus.

Marcus' non-stop waffling drives Bernard crazy. "Stop talking and help me sawing, will you? Why am I always the only one doing all the work?" Guiltily, Marcus starts to saw while Bernard lights a cigarette. But Marcus is clumsy and the saw goes in all directions except through the chain. Impatiently, Bernard takes over and one hour later we have cut it.

"*S'il vous plaît, Monsieur Marcus.* You are welcome." With an exaggeratedly polite gesture, Bernard opens the gate for Marcus who trudges outside with his plastic bags. "Incredible," mumbles Bernard. "Didn't do a thing and yet the first to use the gate."

As we walk back to board up Bob's bunker, Bernard starts up again about Captain Combs. She had the audacity to come down a few days ago in the middle of the night with a film crew from Amtrak. Before evicting everybody, they obviously want to document life underground. Combs even brought a delegation from the Russian Railways with her, all curious to see the problems of their American colleagues. Predictably, Bernard had become furious. "I called her a bitch in front of everybody," Bernard recounts. "Can't you be a bit nicer?" the captain had answered.

"The bitch has a lotta nerve," Bernard continues. "First she steals my key, then she disturbs my sleep in the middle of the night. And then she expects me to be nice and polite? What was I supposed to call her? A butterfly?" The biting way Bernard pronounces "butterfly" sounds even more of a curse than "bitch." Angrily, he is driving the nails extra hard with the hammer into the window frames of Bob's bunker.

"The bitch. How dare she. But her terror game with me won't last long." Bernard tells me about the Coalition's court case against Amtrak. Videotapes have emerged that clearly show Amtrak officers abusing homeless people in Penn Station. "I tell you, Turn, she's on her way out…"

I clean up Bob's bunker, empty the ashtrays, put new candles in the whiskey flasks, and wipe down the table and chairs with window cleaner and kitchen paper. The wads of paper are pitch black and it takes lots of Windex to clean the table to an acceptable level. I make a special corner for my toiletries and hang the towel high to keep it away from rats.

I even dare to touch a few of the piss bottles and throw them away, wrapped in three layers of newspaper and left on the pile of garbage six blocks down. When the candles are burning and the radio is playing, I light a cigarette and pour myself a cup of hot, fresh coffee from the thermos. I am a lucky bastard. A heat wave is hitting New York and the temperature in my room in Brooklyn is in the hundreds. Beneath my window there, young black guys are hanging out all night drinking beer, while yelling "Yo, brother, chill out…" and "Hey man, how's ma nigger doin'…" They slam car doors and play hardcore rap on their ghetto blasters full volume. Here in the tunnel it is cool and peaceful.

Later on that day I go to the South End. Halfway there I meet Joe and Kathy who are putting cans in a shopping cart. They look good. Joe's wrinkled parchment-like skin has become a bit smoother and more tanned. Kathy has glowing cheeks and proudly shows me their new litter of kittens. Friendly, Joe inquires about my wife and family back home. We chat a bit about all sorts of things, but soon get to the upcoming eviction. "It is because of the apartment buildings of Trump," Joe says. "People who buy a place for one million don't want to look at homeless. But they will never kick me out," he says rebelliously. "I wrote that bitch Combs a letter that I would never leave. Over my dead body!"

So Joe and Kathy have also been visited by the evil captain. Joe doesn't trust her for a dime. I try to put him at ease. "If it really gets serious, we'll make a couple of calls and in no time all the networks will be down here," I say confidently. Joe is pessimistic. "Okay, man, that won't help anything. You know what happened on 13th Street? They sent in the tanks." Joe mentions a recent eviction of a squat on the Lower East Side. The squatters had sued the city but had lost the case. They refused, however, to vacate the building voluntarily. The police had arrived with special anti-terrorist units who, backed up by armed personnel carriers, had stormed the building. Journalists had to stay fenced in, five blocks away in a so-called press box. Anyone who ventured outside the box to catch a glimpse of the eviction had his press card confiscated or was beaten up and arrested. Joe looks at me with a serious face.

"Maybe you are right," I say.

"You bet," he says. "I have to go now. Gotta bust some cans."

Frankie is not home, and I continue towards the South End. At the entrance, José, a big Puerto Rican man, is lounging in a garden chair. A refreshing breeze is blowing through the tunnel; outside it is over a hundred degrees. I wave to José, but he gives me the finger and takes a sip of vodka from the bottle resting within arms length. José is still angry because I took his photo once without asking. I tried several times to make up, but with no success. Too bad. Can't be friends with everybody.

A little bit deeper in the tunnels is Little Havana. I am curious to see how Ramon, the former Marxist-Leninist professor, is doing. Maybe he is still in rehab, maybe he's back in the tunnel. A light is burning in his old house, and I knock on the door.

"*Ramon no está aquí,*" someone says. After a few noises, a nervous man with a bat in his hands opens the door. It is Estoban, the unwashed Cuban with the big beard, looking just as bad as before. He still remembers me and we chat a little, but he is clearly not at ease. Looks like I interrupted him in something.

From out of nowhere, a small guy suddenly pops up.

He has a crew cut, a mustache and an aggressive expression in his brown, glassy eyes. "Who the fuck are you?" he says with hostility. I explain who I am. It's only when I tell him that I stay in Bernard's camp, that he starts to become friendly and introduces himself as Julio.

"We just finished working and are taking a break," he says. "We still have to clean ourselves up. Come back in an hour, then we have all the time to talk."

Estoban is sitting on a stretcher, Julio on an icebox when I return later. They offer me a plastic garden chair. Little Havana consists of five wooden shacks around a small open space, like a village square. Two kittens play on a table piled with groceries. "Our new kitties," Julio says proudly. "They are called Peluza and Sin Nombre." The cat without a name jumps on his lap. Bernard gave the kittens to Estoban and Julio. They are Linda's babies.

Little Havana is built on top of, and nearly swamped by, garbage. Rats crawl around in the filth. Julio is questioning me, and I tell him about my travels and show him a *High Times* magazine with an article I wrote about the genocide in Rwanda. He slowly reads it aloud and I have to explain what genocide means. He shakes his head when I tell him about the mass killings. "Wow…That sucks…"

After a lot more questions, I pass the test. Julio has approved of me. Now we have to talk about compensation. Moviemaker Marc Singer also pays him to help to carry lights and heavy batteries. Soon, we have reached an agreement of fifteen bucks a day. Then I can take photos of him and question him about tunnel life. If it is easier, I can also pay in beer and cigarettes. Julio immediately asks for an advance, and sends Estoban out to get "a couple of brewskies."

"I want to know who I am dealing with," Julio explains. "Most reporters here have no respect for our privacy. They think they can just come here, walk over and take a few pictures. Then they go and we never see them back again. And they leave us in our shit."

Estoban returns with a six-pack of Country Club, a cheap but strong beer full off all kinds of artificial additives. Officially, it is not even called beer, but malt liquor. Estoban gives me back exact change. Julio puts a can to his lips and gulps down nearly an entire pint.

"It's fucked up. We are dumped as garbage. We live from garbage and we are treated as garbage. Forgotten and ignored by the world." He takes a second gulp of beer and throws the empty can over his shoulder. "Nobody is accepting empty Country Club cans," he explains. Only the two-for-oners uptown in Harlem will take them.

Julio is twenty-six and has already been homeless for five years. He was born in a Puerto Rican family in the Bronx, but as a kid he grew up on the island. At high school age, he moved back with his father to the U.S., to a town in upstate New York. "And there my life started to fall apart. Crack and coke. The same old story."

Julio opens another brewsky. "When they came out with the slogan 'Crack Kills!'...I tell you, that's not exaggerated. Selling your fucking underwear for a hit...Some people could control their use. I couldn't." Julio says he hasn't used for a year. "I had to stop 'cause I got heart problems. Woke up one morning and my heart was booming crazy. Thought my chest would explode."

The sun is setting and the pillars at the South End bake in a warm, orange glow. Somewhere in the tunnel, a blackbird starts to sing. "There she is," Julio says, and points me at the bird that sits high on top of a T-beam. Julio whistles a few tones and the bird responds. "Same thing every day at this hour. And each morning she awakes me with the same song."

Julio opens his third pint of Country Club. A thundering train rolls by and shakes the houses. Little Havana is only ten meters from an active track.

"Assholes from Amtrak," says Julio when he is audible again above the noise. "They can't just kick us out and bulldoze our homes?" Then he stares at the ground and shakes his head. "Rats, dust, dirt, diesel fumes, what a fucking place to live."

Behind us we hear the rustling of a plastic bag. "Filthy animals!" screams Julio and kicks a big, square bag. Two rats jump out. He takes the bag and inspects the contents. Records of Beethoven, Mozart and Tchaikovsky. Luckily, the rats have not nibbled on the covers. "We deal in records, books, and cans," Julio explains. They find the books and records in the garbage; a lot of literary critics and book reviewers live on the liberal Upper West Side and they get swamped in review copies. Some supers set the books apart to help the homeless. Depending on the quality, a book or record can make anywhere from ten cents to a dollar at the booksellers who have their stands at Broadway.

An old man with a gray hat joins us. Julio introduces him as Getulio, "our kitchen chef." The man gives me a weak handshake. He has dark bags under his sad eyes. Getulio is also from Cuba. He speaks better English than Estoban, but he is the silent type. He withdraws into the kitchen, a shack behind us with an electric stove and a cupboard full of pans.

"Most of the time we cook here. Sometimes we get Chinese take out," Julio tells me. "Only when we're really down and out, we go to a soup kitchen in the neighborhood. We are like a small family here. We take care of each other; we share our food and money. Sometimes we have our quarrels. About stupid things, beer or water. Frankie came over last week to harass us. He told us that we are a bunch of dirty crackheads and that it is because of us that we are all getting kicked out. Fuck him."

A young white man is walking towards us. "Marcy boy!" Julio yells out loudly. "Join us for a beer, man." It is Marc Singer, the British documentary maker. Politely he refuses the beer that

Julio is offering him. Marc has finished shooting, but still comes now and then to see how everybody is doing. Especially after the new developments with Amtrak. Marc absolutely wants to film in case there is an eviction.

He asks Estoban about his leg. Estoban rolls up his pants and shows a few dark spots on his red, inflamed leg. It was a pit bull, says Julio. "The monster. We walked by with our cans. First he bit, then he barked. Not even a warning. Maybe he did not like the sound of rattling cans."

With a flashlight we take a closer look at the wound. It is slowly healing, and shows no sign of an infection. "Stubborn asshole," Julio says. "This time you are lucky, but you should have seen a doctor." Estoban grins sheepishly and goes back to his shack.

Marc tells the latest about Amtrak. He was at Penn Station to have a frank talk with Captain Combs. It was not a nice talk. "Combs thought I wanted to screw her," Marc says. "The bitch is paranoid. She had me body-searched because she thought I was secretly carrying a tape recorder."

Marc understands why Combs hates him. When the captain wanted to film, she got zero cooperation. Bernard had told her to fuck off and Julio told her they only worked with Marc. Combs had hastily concluded that Marc had set all tunnel people against her.

"Honestly, I don't know anything," Marc says. We all laugh at the story.

Marc leaves and Julio opens his fourth can of beer. He is starting to become sentimental and talks about Roxy, the dog he used to have.

"She was a cool puppy," mourns Julio. "But they poisoned her." He has no clue who did it, or what could be the reason behind such a low act. Maybe the poor dog accidentally ate Joe's poisoned meatballs.

"I also had two cats. Rusty and Roger. Also gone. Debby took them when she left me." Debby was Julio's girlfriend. They lived together in his house. "You wanna see it?" Julio asks? "It's behind the wall."

A few hundred meters deeper in the tunnel, is a five foot high wall next to some unused tracks. Behind the wall, there are spaces where more people have built their houses. In front of the wall is an old couch with a few blankets. A rat crawls on the seat, next to a hand that is sticking out from under the blanket.

"Lee, my man, what's up?" Julio calls. Slowly a person rises. It's a skinny white guy, with a long dirty beard and a wild expression in his gaunt eyes. He mumbles something unintelligible and crawls back under the blanket.

"Poor Lee. He is not 100 percent okay," Julio explains. "Makes me sad. We invite him once in a while for a drink or some food. We like to watch over our people. But he always declines. Prefers to be alone on his couch talking to the rats."

I have never been behind the wall because it looked so dirty and dangerous over there. Between the sloppily constructed shacks the ground is strewn with broken TVs, fridges, bikes, and shopping carts. A few rats jump out of a loudspeaker box. All the way at the end of the wall is Julio's house, a wooden cubicle of eight by eight feet. On one side is a small door, only three feet high.

Julio lights a few candles. I have to bend over because the ceiling is low; on top Julio has another story where he sleeps on an old mattress. "I built that story especially for Debby. She wanted more space. And all for fucking nothing." Julio takes another sip and stares sadly at the floor.

The floor is covered with moldy Persian carpets and a few plastic crates to sit on. Except for a little cupboard, the space is empty. Julio takes a small photo album out of the cupboard, the corners eaten away by rats. Some photos are of Julio's cats and dogs, other photos show Debby, a fat girl who smiles in each photo. "She was hanging out with other men," Julio says. "We had a fight. And…um…Yes, there was violence. She is living now with a friend in the Bronx."

"Debby took most of the stuff," Julio explains his frugal interior. "The rest I broke down myself. Pulled out the electricity lines and smashed the alarm and the toaster. I did not want any memories of her."

Julio has now nearly finished the six-pack of malt liquor and his speech starts to slur. His eyes become angry and mean and his words nearly unintelligible. He is now talking about the half-hearted efforts of the homeless organizations to help them. "They just let us rot down here. If they want to help us, then they have to help all the people living in tunnels. And I tell you, they will never do that. Goddamn never," he screams through the tunnel, waving and threatening with his can of beer. "They only do it for the money. They don't give a shit what happens to us."

14. THE ADVENTURES OF FRANKIE, PART 1: FRANKIE IS IN LOVE

"Oh, man, I am so in love." It is evening. I am walking with Frankie on our way out to get water in the park. Our flashlights shine on the tunnel floor so we don't stumble over the tracks and miscellaneous garbage.

Frankie's love is named Vanessa, a girl of seventeen he met last winter round the neighborhood. The poor thing had already had her first abortion, Bernard and Kathy tell me later. Somehow they are very well informed about these things. According to Bernard, the girl is actually only fourteen, but Bernard has a tendency to exaggerate for dramatic effect.

"Three dozen, I repeat, three dozen red roses I sent her for Valentine's Day," says Frankie. "With a note attached: 'I Love You.' Without my name."

I nearly slip on a piece of smooth paper. A centerfold of a porn magazine, showing a black woman with her legs spread. A rat jumps away. Frankie babbles on. "I picked her up after work. She was blushing. I said: Honey, those roses were mine. She kissed me…" Frankie leaves out the details, but reassures me it was a romantic night.

Vanessa has given up her job at a pharmacy and currently works as a counselor at a summer camp in Upstate New York.

In six weeks, after the summer, she will be back in the city. "It's true love, cuz. We gonna marry. Of course we will send you and your wife an invitation."

The day before yesterday the two young lovers bid their farewells. Frankie cried for two days. "Look at my eyes," Frankie says and he points the flashlight towards his face. "They are still red from crying." Frankie is not exaggerating. His penetrating and steely blue eyes are now watery and bloodshot.

Frankie is making preparations to offer Vanessa a future. He is getting his birth certificate, so he can request a new social security card, so he can find a regular job. He would like to work as a bike messenger or a delivery boy for a supermarket.

Frankie looks good. The ugly, white, bald face of last autumn has become lean and tanned. He eats healthier now and works out a bit, so he's lost some weight. His puffed up fat cheeks and chin have gone. He also has new clothes: before Vanessa left, she dragged him into a shop. He now looks like an all-American jock, with a baseball cap, red football sweater, sneakers, and bleached jeans.

"Oh, I wish the summer would fly by," Frankie muses as we fill the jerry cans with water at a fountain in the park. Boats decorated with Chinese lanterns sail on the Hudson. Music and laughter echo across the water. "And I hate to say that. 'Cause I love summer."

15. THE HOMELESS DEBATE OF THE '90S

THE PRETTIFICATION OF
OUR HOMELESS FELLOW CITIZEN

The slapdash folder of the Coalition mentions that:

- One out of five homeless people has a job but cannot afford housing.[5]
- One out of three homeless is a veteran.[6]
- Women and children are the fastest growing segment of the homeless population.[7]

From my own experience and from what the tunnel people have told me about their fellows, combined with data from sociological research and literature, I reach different conclusions:

- More than fifty percent of all homeless have some kind of criminal past, are on parole or are fugitives.[8]
- Most homeless who say they are veterans have hardly seen a battlefield, or have been discharged from the service for all kind of reasons.[9]
- Ninety-five percent of the money you throw in that paper cup will be spent on crack.[10]

It is possible to paint totally different pictures of the homeless population. Advocacy groups such as the Coalition for the Homeless love to portray the homeless as people with whom the public can identify. People tend to help others more if they have things in common. Folks like you and me, who unfortunately became victims of terrible bad luck—a death in the family, a fire in the house, an accident at work. Indeed, there are tragic cases where law-abiding, decent American families lost income and housing and wound up on the street.

This group of all American families is, however, at 1 percent, a tiny minority.[11] The average homeless person has a completely different profile. According to a study from Rossi, 3 out of 4 are single, young, black and male; 30 percent have had psychiatric difficulties in the past; 80 percent have drug or alcohol problems; 40 percent did not finish high school.[12]

"Everybody is one paycheck away from homelessness." It is a slogan that not only Bernard likes to use, but that is repeated over and over like a mantra by homeless organizations to generate sympathy for their clients. Homeless people are in many ways "folks like you and me," writes sociologist Christopher Jencks, "but so are saints and serial killers."[13]

"Lying for justice" has become a generally accepted practice that some people are not even ashamed of. "Sure I'd lie. I'd lie to help the homeless," Jennifer Toth reports in The Mole People, quoting a staff member of the Coalition who was furious because she had openly written about crime, insanity, and drug consumption among tunnel people.[14]

The fact that "prettification" happens amongst outreach workers and homeless organizations is understandable: every lobby group has a tendency to be creative with the facts. If lying serves a higher purpose, and if it is done to defend the interest of "people without a voice," the temptation becomes even harder to resist.

Others, however, question whether it is actually in the interest of the homeless themselves. It creates disbelief, skepticism and irritation among the "worldly." The "believers" on the other hand search for easy solutions while they underestimate the complexity of the problem, according to Jencks and Burt.[15]

Some journalists also take over the "folks-like-you-and-me concept." *New York Times* journalist Walter Goodman heavily criticized the media during the Democratic Convention of 1992. The convention was held in Madison Square Garden, right across from Penn Station, which is home to many homeless people. Weeks beforehand, the police were busy cleaning up the neighborhood by chasing away street people. The Coalition pointed some national TV crews to this clean-up operation, and suddenly homelessness became a huge news item. Poor homeless mothers with cute little kids appeared in front of the cameras to talk about their plight.

"Television news producers can count on advocacy groups to supply them with model victims for viewing purposes, people...untouched by...mental illness, AIDS, domestic violence and lack of education and skills," Goodman writes. "And why should a producer focus on one of the 50 percent of single homeless people who have served time in jail when he can just as easily find someone without a record?"[16]

That same week of the convention, a disturbing report was published about the homeless population in shelters. After anonymous and voluntary urine testing, it appeared that 65 to 80 percent tested positive for drug use in the three preceding days, mostly crack/cocaine. The survey, requested by Mayor

David Dinkins, also found a large number of HIV-positive and mentally ill people. Low skills, little work experience, and prison records were also rife.[17] The report confirmed ugly truths that were until then only heard at Republican cocktail parties.

"Homelessness is a euphemism, a nice way to talk about people who are in fact mentally ill and are addicted to alcohol or drugs," says Al O'Leary, spokesman of the Metropolitan Transit Authority Police. "The homeless have a warning function for people to confirm themselves at the capitalist system," Professor Terry Williams says. These two extremes represent the American political debate. "Conservatives blame the homeless, liberals blame the conservatives," Jencks says pointedly.[18]

DEFINITIONS AND STATISTICS

Statistics on the number of homeless are notoriously inaccurate and are a middle ground between raw estimates—*guesstimates*— and the rare statistical material that is available from shelters, soup kitchens, research, and local governments.

In the mid-'80s, numbers ranged from a few hundred thousand to the incredibly high number of six million. The trouble with counting starts with the difficulties of a basic definition of homelessness. Before the homeless started roaming the streets in large numbers by the end of the '70s, the term homeless was hardly used: The usual term was vagrancy. Even wandering seasonal workers who worked unskilled jobs but could afford a simple hotel on Skid Row were called vagrants.[19]

People began using the more politically correct term "homeless," not simply because of negative stereotyping—wandering, criminal, antisocial, bums—but more to reflect that the *new vagrants* were the result of new demographic and sociological developments. It is tempting to discuss the exact definition of homeless at great length. "Till the moment we enter the House of the Lord, we are all homeless," Father Bill Robinson, a reverend from Brooklyn, told me.[20] Metaphorically speaking, Father Bill is correct, but science and politics need more operational definitions. At the moment, the most widespread definition of homelessness is "not having customary and regular access to a conventional dwelling…that is intended to be used as a sleeping place."

Beyond that, there must be somehow "a private space that has the ability to exclude strangers."[21] Using this definition, the shelter population, although they each have a bed, are considered homeless. Same for the tunnel people, although some of them don't consider themselves to be homeless. Families who are camping out in the highly overcrowded rooms in welfare hotels but still have some privacy are technically not homeless.[22] The alcoholics who live in cheap hotels in rooms of thirty square feet, or the poor black families who are cramped into squats are also not considered homeless. Overlooked in most studies and surveys are the "couch people," those who have lost their homes and are staying on the couches of friends or relatives.[23] To count the homeless population, usually a distinction is made between shelter and street people. Shelters, of course, can provide the exact number of how many people stayed there. The counting of street people, including those who live in the tunnels, is much more complicated. A few surveys, however, have shown that the ratio between shelter and street people is fairly stable and is about fifty/fifty.[24] So by doubling the shelter population, one has a rough estimate of the total homeless population. Of course, there are seasonal fluctuations. On cold winter nights, many homeless street people may decide to sleep in a shelter.

Another distinction is between long-term and short-term homeless. Only a small group, around 20 percent, is homeless for a relatively short period, with a maximum of three months. Sometimes called "crisis homeless," these people normally stay in shelters until they find a solution. Compared with the long-term homeless population, they are also hampered to a lesser extent by drug addiction, mental illness, and low levels of education and work experience. Most of the homeless, however, remain over a year on the streets and are referred to as "the chronically homeless." A return to 'normal' society becomes harder with time.[25] Associated with this distinction are two ways of counting the homeless. One is the PIT (Point-In-Time) count, the actual number of people that are homeless on a certain date. Another method of counting is to look at the number of people who have experienced homelessness over a period of one year, be it a short spell or a long-term situation.[26]

By the end of the '70s, the problem of homelessness had grown to such proportions that Mitch Snyder, the charismatic spokesman of the homeless movement, gave the estimate as three million homeless.[27]

The government and policymakers, however, wanted numbers they could rely on. Finally, in 1984, the department of Housing and Urban Development (HUD), came up with a number of 250 to 300,000 homeless people. This number was derived from hastily executed polls and telephone interviews amongst organizations and experts in all the big cities.

Later, Snyder admitted that his number of three million was greatly inflated: "Here are some numbers. They have no meaning, no value. We mean homeless is not just a small problem, but something of huge proportions."[28]

One of the few efforts to both count and map the homeless population in a scientific way was done in 1985 by sociologist Peter Rossi in Chicago.[29] Interviewers worked in pairs, escorted by off-duty policemen. They checked a great number of randomly chosen blocks as well as all public assessable spaces where homeless people could be expected to be found, such as bus stations and airports, cheap all-night cinemas, vacant houses, dark alleys, porches, and parks. All people were briefly interviewed. Because all respondents got a small fee of five dollars, most of them cooperated.

Rossi counted nearly 3,000 homeless people in the city of Chicago—one out of every 1,000 inhabitants—of whom half stayed in shelters. The other half were out on the streets. This number was close to the estimate of the city, but was significantly lower than the number of 15 to 25,000 used by homeless organizations. Extrapolated to national numbers, it comes close to the HUD estimates.

Another survey dated from 1987, carried out by sociologist Martha Burt for the Urban Institute, a think tank based in Washington, DC. She counted 400,000 homeless people in the whole of America.[30] A HUD survey and other government censuses from 1990 give comparable numbers.[31]

For the city of New York, the Department of Homeless Services came up with a number of 25,000 sheltered homeless in 1994.[32]

Homeless organizations and experts estimated the total number of homeless in New York in 1996 to be somewhere between 40,000 and 120,000.[33]

The Coalition estimates that another 100,000 people are on the edge of homelessness—couch people and families that out of necessity live with two or three other families in small, overcrowded apartments.[34]

HOMELESSNESS THROUGH THE AGES

"Homelessness is not a new problem...It is as old as time," said then Secretary of Health and Human Resources under Reagan, Margaret Heckler. Blaming homelessness on some universal human condition was the perfect justification not to pursue an active policy to tackle the problem.[35]

History and oral tradition have always been full of vagrants, bums, travelers, refugees, beggars, minstrels, fortune-tellers, gypsies, dynamic salesmen, and roving merchants. In short, everyone who was not settled down wandered the world in one way or another. What differs, however, is the way these people were received. Sometimes they were taken in with hospitality, seen as welcome visitors who broke the monotony of daily life with their fascinating tales about exotic places. At other times, they were chased away, ignored, or thrown into jail or labor camps. In their book *Old Men of the Bowery*, Cohen and Sokolovsky quote the historian Gilmore who says—maybe a bit too rosily—that back in the old days, strangers and wanderers were treated with a positive attitude. There was the tradition of unconditional hospitality: "The stranger is viewed as a mysterious person representing a magical, possibly threatening force."[36] Providing hospitality, food, and shelter were seen as effective means to ward off evil curses. To prevent abuse, a three-day limit was set.

Later, there also came a religious component that put a high moral value on frugality and material detachment. According to Cohen and Sokolovsky, "The sanctity of charity to the poor and assisting strangers is a prevalent theme of the New Testament."[37] Monasteries valorized poverty by forsaking worldly possessions. "The Franciscans...who adopted wandering and begging as a mode of living further helped to sanctify begging and vagabondage."[38] After the Protestant Reformation and the centralization of the early European nation states, benevolence and tolerance slowly transformed into repression, for which the centralized government provided the apparatus, and the Protestant religion offered the ideological justification.

Ordinances and laws came into existence to punish vagrancy. Unwilling cases were put into labor camps. Wealth and prosperity during this earthly life were seen by Luther and Calvin as rewards for a righteous and laborious life. Beggars and the poor had no one to blame but themselves, they had strayed from the right path due to their laziness and weak character. These same protestant ethics are still very much alive in the United States today.[39]

In the history of the U.S., most homeless people endured a miserable fate envied by no one. The occurrence of homelessness was like a thermometer for the American economy.[40] Hopper (2003) describes in graphic details the squalor of homeless life in the early twentieth century. Through the ages, however, there has been one type of homeless individual—the hobo—who, just like the cowboy, became an American folk-hero, glorified in both literature (Jack London) and music (Woody Guthrie, Bob Dylan).

In 1923, Nels Anderson, a sociologist who himself spent years on the road, published *The Hobo: The Sociology of the Homeless Man*. His book is a classic in urban anthropology because of the wealth of ethnographic descriptions by an insider. The name hobo is derived from "hoe boys," after the most prevalent piece of equipment in agriculture. The archetypal hobo had a rebellious spirit and was severely afflicted by what the Germans so aptly call "wanderlust." They had their own songs and ballads such as "The Tramp Confession" and "Nothing to Do but Go":

> I'm the wandering son with the nervous feet,
> That never were meant for a steady beat;
> I've had many a job for a while,
> I've been on the bum and I've lived in style;
> And there was the road, stretchin' mile after mile,
> And nothing to do but go.[41]

Hobos had their own magazine, *The Hobo News*, and their own slang with thirty different words to indicate different kind of hobos, bums and vagrants. They had organizations such as the IWW (the Industrial Workers of the World) and the IBWA (the International Brotherhood Welfare Association) that organized yearly meetings. Although the IWW was ridiculed by the bourgeois as an acronym for "I Want Whiskey" or "I Won't Work," it was actually a radical trade union of socialists, anarchists and others who were opposed to the moderate policies of the AFL, the American Federation of Labor. The IBWA was a less politicized organization, focusing more on education and mutual aid. There were colorful characters such as "The King of the Hobos" and "The Millionaire Hobo." The last, a wealthy philanthropist called James Eads How, started the IBWA and also founded Hobo Colleges in Chicago, St. Louis, and other cities around the Midwest and East Coast. There, hobos could learn the rudiments of social sciences, work on their oratory talents, or even get grades in economic science.[42]

The heyday of the hobo was the three first decades of the twentieth century, when exploding industry and agriculture needed thousands of workers. Hobos laid railroad tracks in the expanding West, felled trees in Oregon and Washington, picked fruit and helped with harvests from Dakota to Missouri. They traveled by catching rides on freight trains, moving to wherever there was work. Every big city, especially Chicago and New York, had its own so-called bohemia, a neighborhood with flophouses, brothels, saloons, pawnshops, and employment offices. These were the golden days in the history of homeless, according to Cohen and Sokolovsky. Hobos were never truly broke, could always easily find new jobs, and were idealized and romanticized by the population. Anderson mentions alcoholism and other anti-social behavior in his study, but hobos were never viewed as problematic and needy cases. But with the end of '20s and the onset of the Great Depression, jobs disappeared and wages plummeted. The once-bustling bohemia changed into a run-down neighborhood. At the depth of the crisis, the number of homeless reached record levels. In a 1933 census, one and a half million were counted.[43]

"It is sad to listen to the noises of a street that had its spirit broken," writes historian Bendiner about New York's hobohemia, the Bowery.[44] "It is pathetic to see beggars where rebels once shouted, sang and whored."

THE GROWTH OF HOMELESSNESS IN THE '80S

The economy started the bumpy road to recovery in 1936, and the millions of jobless slowly found their way back in the work-force aided by Roosevelt's New Deal. The war industry absorbed the last unemployed. The booming post-war economy and Truman's Fair Deal reduced the national numbers of homeless to maybe a few thousand. Truman introduced legislation to help returning veterans—the G.I. Bill of Rights, the Veteran Administration, Social Security, and pension plans—and laid the foundations for what was later to become Medicare. The few thousands who still roamed the streets could be sheltered in churches, missions, and an abundance of cheap hotels.

Beginning in the late '70s, the ranks of homeless started to swell again, only to explode in the early '80s. It became clear that it was a new and huge problem. People pointed to the Reagan administration as the main culprit, as it steadily cut social programs and mental health care. The reality was much more complicated.

One of the best analyses appeared in 1994 in the publication

The Homeless,[45] written by sociologist Christopher Jencks, who had already made a name for himself as a deep and pragmatic thinker with his book *Rethinking Social Policy*.

According to Jencks, deinstitutionalization of mental health care, a tightening of the labor market, the disintegration of traditional family structures, budget cuts for social programs, the crack epidemic, and finally the worsening housing market caused the most vulnerable people to cross that thin line from extreme poverty into homelessness.

The number of people with mental health problems among the homeless is remarkably high. In Rossi's study of the homeless in Chicago, it appeared that 30 percent of the homeless had been institutionalized in the past.[46] Jencks estimates that one third of the current homeless population would be in an institution were the pre-Reagan health policies still in effect.

The deinstitutionalization of psychiatric care is a long process that had already begun in the '50s. New medicines appeared on the market that made outpatient treatment possible.[47] Some patients benefited from this treatment more than they would have from a lengthy isolation in an asylum. For others, however, it had disastrous results. In more progressive psychiatric circles, mental hospitals were considered repressive government institutions.[48] According to this school of thinking, mental disorders did not exist; rather, mental health was a relative concept that existed only in a certain social and cultural context.

At the introduction of Medicaid and SSI in the '60s and '70s, patients began to enter federal hospitals or private clinics that received Medicaid and SSI payments directly, which state-run hospitals did not. Sufficient care was not taken, however, and many patients were declared cured and sent packing. At the end of the '70s, progressive forces successfully lobbied for the restriction of involuntary commitment, and many more of the mentally ill were released into the streets. Federal and local governments with increasingly tight budgets welcomed these developments.

Then came the drastic budget cuts of the Reagan administration. Between 1981 and 1983, the eligibility standards to receive federal disability benefits were severely tightened. About three hundred thousand people, among them roughly one hundred thousand with mental problems, were dropped from the rolls. Most of them did not find work and wound up on the streets. According to Jencks, "this assault on the disabled was one of the low points of modern American social policy."[49]

Rising unemployment caused a new wave of homelessness. In the early '70s, there were one million unemployed single men living below the poverty level. By 1984, this population of the potentially homeless had risen to three million, of whom one third were black.[50]

These growing numbers of poor have been exacerbated by the disappearance of jobs requiring unskilled labor. A new wave of Latino immigrants, partly caused by the civil wars in Central America, put even more pressure on the labor market. According to anthropologist Kim Hopper, 279,000 jobs disappeared in New York alone due to outsourcing to low-wage countries, international competition, deregulation of labor laws, and automation.[51]

Over time, the American economy has changed from an industrial to service-oriented one. According to Hopper, the number of service-oriented jobs rose 60 percent in the period from the early '70s to the late '80s while industrial jobs decreased by 15 percent. The remaining industrial jobs required higher levels of education or experience.

Those able to find jobs were confronted with lower wages due to competition on the labor market: a new wave of legal and illegal immigrants, mostly Latinos and Asians, were willing to work eighty hour weeks in sweatshops.

Day labor also became harder to get. There used to be many places in Manhattan—the Meat Market district, the Bowery, 125th Street in Harlem—where early morning job seekers assembled. There they were picked up by middlemen who brought them to the docks, the construction sites, and the freight terminals where extra hands were always needed. These informal recruitment places for temp workers have all but disappeared.

Although the average income for women, especially black women, rose in the '70s and '80s to become more equal to that of men,[52] the number of single mothers living below poverty levels doubled.[53] The Republican wave, spearheaded by Newt Gingrich with his manifesto "Contract with America," reasoned that welfare and child support just encouraged people to have more children. When benefits were slashed, it did not achieve the desired result of fewer single mothers, resulting only in poorer ones. Between 1980 and 1990, their spending power was cut in half.

There was small economic upheaval in the mid-'80s, but the number of homeless kept rising. According to Jencks, this is when the crack factor came into existence. The new drug appeared on the scene around this time, and had a devastating effect on the poor black communities as if it were a chemical weapon specially designed to eliminate the poor black underclass. More than half of the black population subscribes to this conspiracy theory. "The increasing popular view…is that they, as poor people are…superfluous and expendable, and that they are being killed off in a sort of triage operation," writes Williams in *Crackhouse*.[54] In the '90s in New York, it was easier and cheaper to get crack than to buy the relatively harmless marijuana.[55]

Before this, alcohol had been the traditional drug of choice for the down and out. For a few bucks, one could buy a six-pack of beer, a flask of whiskey, or a bottle of Night Train—the cheap, strong wine traditionally favored by vagrants. A small bag of weed cost only five dollars. Heroin and cocaine, with street prices of fifty to sixty dollars for a portion, were out of reach for the poor. In surveys among the shelter population in the early '80s, no one even bothered to research the prevalence of these drugs. By the mid-'80s, however, the strongly addictive crack came onto the market in small capsules or vials of ten dollars. Later, the prices dropped even further to three dollars a portion.

Heavy smokers don't know when to stop and can consume dozens of portions a day. Dealing crack became a common survival strategy in the poverty-stricken inner cities. Its use spread explosively within a few years.

Another plague that hit at around the same time was the AIDS epidemic. Just like crack, it hit hardest amongst the poor underclass. Blacks have an HIV rate three times higher than whites.[56]

In the mid-'80s, when infection rates soared, and ignorance and hysteria soared even higher, evictions of HIV-positive tenants were common. Landlords didn't want infected people living in their properties. People got fired for having the virus. Those able to hang onto their homes and jobs were confronted with sky-high bills for medicines and care. Those who were hospitalized could at a certain point no longer afford it. The New York State Department of Health concluded in 1987 that 9 percent of the homeless population was HIV-positive.[57] The Coalition estimates that in 1994, 20 to 30 percent of the New York homeless population was infected.[58] Finally, there is the relationship between housing and homelessness. It is an extremely complicated discussion in which rent control, the real estate market, federal housing subsidies, and low income housing projects have to be taken into account. Some advocacy groups say that federal cutbacks on housing subsidies are the main reason for the increase of homelessness. On the other end of the spectrum, conservatives state that the housing subsidies proposed by progressives are to blame.[59]

The Coalition mentions in its 1994 annual report that in New York alone, one million cheap apartments, or so-called single room occupancy (SRO) units, disappeared during the '70s and '80s. The city had decided to subsidize landlords to fix up their dilapidated buildings. Beautiful but expensive apartments were the result.[60]

According to Jencks, any direct relationship is hard to establish. Rather, he focuses on what he calls the "destruction of Skid Row." Skid Row, with its abundance of cheap rooms and hotels, was traditionally a safe heaven and refuge for the poorest of the poor who could not afford an apartment.

After World War II, the vagrant population dwindled and so did its favorite kind of lodging houses—the so-called cage and cubicle hotels which got the name because the rooms of 30 square feet aren't much bigger than birdcages, and often have a ceiling of chicken wire. Most of these flophouses were torn down, because of gentrification, new building regulations, and the economic laws of supply and demand and were not replaced. Jencks states that between the 1970s and 1990s, some four hundred thousand cheap rooms disappeared this way.

The few remaining flophouses could thus raise their rents, so by 1994, a night at the Sunshine Hotel on the Bowery, one of the last remaining cage hotels, cost about eight bucks. A comparison of spending power and wages: in the '60s, ten hours of work at minimum wage could pay for one month of rent. By 1994, it had risen to forty to sixty hours. In the '60s, a bed for one night was a quarter of the price for a six-pack of beer. Now a room costs twice as much as a six-pack, "making oblivion cheaper than privacy," writes Jencks.[61] The cage hotels were not an ideal place to live, but were still more humane than the shelters.[62] In interviews with homeless people, the prison scores higher on issues like personal safety, food quality, privacy, and cleanliness. It is only on the point of freedom that a shelter scores higher.[63]

The above chapter is a discussion of external factors. But human beings are not passive objects riding the waves of fate. In part, each of us is responsible for his or her own fate, even the homeless. How big a part we play is, of course, the question. It is the age-old metaphysical debate between voluntarism and determinism, which roughly translates in our modern days into the political debate between the right and the left.

16. THE TRULY CHOSEN

Bernard was right. Tony hasn't changed a bit—still full of plans to conquer the world with his designs. Now, his ambitions have become even bigger. His designs will not only be on T-shirts, but on ties, socks, pajamas, and yes, even on wallpaper. One evening I am in his bunker, and Tony shows me his latest designs. Before, I had seen orchids and marijuana plants. These are inspired by tropical fish with big fluttering tails that Tony has colored with

1. Thursday Morning, 5:30 AM: Bernard starts canning.

2. Bernard gives food away to a homeless friend.

3. Bernard and Tony sort bags of cans.

4. Bernard and Tony walk with bags of cans beneath the self-portrait of graffiti artist Chris Pape.

5. Sunlight filters through the grates at Bernard's camp.

6. Bernard makes coffee while Tony watches on.

7. Tony finds some cans in the garbage.

8. Tony pushes his merrily decorated shopping cart.

9. Tony sorts empty bottles in the tunnel.

10. Tony on workfare in the Bronx.

11. Little Havana: Poncho watches TV while Julio looks on.

12. The South End: Julio drags a record player to his shack. Poncho heads out.

13. Christmas Eve: Police at an emergency exit after a suicide on the train tracks.

14. Christmas Day: At his fire, Bernard enjoys some cheese and a good glass of wine.

15. Sergeant Bryan Henry from Metro North Police engages in a discussion with a homeless man he found on "Burma Road," a hot and dark alley seven stories under Grand Central Station.

16. Little Havana at their first meeting at Project Renewal. From left to right: Hugo, Estoban, Poncho, Julio, Getulio. Behind the table is Dov Waisman.

17. Grave and votive candle for Pelusa, Julio's favorite cat.

18. Lee sleeps on his couch.

19. The Kool-Aid Kid has a shave at Bernard's camp.

20. Marcus has dinner in his den.

21. Kathy in her bunker with most of her cats.

22. Christmas Eve: Joe patches up the wounded Lady Bug with duct tape.

23. Frankie starts a working day.

24. Frankie collects empty cans at a building near the West Side Highway.

25. Frankie returns his empties to WeCan redemption center.

26. Fatima, Ment, and Jazzy on a Friday Night in Frankie's place.

27. Bob and Bernard working. Bob ties up a bag with empty cans.

28. Bernard and Bob serving dinner in the tunnel.

SUMMER 1997: THE TUNNEL PEOPLE IN THEIR
NEW APARTMENTS.

29. Bernard in Harlem.

30. Bob in the Holland House.

31. Poncho in the Bronx.

32. Ment, Jazzy, Fatima, Brian Jr., and Frankie on the Upper West
Side.

33. Bernard in the nearly empty tunnel, posing by the portrait Chris Pape made of him nearly twenty years ago *(January 2010)*.

34. The South End, where all constructions have been torn down. During a very cold winter, a stalactite has formed where Little Havana once stood *(January 2010)*.

markers in all colors of the rainbow. "Actually, you're looking at forty-thousand-dollar pieces," he says. He closes his sketchbook with a bang and a significant expression. After the fire, Tony moved into a new bunker, adjacent to Bob's. In fact, it is actually two bunkers joined together. The first one is the entrance that he uses as storage space. It is now full of bags, cans, and cases of bottles that still need to be sorted out.

Tony lost all of his possessions in the fire, but he has managed to fill up his sleeping room with new junk in no time. The walls are covered with clothes hangers carrying sweaters and coats, paintings of poetic rock landscapes with rippling streams, and the colorful calendars given away by Chinese restaurants.

The central point in Tony's place is a small table in the corner. A mirror and two candles sparsely light his room; an extravagant and huge ashtray, filled to the rim with cigarette butts, takes up the rest of the table. With a small statue of the Madonna beside it, the ashtray looks like an altar dedicated to the Nicotine God.

Tony sits on the edge of his bed and lights a cigarette. Maybe he is waiting for a spontaneous offer from my side to invest money in his T-shirt business. To get me in a good mood, he offers to lend me a pile of porn magazines that are strewn on the floor.

Like most people in the tunnel, Tony looks a lot healthier than he did last autumn. He wears shorts that are held up by big red suspenders stretched over his muscular and very hairy chest. His hair is short and he has a gray stubbly beard. Tony seems very pleased with his new look: with more fashionable shorts, he could actually join the delegation of middle-aged leather boys in the gay pride parade that is happening one of these days in Manhattan. Tony goes there every year to collect cans and sell his junk to bystanders.

Tony feels, and correctly so, that I don't want to discuss his T-shirt business proposals and starts to talk about the situation at his sister's on the Lower East Side. The breasts of his niece are slowly budding, and suddenly all the boys in the neighborhood are after her.

She loves the attention, and has already been through a dozen boyfriends in a couple of months. But for Uncle Tony, she has less attention now. Even worse, she brings her new boyfriends home and they take Tony's lazy chair. The days of watching TV in peace are over. Tony got mad at his sister. "Do you know what your daughter is?" he had screamed at her last spring. "The same as our mother. She died from TB. And you know what kind of disease that is. It is a disease for prostitutes."

Infuriated, Tony's sister had kicked him out of her home. Tony was offended and stayed completely out of touch for months until she became concerned. "She had called all the morgues in the city to see if they had found me," Tony laughs. "She thought I was already buried at Potter's Field." In Potter's Field, prisoners from Riker's Island bury unclaimed and unidentified bodies in graves marked only by a number.

When Tony had decided that his sister had learnt her lesson, he showed up at her door. She burst into tears at seeing her missing brother again. Since then, Tony is treated with respect again and he's got his spot back in front of the TV. "Nobody fools around with me," he says confidently. It sounds like a warning.

Tony pours milk in a bowl for his cats. Proudly he shows me his new litter of kittens in a box in the corner. The milk bowl is too high for the cats, so he uses a sugar pot that they can step up onto. Sometimes a kitten slips and falls head-first into the milk. Tony then carefully pulls it out by its tail, and strokes its head tenderly. The mewing attracts more cats, and soon his space is so crowded with cats you can't walk without stepping on an animal. Even Linda and Batman, Bernard's newest cat, stick their heads around the corner. Tony gets a packet of drumsticks out of a plastic bag and feeds the hungry newcomers. Then he put his own groceries, half a loaf of bread and cheese, next to the milk bowl in between the cats.

"All right," he says with satisfaction. "No rat dares to touch that."

At the moment a very fat rat is living under his bed, Tony says, but the rat hasn't shown up for a few days. "The mouses, they don't have no mercy on nothing. Newspapers, books, clothes, yes, even steel and concrete."

With their bellies now full, the well-fed cats start to purr contentedly on Tony's feet. He pats them encouragingly on their backs. "Come on, cats. Go get some mouses."

"That idiot Tony," Bernard raves next morning while we sort out the bags at Pedro and Harvey's. Tony had complained that the cheese and bread disappeared. "How long he has been living now in the tunnel?" Bernard is in a foul mood and goes on about other annoying stuff. Angel, another super across the street, had been on holiday. His replacement had no experience. He left the piles of old newspapers on the sidewalk while putting the garbage cans in the street. The exact reverse of the official Sanitation regulations. Bernard had offered his help, explaining that he had worked the block for over five years. The new super looked at him suspiciously and had accepted Bernard's help only with the greatest reluctance. It was only later, when he saw Bernard chatting at ease with Harvey and Pedro, that he realized that Bernard was a reliable and respected worker. Ashamed of his prejudices, the new super had offered Bernard a few bucks for his help.

"Just leave it," Bernard had told him, deeply offended. "That one was on me."

Angrily, Bernard straightens out a crushed cola can. "I don't understand why these assholes are bothering us," he says indignantly. "Same thing last time at the supermarket. I wanted to put my cans in the machine but the manager said it was broken. I said: 'Cut the crap, just plug it in and turn on the switch.' Another time I am sorting out bags, some bitch in a pantsuit walks up, and tells me I am stealing city property. I didn't say a word, I just looked at her. The people don't understand. They should be happy we do this work. Since can recycling started, petty crime decreased by half and the streets look a lot cleaner."

Maybe the lady in the pantsuit was confused with the old paper recycling. Since the prices of old paper tripled in early 1995, up to eighty dollars for a metric ton, a new type of scavenger popped up. They drive their vans around in the early morning to take the old paper and cardboard before it can be picked up by the cleaning crews. The sanitation department also sells the old paper, and in this way loses millions of dollars a year. In the summer of 1995, the city started to take measures against these entrepreneurs. "It's three o'clock in the morning. Do you know where your garbage hangs out?" was the headline of a *Times* article about the crew of paper thieves who had been arrested.

While we are working the garbage, Bernard's name is called. Behind us is a sloppy man with greasy, curly hair that sticks out at all sides. Around his neck hangs a big video camera. He is wearing a gray jogging suit with oily stains and annoyingly flashy cowboy boots over his pants. Pieces of egg yolk are sticking in his mustache. "Jesus, there is that idiot again," Bernard says with irritation. The man introduces himself as a moviemaker from the neighborhood. When he saw homeless people rummaging through the garbage, he got the idea of making a documentary about the "street-combers of Manhattan."

"I thought you would be here last week," Bernard says sternly.

"I am sorry, I overslept," the greasy moviemaker says. "Do you mind if I start now?" Bernard looks annoyed.

"Do what you gotta do," he says brusquely. This is the first time I've seen Bernard irritated when someone with a camera is around. Usually, the vain Bernard loves to cooperate with any and all media. But this man manages to drive everybody crazy. While talking to us, he doesn't even remove his Walkman's headphones from his ears. He shows off his fancy camera, plays with all its gadgets and brags about how expensive it was. Bernard also has a problem with the fact that it is not clear for whom he's actually working. Bernard prefers to work with European networks with exotic names. They pay better and show more respect than their American counterparts.

"So, what do you like about canning?" the man asks, and nearly pushes his camera into Bernard's face. Bernard has to step backwards, and nearly trips over the garbage bags he is standing next to. The guy has told me to stop working, so Pedro, Harvey, and I watch the whole scene from the side.

"Canning teaches me about people," Bernard replies routinely, clearly bored.

"How do you mean?" the moviemaker asks, and proceeds to order Harvey and Pedro to shut up.

"Canning is my independence. You see, at this level, complacency is the greatest danger." Bernard has his script ready. I have heard it before and go to get coffee.

"So, what do you like about canning?" I hear when I return fifteen minutes later. The moviemaker has forgotten to switch on the audio button and has to start all over. Like an experienced anchorman doing a stand-up in a far away country, Bernard poses once again between the garbage bags and repeats the philosophy behind canning patiently for the fourth or fifth time.

"The asshole was a fucking faggot," Bernard swears after we walk back, delayed for a full hour by the filming. "I tell you, Tut, you could smell it from half a mile. Rude motherfucker. The way he told the supers to shut up. The nerve. How the fuck he dares. And then he invites me back home to watch the footage. Fuckin' dirty-ass faggot. Really thinks I am crazy."

Since the summer, "faggot" and, when referring to females, "bitch," are Bernard's most favored expletives. For extreme cases, he uses the even more offending "closet faggot." Bob is a faggot; Tony, of course, is also one and the same for the sleazy Manny. The two-for-oner Pier John is a closet faggot, although Bernard does not really mean that in too negative of a way because the two have become good friends. They work together a lot, and Bernard is even thinking of becoming a full-time business partner with John.

Bernard also suspects Harvey is a closet faggot. Marcus and Frankie might not be faggots, but at least they are morons of the first class. A moron is bit more stupid than an idiot. And because faggots and morons are subcategories of idiots, according to Bernard nearly the whole world's population consists of idiots. I once asked him about the often-mentioned brotherhood in the tunnel, while he consistently referred to all his fellow tunnel dwellers as assholes, idiots, morons, scumbags, and dickheads.

"Look around and think!" he answered sternly. "Do you know a better word for them?" I thought of all the tricks pulled by Tony,

Burk, Marcus, and Frankie and could not come up with a better word.

Later that morning, Bernard is relaxing in one of the waiting-room chairs near the tracks. The sunlight falls gently through the grate, and Bernard enjoys the warm rays while drinking a cup of tea. The radio softly plays "LA Woman" by the Doors, and up top in the park, the birds are singing their songs. Bernard is in a good mood, and offers the thermos of fresh coffee he made for me. I ask him about the sensitive subject of brotherhood.

"Well, brotherhood and sense of community," Bernard muses. "I never considered this a real community. Everybody contributed something to the welfare of others, but that was about it. We had our fights and disputes, but we tried to dismiss them and then moved on." Bernard is talking in the past tense about the time when most of the bunkers were inhabited. He realizes that soon tunnel life will be finished for him as for them. "Well, brotherhood, yes, in a way there was. We live in the most racist city in the world, but nobody down here ever got any preferential treatment because of his race or color. One time Willy and Sheila had an argument with Bob."

Willy and Sheila were a black couple, explains Bernard. Willy was addicted to crack; Sheila also smoked, but was more of an alcoholic. Three years ago, they left the tunnel. Willy soon developed the first symptoms of AIDS and had died in the meantime. Sheila went on to live together with a three-hundred-pound lesbian in a shelter in the Bronx.

"Sheila once called Bob 'white trash,'" Bernard continues. "I said: 'Sheila, you don't know nothing! Later when the snowflakes come down through the grate, we all depend on each other.' It is sad," Bernard sighs. "A lot of people down here started to cultivate their pettiness. A bunch of lying, cheating assholes. They had nothing to hold onto. They had crawled down here out of shame. They jumped on every distraction, they grabbed every chance to get high. And in the end, all had to prove they could leave the tunnel faster than me. To go where? I tell you, rushing to their downfall." Bernard speaks with a bitter tone in his voice.

"They did not master the existence down here, let alone life up top. Basically there is only more chaos there."

"Victims of society? Fuck it! They're no more victims than anyone else. Their existence down here was their own choice. But they never could accept that. They never appreciated the lessons of the tunnel. And most insulting: They never realized who they really were. But basically, they were the truly chosen."

Bernard talks softly, but with conviction. Disappointment rumbles in his voice. "All creatures on earth are here to express a certain aspect of the mystery of life. But they never understood that. They sidetracked and got lost."

"Look around you, Duke, and feel the vibes. Peace, tranquility, quiet. Everything in the universe consists basically of vibrations. And if you know anything about religion, it is telling that all prophets secluded themselves in the desert or wilderness. There was a reason for it. No, don't worry, I don't consider myself a prophet. I make no claim to uniqueness. But tell me honest, Dune, even you sleep better here than in Brooklyn?"

I can't deny it. Bernard is right.

17. FRANKIE'S ADVENTURES, PART 2:
FRANKIE CHECKS OUT ASSES

"Hmmm, nice fat ass," Frankie audibly growls when a fat Puerto Rican lady in fluorescent pink spandex pants walks by. "I like 'em big and fat."

I am canning with Frankie and we take a break having just collected and redeemed four bags of empties. Frankie knows good garbage addresses with cans in abundance, so we filled up our bags in no time.

We are sitting on the sidewalk, drinking coffee, eating burgers, and watching girls. "You see that girl on the other side of the street? Vanessa has the same kind of tits." Hawk-eyed Frankie has spotted a girl two hundred feet away, and I have to look very hard to find her. Frankie loves big-breasted girls with large behinds. A beautiful slender girl walks by in a tight leather mini-skirt. I point her out to Frankie, who is taking a bite out of his Big Mac.

"Naw. Too skinny. They gotta have some meat around their bones," he says and wipes a blob of mayonnaise from his mouth. In the meantime, he has commented on a dozen girls and compared their body parts with those of Vanessa. "See that girl? Just my girl. Same hair. Only Vanessa has shorter legs. And that one over there? Vanessa's ass is just as wide. Only more rounded." He sighs deeply. "I swear to God, she has an ass like this." With both hands, he indicates her measurements below the belt, with the same gestures a fisherman uses to indicate the size of the giant pike he caught.

Slowly, I start to make a composite image of Vanessa as a short-legged, big-breasted vamp with a huge bottom. On the other side a flashy girl walks by, with heavy make-up and layers of fat rolling over jean shorts that are way too tight. "Does she look like that?" I inquire carefully.

"That's a dirty skeezer, idiot," Frankie says, offended. I look at him puzzled. "A skeezer is when, ahem," Frankie thinks, "um, look, when a lady offers certain sexual services in exchange for monetary means, you understand?"

I am not used to such diplomatic language, and Frankie sees it in my surprised face. "It's like, like, if this bitch sucked my dick for three bucks, then it's a fuckin' skeezer," he corrects himself.

Frankie counts his money. In half a day, we made over sixty dollars and he has enough for the present he wants to buy for Vanessa. Her birthday is in a few days, and he wants to send her a big teddy bear. The bear has a birthday card in its claws. If you open the card, red lights in the shape of a heart will light up. "She loves bears," he sighs.

18. KICKED OUT OF THE TUNNEL

It is the Fourth of July. America goes to picnic. Riverside Park looks like a Rwandan refugee camp. Black and brown people sit on blankets around fires, children cry, the sound of explosions fills the air, and a thick layer of smoke hovers above the ground. Homeless people forage in the midst of the crowd, picking up cans that are sometimes still being consumed.

It is not much nicer in the tunnel. The greasy fumes of hotdogs and burnt burgers enter through the grates to mix with gunpowder smoke from heavy firecrackers and other fireworks thrown down by kids. Huge explosions thunder through the tunnel.

Bernard has now been in a terrible mood for a few days straight. He is unapproachable and grumpy, and I start to get tired of him. He whines and nags all the time like an old woman and bombards me with his folksy wisdom, expressions he probably learned from his mother in the Deep South. "A watched pot never boils" is one of his favorites and it drives me crazy. This morning, he said it three times as I lifted the lid of the pot to see if the coffee was ready. "You'll never make Boy Scouts," is another annoying Bernardism he tells me when I throw the wrong piece of wood on the fire.

Otherwise, he can only rant and rave and curse and complain about everybody, about Burk, Tony, and the Kool-Aid Kid who still pops up once in a while and empties and dirties all the pans. Bernard is getting to be a repetitive bore, and I even stop taking notes.

A new development is that Margaret, and journalists in general, have started to get on his nerves. Since the book *The Mole People* has been released in Germany, there has been an invasion of Teutonic journalists brought down by Margaret. This week alone, we've already seen three German TV-crews.

Yesterday he yelled at me for giving a copy of the gate key to Marcus. The latter had asked me politely, since Bernard refused to give him one. *"Il pense qu'il est le Roi,"* Marcus had whispered softly.

If Marcus had only been discreet, as I begged him, there

wouldn't have been any problems. But he opened the gate for everybody who wanted to enter. Bernard had bumped into two Mexicans performing anal sex on the stairs. Marcus had let them in. "Today you got two, tomorrow four and after tomorrow eight. Before you know it there will be a Mexican village down here and gone is the peace," Bernard had yelled at me. "And by the way, I am the one making the rules down here. I am the one responsible. In the meantime, everybody just does what he wants. I'm getting sick of it." Bernard had not asked me to return my key, but it was close.

Evening falls, the explosions become less frequent, and I make another pot of coffee. I start a fire, but when I put the rattling kettle on the grill, Bernard angrily comes out of his bunker. "Goddammit," he screams. "It looks like there is a curse in the tunnel. Just relaxing has become an impossible challenge."

I have to chuckle on the inside. Bernard's efforts to smoke crack in peace are sometimes pure slapstick. Once, he sat at a quiet spot in the park looking out over the Hudson. Just at the very moment when he wanted to light his stem, a gay man popped out of the brushes and begged to suck him.

"And are you making another pot of coffee again?" Bernard goes on. "This morning you already finished one goddamn whole pot." He should not have told me that. Now I am offended. After all, I never nag him about his crack habit. Besides, I always provide plenty of wood, water, and coffee. Sulking, I go up top and decide to stay away a few days.

A few days later, Bernard is walking towards me as I enter the tunnel. The grouchy expression on his face makes me expect the worst. "Bad news, Tut," he says bluntly. "Bob is back. And you know the deal."

Bob was staying at the YMCA in Brooklyn, but lost his SSI and Medicaid and is back on the streets. Obviously, he blew it over there. The tunnel is the only place left for him. Bernard promised Bob to always keep his spot open.

"Can't we fix up another bunker?" I ask carefully. "Forget it," he says laughing haughtily. "Impossible."

We sit at the fire and Tony joins us. Bernard starts to rave and rant at the Germans. "Three times they came down the last days. They gave me ten dollars. I am not used to that from Europeans. What a goddamn fucking offense. They ordered me to be at We-Can at seven o'clock in the morning for some extra shooting. I did not show up." Tony listens and nods approvingly.

"And Margaret, she is also finished. For four years I carried her tripod. Next week her book is going to print and still she yells seven times a week through the grill. She was going to give me a couple of hundred bucks so I could start two-for oneing, now suddenly she doesn't have any money. And Jennifer Toth, she also is not welcome here anymore. She can't even spell my name right. And that's just the smallest error in her book. And Dree Andrea: she has been in town a few times now and has not even bothered to say hi to me. And Terry Williams, he still owes me two hundred dollars if his TV-piece got aired. Never heard from him. And Chris fucking Pape, he shows up every week on my doorstep with another Japanese film crew. Playing big shot artist, but never even bought me a hamburger."

"Damn it," concludes Bernard. "From now on, everybody who wants to shoot a doc here will pay me 250 dollars a day. Flat rate! Just the usual stuff at the grill. If they want to film me up top collecting cans, then it's another hundred extra."

Bernard has had it. I wonder what I did wrong. Maybe I took his hospitality for granted. Bernard evades the question when I ask, and goes on about journalists in general. "Goddamn, I totally understand that every journalist needs a healthy dose of opportunism, but if they start to exploit us, then they go too far. They all think there is something to gain in this life."

"Yeah," grumbles Tony the yes-man.

"But in the end they will meet themselves," Bernard continues. "Because there is nothing to gain. It is all about purification of the soul and a good conscience. I tell you, Turn, all these folks will wind up with bad karma. Look what happened with *Newsday*." Once, Bernard was taking a nap when he woke up to the noise of a heavy generator. He opened the door and was blinded by big floodlights. "Who the fuck are you and what the fuck are you doing here?" he had screamed.

"We have permission from Amtrak," the *Newsday* crew had answered.

"But not to take photos of my kitchen and my living room," Bernard had angrily responded, and slammed the door in their faces.

A few days later, Bernard saw himself in *Newsday* portrayed as Cerberus, the Three-headed Hell Hound guarding the gates of Hades. A few weeks later, *Newsday* went bankrupt.

"They all think they can fuck with us. They all think they're so smart with their college education. Us, they consider us a bunch of mentally-ill crackheads."

"You're right, B," Tony adds. "They all think we are crazy. But just wait till my designs are on the market. Then I will have the last laugh." I go back to Brooklyn. I can finish my story, Bernard promises, but I lost Bob's bunker.

Kathy and Joe comfort me when I tell them Bernard is acting up and that I lost my space. "Bernard is getting nervous," explains Joe. "He's started to realize he is no longer the mayor."

"He has tunnel fever," gossips Kathy. "He is not coming out during the day. Only at night, to collect cans."

I move my activities to the South End, but stop by now and then at Bernard's camp. Life goes on there as usual. Tony is in the best of moods and enjoys the summer. He has decorated his shopping cart with flags, teddy bears, and all kind of little toys and dolls. When he walks down the street with his bare chest, humming and singing Puerto Rican songs, he leaves a trail of smiling people behind him.

Tony had to go on workfare: it's a new program of Mayor Giuliani's that forces people on welfare to do at least seventy hours of community service monthly. I once went to take a look when Tony was supposed to be sweeping the Bronx streets at 6:30 in the morning. Tony arrived whistling, and two hours too late. He stopped working after half a day. "Waste of time. Let them keep my welfare. I make more money with cans." Since then he's started to work as a two-for-oner at Sloan's supermarket on 96th Street. He is also finally taking care of the thousands of empty glass bottles that had slowly accumulated in the tunnel. He hired Burk, who spent one full day bringing all the bottles in shopping carts to WeCan. Burk got paid just seven dollars, Bernard tells me shaking his head. Tony put the remaining eighty dollars in his pocket.

Bernard still has his bad moods, and is now focusing all of his ire on Bob and Margaret. Bob has proven worthy of his old nickname "Captain Chaos" in all its honor and glory. Bernard is slowly realizing that he has invited in a Trojan Horse. After not touching the stem for a few months, Bob is back at his old habits and performing any trick as long as it will pay for a hit. One time I visit and see Bob pacing restlessly from his bunker to the row of waiting room chairs and the tracks where he sits down for a while and deeply inhales a cigarette. When I show up, he gives me a hug to thank me for the pack of coffee I left for him at his bunker. "Man, you don't even know how much I appreciated that," he says with his loud, raspy voice. Being a heavy smoker and coffee drinker myself creates a bond with Bob. "If I could choose between a hit and a coffee in the morning, really, I would take the coffee."

Bernard says mockingly. "Oh yeah, Bob, shall we try that one of these days? I will bring you for breakfast a tray with a thermos of coffee and a couple of dime bags. Then we will see what you choose."

"Come on Bernard, don't be an asshole," Bob says, annoyed. "You know damn well about that time I still had some dime bags, but first I had my coffee."

Bernard laughs and sits on the waiting chairs. "I swear to God," Bob says solemnly to me. "It really happened. I had smoked so much that night," he explains the rare event, "I just couldn't get higher..." I nod as if to say I take him at his word. Immediately Bob jumps on the opportunity, and asks if I can lend him a ten, or even better, a twenty. "In a few days I will get my SSI again," he tries to convince me. His clear blue eyes get a matte gloss to them when I have to disappoint him.

"Listen, Tut, there are two things in life that will never change," whispers Bernard after Bob has retreated to his bunker. "And that is your mother, and that is Bob." He sighs. "It is hopeless. The whole day he is crawling around and brooding on schemes to get money. I can't show up with him anywhere anymore. He owes WeCan three hundred dollars, yesterday he managed to get thirty bucks out of Pier John, and he also owes Tony. I am sure he scammed the YMCA as well. He had a TV there, a pool, a billiard table, AC, you don't leave that for nothing."

Bernard sighs again and starts to scold Margaret now. In the last week she has left ten messages on his voicemail. Four times she has called through the intercom, exactly at the rare, quiet moments when Bernard wanted to relax and smoke a pipe. Poor Margaret really blew it. On top of that, she has offended him to the very depths of his soul. There was an article about the upcoming tunnel eviction in *The Spirit*, a free weekly magazine on the West Side. The writers of the article had met Margaret, Marc and me and mentioned in their piece a photographer, a filmmaker and an anthropologist, "who, apparently fascinated by the dwellers, circled the dim caverns." Bernard had had a friendly chat with the writers, and had told them that he couldn't turn his ass anymore "without bumping into some bozo with a camera and a note pad." Margaret had taken it personally, but was even angrier about Bernard talking to competing journalists. "You are just addicted to media attention," she had accused him. He answered that no one had an exclusive copyright to him, and that he was free to talk to anyone he liked.

19. LITTLE HAVANA REVISITED

Sometime in mid-July, it is the hottest day of the year. The temperature has risen into the hundreds and the radio implores everybody to stay inside near the AC and only go outside for emergencies. After a boiling-hot bike ride from Brooklyn, a fresh wave of cool airs welcomes me when I enter the tunnel's South End. Every Saturday and Sunday, I wake Julio up at 11:30 and we go out together.

On Saturdays, he sells the books he's found on the streets to the vendors at Broadway. Sundays are his can days. In the summer, there are free rock concerts in Central Park as well, so Julio can combine work with pleasure.

Slowly, I get to know the other inhabitants of Little Havana. Poncho is a big and jolly black Cuban, who just like Estoban came with the Mariel Boatlift to the Promised Land. Hugo is a shy Peruvian who has slick black hair and wears glasses with thick frames. He immigrated to the U.S. with his family as a kid.

Little Havana is still sleeping when I get to Julio's house and knock on his door. After a few knocks, he crawls out of the door with a creased face. "Excuse my appearance," he mumbles. He washes his face with some water and joins me on a chair. "It got late last night."

A few pigeons sit on the wall and the ground amidst the garbage. Julio gets some bread to feed them. Almost immediately rats come out, and chase the pigeons away. "Dirty rats," mutters Julio. "You can't even feed the pigeons anymore. What a life. The tunnel also is falling apart." He points at some cracks along the tunnel walls. Last night some pieces fell onto his roof.

Julio is in a sad mood. Yesterday they had a fight about the fridge. In the end, Getulio smashed it. "We call ourselves a family and then it's even more sad that we fight about these things. People here can't talk things out. They have to grab a bat." Lately, they've had a lot of fights. Most of the time it is about electricity. The one tiny cable that provides the electricity for Little Havana has limited capacity. The TV they got only recently eats up energy. There are always problems when Getulio is making an espresso on his electric heater, while Poncho is just watching a baseball game.

"I don't understand," mourns Julio. "I'm glad I no longer have electricity. Only a small radio, but the batteries are dead. The whole day you have all this noise around you, and even then people go to sleep with the radio on. Can you imagine? What kinda dreams you gonna have?"

We walk past Lee, concentrated on building something that looks like a model of Stonehenge with old batteries. He does not answer our greeting. "Last night he was talking about milky ways, galaxies, and black holes," Julio says. "Didn't make any sense. But he went on and on."

Outside, the heat knocks us out. The asphalt is sticky when we make our way to the supermarket to redeem some cans. The streets are deserted. It is obviously not a day to work. One by one, Julio slowly puts the cans in the machine. We decide to get a bag of ice and a case of beer and have an easy day.

Back in the tunnel, Poncho, Estoban, and Hugo have woken up and are sitting around the TV. "Boys, let's call it a day," Julio says. Little Havana screams with joy as Julio unpacks the beer and puts it with some ice in the cooler. We get a few extra chairs and soon everybody is watching the ball game and sipping a cold beer.

Julio muses about tunnel life. "I get sick of the way people look down on us. I walk on the streets, I see guys with pretty girls eating in restaurants; they wear nice clothes and drive in fast cars. Damn, I think, I want that too. But it is difficult to find a job. Try to explain to a boss that you have been homeless for four years. Nobody will take you. And how can I keep myself clean down here? I can't even appear decently at a job interview."

Hugo listens and nods. "Being homeless is a vicious circle," he says. "The longer you are homeless, the harder it is to break out of it."

Hugo became homeless seven years ago. Drugs were the reason. Before, he used to work as a doorman at fancy hotels like the Marriott and the Hilton. Hugo started to snort coke but could not control it. He decided to temporarily stop working. "I was afraid I would be caught using drugs at work. Then I would have fucked up completely." He explains that all hotels keep a blacklist of ex-employees that use drugs or are unreliable. Hugo sighs. "At that time I had never heard of rehab and assistance programs. It sounds ridiculous, but I figured that there was only one way to get out of it. I gave up my apartment and of all things, I joined the fucking navy."

Hugo went through boot camp a few months with no problems. Just before the graduation there was a final test. "I made an unforgivable mistake. The night before we had a party. The next day there was a compulsory piss test. They found traces of cocaine." Hugo got an Entry Level Discharge. His family was embarrassed and wanted nothing to do with him anymore. In his first weeks of homelessness, Hugo stayed with friends. "I had a whole schedule. Two days here, three days there. But in the end it did not work out. I had to pay ten bucks for a place on the goddamn couch. I had an argument and I was kicked out. It was fucking scary. I didn't know what to do, where to go. For three days I rode the subway, up and down with the *Seven* from Times Square to Queens and the other way around. I slept sitting up on a bench."

Hugo gets a painful look when he talks about that period. "Yeah, I was fucked up. I did not know about shelters, had never heard about soup kitchens. Another homeless person in the subway had to explain that to me. He told me about a shelter, on Ward Island, near Riker's. But to go there, you had to walk through a bad neighborhood. One time I was mugged by a bunch of blacks. I said 'Yo, I'm homeless!' But they did not believe me. They nearly stabbed me when they couldn't find money. In the shelter they stole my last clothes. My only winter coat. I finally went to sleep at La Guardia airport. They leave you alone as long as you move at seven in the morning."

During the day, Hugo made money handing out fliers for fortune-tellers and clairvoyants. If he worked hard, he could make twenty, thirty dollars a day. "I worked for every gypsy and fortune-teller in town. It was always the same. The first days were okay, then they started to get difficult: 'We pay you tomorrow.' Then I knew what time it was and I was gone."

Later, Hugo distributed fliers for strip clubs: The Kit Kat Club at Times Square and the Pink Poodle Bar on the East Side. "It was zero degrees," he remembers. "The steady crew stayed home. When it got warmer, they returned. The boss told them they could fuck off and take me as an example."

Because he worked the nightshift, he slept during the day at Saint James Church on the Upper East Side. "You could sleep there as long as you sat upright. They even set apart a special

section for us." When this sleeping spot became too popular and
the church was flooded with the homeless, the pastor put an
end to it. After that, Hugo slept all over the place: on porches
of banks, in a hallway at a hospital, in burnt-out houses and
parking lots. He finally wound up at the so-called Rotunda at
Riverside Park.

The Rotunda is a half-covered open space in the park where
a small colony of homeless was camping out. During the day,
churches from the neighborhood came to bring soup and sandwiches. Hugo slept in a huge fridge he had found on the street.
"It was just a small house," he smiles. There, he met Julio who
slept next to him in a cardboard box.

In the winter of 1991 the park police cleaned up the Rotunda.
Julio and Hugo went to sleep in the park. "During the day we had
to hide our blankets in the bushes," recounts Hugo. "If the park
police found them, they threw them away. And then you just
had to see how to spend the night. The next day we had to go
to Times Square where the Coalition was handing out blankets."
In the end, Julio and Hugo found the tunnel and befriended the
Cubans. "If you compare this with where I used to sleep, this
tops everything...Privacy, electricity, your own little house. The
only thing that lacks is room service."

Yesterday's heat has transformed into oppressive humidity, and
dark clouds pack the sky as I walk with Julio and Estoban towards
Central Park. Julio knows the park like the back of his hand, as
he slept there for months before he came to the rotunda. He
poses for a photo in front of the Dakota at the spot where John
Lennon was shot. Fans still bring fresh flowers. Then Julio takes
me to Strawberry Field, a spot in the park named after the dead
Beatle.

Like a experienced tour guide, Julio shows me all the corners
of the park: the watch tower, where bird watchers are observing
the rare peregrine falcon; the Ramble, a rocky part of the park
where gays and rent boys are cruising; the lake on the South
Side where Julio used to sleep at an entrance of the subway till
the park police kicked him out; the spot where puppet players

do their show mimicking the Sisters Sledge; the roller skating rink, where kids perform acrobatic tours in front of an audience of tourists, yuppies and bums.

Julio loves the park and nature in general. "If it wasn't for the park, I would have gone crazy in the tunnel," he says, as he inspects every garbage bin for empty cans with the taciturn Estoban. "I need to get away once in a while from the rats and the garbage to walk around the trees and the squirrels."

People are arriving at the Rumsey Baseball Field, an open space with a grandstand where the summer concerts take place. Today the audience is mostly black, since the Brooklyn based Haitian/Jamaican group Vodou 155 is playing. People are carrying big protest signs to draw attention to the case of black journalist and activist Mumia Abu Jamal, who has been on death row for years.

"Wow, that sucks," says Julio when I explain who Jamal is and that he is accused of killing a cop. Julio has had very little education, in fact he's nearly illiterate, unlike Poncho, who reads the *Times* everyday. I love discussing Castro, O.J. Simpson, and Bosnia with Poncho.

"I tell you, crazy, crazy people. This Karadzic, crazy man, just like Castro," he always says whenever we talk about Bosnia. Poncho is of the opinion that NATO should bomb the Serbs into oblivion. That actually happens a few weeks later and Poncho is clapping his hands with joy. "What did I tell you…Boom, boom, boom!" Poncho has followed the bombardments live on CNN from the tunnel. Julio doesn't understand much of the war in Bosnia, but thinks that the snipers in Sarajevo suck.

"Be quiet, you guys," calls Julio to the dozens of sparrows that jump around him. "There is enough for everybody." We are sitting on the side of a low wall, feeding the birds with bread. Julio has hung his can bag strategically on a garbage bin next to the pizza and beer stand.

There is not much to do. The people who want to throw an empty can away deposit it in Julio's bag. Then, very nicely, we say thank you. When someone throws a can in the garbage bin, we demonstratively take it out and put it the right bag. Estoban in the meantime is walking around the audience and collecting cans over there.

We had bought some cheap beers at the supermarket and smuggled them in the bag with the empties. Since Julio knows the guys from the beer stand and always helps them clean up, they don't make an issue of it. They even give us a bag of ice.

Meanwhile Julio has discovered an ant colony and throws crumbs at the entrance. When the crumbs are too big, Julio helps the ants and pulverizes the crumbs into smaller pieces. He happily he watches how the insects take their bread to their underground home. The band starts to play and Julio stands in-between the audience with a can of beer in his hand. He is mesmerized by the beautiful Haitian singers, dressed in long skirts and tight T-shirts, who swing to the rhythm. The sky gets darker and turns a nasty green color. Thunder booms, and when the raindrops start to fall, the organization decides to cancel the concert. Julio screams that they have to go on and waves aggressively with his can of beer. When the downpour starts, everybody runs for shelter under the grandstand or at the food stalls. Everyone except Julio. He has taken off his shirt and catches the raindrops in his wide-open mouth while performing a wild rain dance.

Estoban looks warily at Julio who is now dancing like a maniac and nearly falls in the mud. It is a heavy, but very short, rainstorm and in a while the sun breaks through the clouds. The band gets the plastic protection sleeves off of their guitars and boxes, and start to play again. Julio is ecstatic.

"Fucking amazing," he yells at me. "Fucking asshole," he yells, when I point out another homeless man who is sneakily stealing our cans from the bag. In a split second, the dancing maniac has turned into an aggressive street kid protecting his turf. He grabs the can thief by his shirt and curses at him with terrible words. The can man, a short, stocky Mexican in a dirty leather coat, trembles with fear when Julio takes back his stolen cans, and a lot of extra ones from the Mexican as well.

"And now get the fuck outta here," he screams at the Mexican who walks away with drooping shoulders. When Julio counts the extra cans, he has a contented expression on his face. He has nearly doubled his harvest. "What was that idiot thinking? Last week they also stole a bag off me when I didn't watch it for a moment. Won't happen again."

We are back in the tunnel. The cans have been redeemed, we got more beer and pizza, and Julio also got a bag of weed. We smoke a reefer with Hugo and Poncho and discuss the looming eviction. A few Amtrak officers had shown up in the tunnel, shouting with a bullhorn that it was time for everybody to move. Nobody has heard anything from the Coalition. They had come to the tunnel a few weeks earlier and promised to follow up, but they never returned. Little Havana is worried. They feel deserted by everybody.

In the next week, the Coalition finally turns up. They are slowly winning the trust and confidence of Little Havana. Margaret and I have put aside our mutual antipathy and try to help the Coalition a bit by convincing the tunnel people that this time the eviction is for real. If they don't want to wind up on the street, they should look into the alternative housing program offered to them.

20. THE ADVENTURES OF FRANKIE, PART 3: KATHY AND JOE COMPLAIN ABOUT FRANKIE

"Me and Joe, we don't talk no more," Frankie says curtly. Why, he does not want to explain. After a day canning with him, we walk back through the park. Kathy and Joe are sitting on a bench, enjoying the nice weather, and wave affably back when I greet them. After doing a small photo assignment for Kathy, portraits of all her cats, we are now friends. Frankie looks at the ground, ignoring them, while he drags his rattling shopping cart behind him. After I help Frankie get his cart into the tunnel, I walk back to the park to join Kathy and Joe. "It is all because of Frankie," Kathy tells me indignantly. "He'll get us all kicked out." Joe is silent, but nods in agreement. Only now, in the broad daylight, do I see that his arms are covered with huge scars.

"He invites minors in the tunnel, they drink and party all through the night. At this moment, there are already three kids staying over." Kathy sighs. "Where will it end?"

Indeed it has become rather crowded at Frankie's. When I picked him up this morning to go canning, I stumbled over the sleeping bodies of three kids who were lying on mattresses strewn all over the floor. Frankie told me that one had run away from home, and that the other two had been kicked out by their parents.

"Yeah," Joe says. "That's why we haven't cut the lock yet at the parking garage. It would be crowded with mothers getting their kids out of the tunnel."

"That's right," Kathy says. "The mothers pay Frankie so their kids can stay there. On top of that, the kids also pay Frankie for food and shelter." It doesn't sound logical, but Kathy affirms it with a self-assured nod. "He only works Fridays," Kathy gossips. "Even me and Joe can't afford that."

Kathy tells me the Coalition came by. Mary Brosnahan told them they will get alternative housing. Margaret and Mary also reassured Kathy that she will be able to keep all her cats. "They only help people who behave well," Kathy says in her hoarse voice. "Me and Joe. And Ozzy. But not Frankie. He's a pyromaniac and a sex addict."

Frankie is a pyromaniac because he once burnt down the shack of an abusive Mexican. Now he has started to burn the garbage around his place. Sometimes Joe and Kathy's bunker is covered in thick smoke. And Frankie is a sex maniac because he makes a lot of noise when making love to his ex-girlfriend. Her name is Maria, and she is a very fat Puerto Rican girl. She still lives with her parents, but moved in with Frankie because she thinks it's cozy down there. "Sex with my ex," Frankie had chuckled. "She loves to get laid. When we fuck, the bunkers shake."

21. SEARCHING FOR MOLE PEOPLE

"Chief Exterminator MTA" is printed on P.C. Taylor's business card. He's boss of the department for the elimination of rats and cockroaches in New York's huge subway system, the Metropolitan Transit Authority. He is also responsible for cleaning and maintenance. A total of 714 miles of tracks and 6,000 trains, P.C. Taylor tells me enthusiastically.

"I know you journalists love numbers. Here you got a few more," he says and hands me a paper with some mind-boggling numbers: 10,675 signals; 469 stations; 87 miles of platforms. And all over that huge system, smoking is strictly prohibited. Every passenger is bombarded by big posters that scream with bold capitals: don't even think of smoking. P.C.'s office, hidden deep down inside the gigantic subway station at Times Square, is the only exception to this rule.

At his ease, he leans backwards, packs his pipe and tells me about his work. "We put down bowls with rat poison, mixed with peanut butter so the rats don't taste it. The tunnel people are eating it. I wrote the producer of the poison to see if it could be dangerous. Thank God not. An adult has to eat at least a pound of it."

I wound up at P.C. Taylor's because I wanted to see the homeless situation in the other tunnels. The French journalist Sabine had told me last autumn that Bernard's tunnel was the Fifth Avenue of tunnels compared to what she had seen in the subway. She had been there a few times, with P.C., and also with the Transit Police. After budget cuts, however, there are no more Transit Police and NYPD's public information staff is seriously reduced. No more guided underground tours with police protection for journalists.

I don't feel like going down by myself to search the subway tunnels with only a small flashlight. It is crazy dangerous because of the trains and the third rail that can kill instantly with its six hundred volts, but more so because of the people down there, the so-called mole people who are considerably less sophisticated than the ones in our Amtrak tunnel. "Whatever you do," Bernard had warned me stringently, "never, I say never, go down in the subway tunnels on your own." In this case, I listen to the stubborn Bernard, and I have put my cards on P.C. to take me to the mole people. Although my quest does not yield many of them, I meet the most interesting authorities and aid workers.

"Mole people" is in fact a pejorative name for tunnel people. Coined by the homeless themselves, they whispered that some people had been down so deep, and for so long, that they could not stand sunlight any more and could produce only a weird squeaking instead of talking. The term was first used in a sensational headline from *New York Newsday*, and became common after Jennifer Toth's book *The Mole People*.

Among experts, mole people are a subset of tunnel people who live several stories underground or dwell in the inhospitable labyrinth of subway tunnels. Due to disease, alcohol, and drug addiction, most are in a desperate state.

P.C. lights his pipe with a wooden match and blows out big blue clouds of smoke. He prefers the term "tunnel people." Nobody knows exactly how many there are. Estimates range from a few hundred to many thousands. There are also big fluctuations by season. In the summer, most subway tunnels are even hotter and more humid than outside. In wintertime, when it is getting cold, many homeless people leave the parks and streets and go down into the relatively warm subway system.

According to P.C., the number has fallen drastically over the years. He deduces this from the occurrence of track fires, both the fires made by the homeless to warm themselves and the accidental fires that start when the homeless leave stuff behind that is ignited by contact with the third rail. There used to be a few of them every day. Over the last year, there were only nine or ten. Since the early '90s, when the tunnel population peaked, the authorities have been using a two-track approach to tackle the problem: the Transit Police evict tunnel people because they are trespassing and constitute a danger to themselves and MTA passengers. At the same time, outreach workers patiently try to convince the homeless to leave the tunnels and help them find services such as shelters and rehab.

Some organizations, like the Bowery Residents Committee and Housing Works, have special teams that focus on tunnel people. The Transit Authority has its own program, MTA/Connections. The New York City Police Department has also its own homeless outreach unit.

"It's a sad world down there," P.C. says. "In 1994, we had three fatal accidents in one day. A stray dog, a maintenance worker who was hit by a train, and a homeless person who got electrocuted." The incident with the dog became headline news in the tabloids. According to the *New York Post*, the dog was walking along the tracks and refused to move out of the way of the subway train that had slowed down to a crawl. The driver had hooted his horn a few times, but to no avail. Finally, he hit the throttle, rode over the dog, and left it in pieces.

P.C. continues. "Two hundred people called the MTA to protest the dog being killed. We got an avalanche of mail, we got problems with the Animal Protection Agency and Animal Rights Groups. We got twelve reactions regarding the killed maintenance worker. And nobody was interested in the homeless."

P.C. gives me a green and orange fluorescent vest. I can join one of his cleaning crews tonight. I meet them at midnight. With their yellow helmets, white mouth masks, latex gloves, orange ear protectors and the big spray can of disinfectant on their backs, they look like Ghostbusters. The few passengers that are still around at this hour look at us rather concerned. The crew works all through the night and normally cleans two or three stations.

Through shutters in the street, they enter the emergency exits and clean all the mess they find on their way down. The hygienic precautionary measures are necessary, since they stumble upon infected needles and excrement. They also always work with a police escort.

"If we would work on our own, we could be attacked by mole people," says Skinny, the most talkative of the whole crew. "Us they see as the enemy. Understandably, because we throw away the last possessions they still have in this world."

Skinny works two jobs: during the day he works as an outreach worker at a rehab in Brooklyn, at night as a cleaner for P.C. Sometimes he meets his clients, crack and heroin addicts, in the tunnels. "We see the lowest of the low. Pieces of misery," Skinny says.

"Two-legged rats, we call 'em," remarks the youngest of the crew. He wears heavy golden chains around his neck and four huge rings on each hand. It must be difficult to put on his latex gloves. "Shut up, Gold Finger," Skinny says. He doesn't think it's funny. "One time we were cleaning a huge pile of garbage. The garbage started to move and a man crawled out under it. We told him he could not stay there. 'I am too sick to leave,' he stuttered. He was taken to a hospital. A week later we heard he had died from AIDS." Skinny sighs. "Some people come down here to die in peace. And we, we clean them up." Every year, they find a few dead bodies.

After a few transfers, we arrive at Delancey Street station on the Lower East Side. We wait for the police at a shutter in the street. Nearby is an emergency exit they call "The Club" because it is close to a disco. "They were dealing heroin in the open," Skinny says. "The dealer had put all his stuff very neatly on a cardboard box. You could even rent needles."

The police arrive and the shutter is opened with a special key. With guns drawn, the cops go down first and return a few minutes later. All clear down there, they tell us and the crew starts working. The staircase leading down to the subway has an unbearably heavy stench of urine. Routinely, the crews spray the disinfectant into every corner and throw away old newspapers, blankets and cardboard, filling the garbage bags they have brought along. When I come up, there is bad news. The cops have found out that I need additional permission from the NYPD. "I'm sorry, kid, but you gotta go," a cop says. Too bad, but I have to leave Skinny, Gold Finger, and their buddies.

The labyrinth under Grand Central is seven stories deep, and has hundreds of stairways, alleys, and kilometers of tunnels that are said not to be in use. The total surface is as big as twelve football fields. At night, scores of homeless descended from the waiting rooms and platforms to their netherworld. During the day they hung around among the crowds of passengers commuting from the suburbs to their offices mid-town. At the moment, there are only a handful of homeless who remain. This is in great part thanks to the five-year efforts of police Sergeant Bryan Henry.

Sergeant Henry is a big black man with penetrating yet warm brown eyes that command authority. When Metro North started an outreach program to handle the homeless problem in the early '90s, Henry volunteered right away. On his own and armed only with a big flashlight, he went down into the dark caves every day. He managed to clean up the whole area with a mixture of arguments, understanding and, if necessary, force. A lot of tunnel people entered help programs thanks to Henry's intervention.

"I studied Eastern philosophy. My karma lacks compassion. I try to compensate for that through my work," Henry explains his tireless efforts. "It's pretty simple. For the same token, I could have been one of these people myself. I try never to forget that."

Henry tells me stories about the old situation. "Up in the station here, we had a whole colony of homeless," he says. "In the end, it became more comfortable than a shelter. At night, the police were patrolling in between the benches where people slept. In the morning, you had three homeless organizations handing out coffee, sandwiches and donuts. Room service and police protection. Everybody had his friends, the prostitutes had their clients on their doorsteps. Pickpockets and con artists got a wave of new, fresh victims every day. Dealers and liquor stores around the corner. A self-sufficient community came into being and with its well organized infrastructure attracted even more homeless like a magnet. But the commuters felt unsafe and started to take their cars. Slowly, we broke down that whole network. You sometimes see people coming back, but they never stay long. There is nothing to do, their friends aren't there any more, the action has gone. They realize the party is over."[64]

Some homeless moved on to other places, others went to rehab, hospitals and shelters and got more or less back on track.

Sometimes I meet a former homeless from the tunnels and the station, now well dressed and clean. They thank me for keeping them from going under," Henry says. "That's why I do this work. It gives me intense satisfaction to save a life."

An excursion with Bryan Henry is no problem and he takes me on his daily search for the few remaining mole people. At the end of a platform, we take an elevator down three stories. Then Henry leads me through dark passages and rusty stairwells, along hissing and leaking steam pipes even deeper down into the station. Finally we reach our final destination, 'Burma Road,' a popular spot for the homeless. It is a long passageway seven stories below ground, named for its unbearable heat and humidity. The construction of the Burma Railroad by Allied POW's in the extreme climatic conditions took thousands of lives.

"Be quiet for a moment," Henry says. "He has to be up here." Henry points at the ceiling. Maintenance workers have recently spotted a mole man. Henry has also seen the man a few times, but he always slips away. "Sometimes it's like playing cat and mouse," he says.

Henry opens a metal door with a demolished lock, and climbs a metal ladder. We enter a small crevice. There, a black man sleeps on a bed of blankets and cardboard. "Good morning," Henry calls out. Disturbed, the man turns himself over. They know each other.

"Damn it, Bryan," he mumbles. "Why do you have to bring all these journalists here?"

"You tell him," Henry says to me. I try to convince the homeless man of the social relevance of journalism. He is not impressed, turns over another time and pulls the blanket over his head.

"Shall we get up?" Henry says, still friendly. "This is not a place for the homeless."

"Fuck it," we hear from under the blanket. "I am not homeless, I'm just a struggling man. I am only taking a nap here because I am depressed."

"Come on, guy, you are homeless and we can bring you to a place where they can help you."

"Goddammit. Leave me alone, Bryan. I don't need help."

"Be serious, man."

"Okay, okay, go ahead and arrest me. That's what you like to do, eh? You represent the establishment. It's a cultural thing, you know. You don't understand."

"Stop bullshitting around," Henry tells him, now impatient. "Just get up." The man rises and makes a threatening movement towards Sergeant Henry. He is naked except for a pair of loose, red briefs.

"Stop it right there!" Henry barks, while putting his hand on his Glock. "I'm the one who's in control here! Get dressed and follow me. Slowly."

Henry calls a few colleagues on his radio, and grumbling, the man follows him down the stairs. While we are waiting on Burma Road for the reinforcements, the man is still protesting, now calling on traditional tribal structures in Africa to defend himself. Henry listens to the confused discourse with a smile.

"Hey, that's the phone guy," the two cops say when they arrive. They handcuff the man. "We've been after him for some time."

The man is a con artist who watches and memorizes the secret credit card codes people punch in on pay phones. He then sells these codes to other people. The unsuspecting owner has to foot a hefty bill at the end of the month. It's a popular scam in New York.

Henry sighs as we descend another level. "He will be held a few days at a police station, then he is free and will come down here again. With that bullshit about African culture he tries to put up a façade of dignity. Obviously he is mentally ill, but not crazy enough for involuntary confinement. A Catch-22 situation. He refuses help, and I cannot force him to accept help. Just letting him stay is also not possible, because next week he will be joined by ten others."

Deeper under Grand Central, we enter deserted tunnels barely illuminated by a few fluorescent lights. It used to be pitch black, Henry tells me. He points me to the places where groups used to live. One spot was known as "The Condos." It is a platform on top of a subterranean cliff about thirty feet high with trains passing under it. They were pretty organized in the Condos, Henry says. They washed their clothes with water that leaked from the pipes, and dried it on the hot steam pipes. They tapped electricity from the emergency lights. The Condo inhabitants stole heavy copper wiring from signals and switches to sell as scrap metal. Once in a while a train derailed.

"Too bad they had to go," Henry says. "But they couldn't stay. This environment is unfit for human dwellings. Rats, high-voltage wires, asbestos, fine metal dust. If you break a leg and nobody finds you, no doubt you will die like an animal."

Once, Henry found a woman unconscious and naked. She had been raped and robbed of all her clothes. "If we hadn't found her, she would have died there. I got blankets for her and brought her to the hospital. It turns out she was four months pregnant. Addicted to crack and mentally ill. She had already had two kids that had been taken away from her by Child Protective Services."

One night, his work almost killed him. He had crawled through a small hole under a platform. The people living there lit some newspapers and garbage to stop him. If he hadn't found the exit as fast as he had, he would have suffocated in the smoke.

Henry shows me the deserted platform. The hole is now bricked up. In total, Metro North has spent a few million on metal fencing, strong locks and chains, the closing up of empty spaces, and installing lights. Henry has actually made his own job obsolete. "I rarely meet people here. You were lucky we met the phone guy."

A maintenance worker repairing a steam pipe confirms it. "Long time ago we saw someone. It has become a lot safer since Henry cleaned it up down here." The worker was once chased by a furious mole man with a knife because he had accidentally stepped on his feet.

Upstairs in Henry's office I see medals, decorations, awards and group portraits with high level politicians. "They think it is cool to pose with a negro in a uniform for the photo," Henry says with a wink. Everyone, not just fellow policemen and politicians but aid workers and the homeless as well respects the Sergeant, who only a year ago was still a lieutenant.

Bernard has a different opinion. "Since Bryan was promoted to Sergeant, he thinks he's a big shot," he said. "I tell you, Tune, he doesn't understand a damn thing." The two had met just once. A TV crew had arranged the meeting under Grand Central. "Why is someone with your abilities living in the tunnels?" Henry had asked. Bernard had been deeply offended.

"I balance between a social worker and a police officer," Henry says. "My primary task is to make Grand Central safe for everybody. But I try to do that as humanely as possible. The homeless associate a uniform only with cruelty and repression. After they meet me, they know it also can be different."

Henry talks about a girl who sometimes slept in the tunnels, other times slept in the waiting room of the station. "She was a sad case, but you could really laugh with her. She always performed crazy imitations of me. Everybody at the station mourned when she was killed."

The girl was a prostitute with a boyfriend who dealt crack in the Bronx. When he found out she was HIV-positive, he stabbed her, cut her body up into pieces and put the remains in suitcases on the street.

"We couldn't just dump her like a piece of garbage in Potter's Field," Henry says. He organized a small memorial and gave the eulogy. "I told them that the girl had been a free spirit who had chosen her lifestyle. Even if her life represented everything that is completely rejected by society, we could at least learn one thing from her: no matter what you do, what people want you to do, you're born alone and you die alone. And in between these moments everybody makes his own choices."

"Homelessness is terrible," Henry muses. "It kills you. You are set on fire by gangs, you die slowly from AIDS." Henry started to work for the police force as a paramedic, and knows the symptoms very well. Besides tuberculosis and pneumonia, meningitis is common. Sometimes he meets people like that in the tunnel. "They have crawled away to die, they don't know what is happening and go into a coma. In that sense it's a merciful death."

Septic shock is also common. "The body has so many infections, internal lesions, and subcutaneous ulcers that at some point the immune system can't handle it anymore. Blood poisoning is the result. One minute the victim is alive and kicking, and then within a few hours he is completely dead."

Food poisoning also happens frequently, says Henry. "Nobody has exact data about this, but for people with low resistance, it can be fatal. Homeless like to brag that they ate an excellent lobster from a garbage can but will never tell you how often they fell sick."

Henry's voice softens. "Slowly, as a homeless person, you are robbed of all your dignity, you lose self confidence and self respect. People yell at you 'Go get a job!' But those kind of people will never hire you. There are completely separate medical and legal systems. In the hospitals, you wind up with minimal care in the pauper's section; doormen, cops and security men beat you up and you can't sue them for assault. Really, it's a tale of two cities."

22. THE ADVENTURES OF FRANKIE, PART 4:
A BABY IN THE TUNNEL

"Shoes out," Frankie call out sternly as I am about to enter. Visitors who have braved an alley drenched with dog piss and shit are no longer allowed to smudge the floor of his living room with their soiled shoes. "I don't want this place to become a junkie hole," Frankie explains the new policy.

Five people now live in Frankie's place. The maximum capacity has definitely been reached, so there is a need for new house rules. Ment moved in again. He is a free man now, released after doing his time for what he says was a robbery.

Ment doesn't want to talk about his time in jail. "It was okay," is all he says.

Fat Maria also seems to have become a permanent resident. Frankie just can't keep waiting and yearning for Vanessa until she comes back. "A man gotta do his thing," Frankie justifies his unfaithfulness. Ment has brought his new girlfriend to live there as well. Her name is Fatima; she is a beautiful nineteen-year-old girl with Greek and African roots. The two are hopelessly in love, and make out on Frankie's couch like two love birds.

Number five is Jazzy, Fatima's eighteen-month-old baby girl. The father has left them, and now Ment has become godfather. Frankie plays the sugar daddy to Jazzy who is crawling on all fours in the living room. He grabs the toddler by her feet and swings her above his head. "Stop it," Fatima cries, terrified. Jazzy screams happily at the fun. "Yo, the rug monkey loves it," Frankie laughs.

Tonight it is party time. Long strips of condoms hang like garlands from the ceiling. The speakers blast loud rap music, and Frankie and Ment toast with their 40's of Miller. Fatima and Maria are dancing like Go-Go girls on top of the speakers in their tight T-shirts. Their heavy breasts shake with the rhythm. Fatima has huge stretch marks under her belly button. Jazzy must have been a tough delivery.

"Stop it," Maria cries at Frankie. He has a black bra, a souvenir from Vanessa, wrapped around his head and is now pinching Maria's huge ass. Jazzy has been tied up in a buggy with a pacifier in her mouth. She looks around dazed.

Kathy enters. They are friends again. "A cat is dying," she sobs when Ment has turned down the music. Down in their bunker, the big red tomcat with the torn ears is rattling like an old man. Kathy has put a blanket over him. "Let him die in peace," Ment says. We watch the dying cat; there is nothing we can do. Joe is lying exhausted on his bed. Three days ago, he had a small stroke. Frankie and Ment carried him out of the tunnel and brought him to the hospital where he spent only one day. "This is no life," Kathy says with a hoarse voice and points at Joe. "He doesn't care about his heart condition. All he does is drink. He only works one day a month. We both live on my SSI now."

The cat passes away with one last cough, and Kathy pulls the blanket to cover its body. "Time to move out," she sighs. "I am sick of the tunnel. I want a space where I can wash myself."

23. AID WORKERS VS. MOLE PEOPLE

"In the beginning we were hesitant to advertise our program," says Victoria Mason-Ailey, the spokesperson for the MTA/Connections program. We are sitting in her office on the twentieth floor on Lexington Avenue. "We were afraid our passengers would think it was a waste of time and money. After all, we are in the public transportation business, not in the social work sector. But it is in everybody's interest, both our maintenance workers as well our passengers, not to tolerate homeless in the tunnels. A few years ago, we had a few dozen accidents with homeless in the subway tunnels every year. But over the past eight months, we've had only five accidents. Still five too many, but we are going in the right direction."

"And you should hear the passengers curse when a tunnel person is run over. They don't care about a dead homeless person but hate the subway because it has a one hour delay."

The program started in 1990 and currently employs twenty people—psychologists, doctors, paramedics, and drug counselors. The program operates not only in all subway tunnels, stations and platforms, but also in railroad terminals like Penn and Grand Central. An estimated two thousand homeless people are on the rolls as clients. Every year, the program costs about one million dollars. Although there are big budget cuts scheduled in all MTA departments, the board has already assured Mason-Ailey that the Connections program will not be scrapped.

"A recent survey among passengers showed that the feeling of security has greatly increased now the biggest congregations of homeless on stations and platforms are gone," says Mason-Ailey. "It rarely happened, but there was always that fear of that one crazy homeless person who would push you in front of the train."

The MTA/Connections program has a dual approach. On the one hand there is the outreach component, making contact with the homeless to convince them they need professional help. Teams of two people go out, sometimes with police escort, and search for the homeless in stations, platforms and tunnels. The teams have special track training.

"You have to understand the subway signals," Mason-Ailey explains. "You have to know how to deal with the third rail, feel the air flow of approaching trains. When you are looking for homeless, you are easily distracted and it can happen that a train suddenly appears out of nowhere. In my opinion, it was crazy that these two from Housing Works took the secretary of housing down in the tunnels," she says, shaking her head.

By returning on a regular basis, the teams try to gain the trust of the homeless. They always leave a business card, in case the homeless person wants to call the outreach workers. If he or she does decide it is time to accept help, the teams can refer them to the appropriate organizations: MTA/Connections cooperates closely with groups that specialize in helping people deal with drug, alcohol, AIDS, or psychiatric problems, as well as all city hospitals.[65]

The second component in the program is the so-called "case management." Once a client is receiving assistance, whether they are in a clinic, are back on welfare, or have received alternative housing, it must be checked to ensure they are fulfilling their new tasks and obligations and not sliding back down into old habits.

"We even have to visit Clifford every month and tell him that he needs to pay the rent on time and has to fill in his welfare paper at the end of the month," Mason-Ailey says. Clifford is the poster boy for MTA / Connections, a success story described on the program's flier. Mason-Ailey shows me a *New York Newsday* article. "His Life was Like a Box of Grenades," the headlines scream sensationally, a variation of Forrest Gump's "Life is Like a Box of Chocolates."

Clifford was the ultimate mole man. In pitch dark tunnels, Clifford was shooting up heroin with blunt and bent needles, using the one arm that was OK to inject it into his other arm that was partially paralyzed. That's to say, if he wasn't suffering delirium tremens from drinking cheap vodka and whiskey. Six stories deep under Grand Central, he had crawled away so as not to face his shattered life. Thanks to the efforts of two outreach workers from MTA/Connections, as well as Sergeant Bryan Henry and a fellow homeless man, Clifford saw the light again. He successfully made it through rehab, got his identity papers back, and could apply for welfare. Now Clifford lives in an apartment in Brooklyn, the proud owner of a doorbell and his nameplate on the door.

The program has become so effective that Amtrak now has consulted MTA/Connections to help with their problem with the homeless of Penn Station. Under new regulations, the police can evict the homeless from the Amtrak stations if they become a nuisance. Apart from a prohibition of urinating in public, panhandling, playing loud music and selling merchandise, it is currently also forbidden to sleep lying flat. But the homeless are very inventive, Mason-Ailey explains. "They found out pretty fast that the police could not intervene if they slept sitting straight up. And those that wanted to lie down just went one story below, to the waiting room of the New Jersey Transit where the NYPD doesn't have jurisdiction. In no time, Penn was crowded again with homeless who were sleeping side-by-side, sitting up with their garbage bags. No regular traveler dared to sit between them anymore. In these situations we can offer our services and make a difference."

"If we accept that people will settle down in the tunnels, we are only pushing the problem farther down into the deep," says Shary Siegel. "And with every day someone lives on the street, it is harder to get him back."

Shary Siegel is the coordinator from the MTA/Connections teams. Mason-Ailey introduced us because I want to join her tunnel teams. Siegel's office is on Columbus Circle, from her window at the 30th story you have a view over the whole of Central Park.

Siegel finishes a phone call with the assistant of Secretary Cisneros, and tells an outreach team to make sure Clifford hands in his welfare forms in time. She runs her hands through her messy hair, and apologizes for making me wait so long.

"It's a complete madhouse here," she sighs when a staff member puts a pile of new faxes on her desk. Siegel draws the organizational structure of MTA/Connections for me on a big sheet of paper: where the money is coming from; which organizations are involved; which federal, state, and city institutions are currently giving grants; to whom to they must report; who has the final decision making power. By the end of it, she has drawn a cryptic chart with arrows and dotted lines and acronyms written all over it: DHS; BRC; HUD; HHC; BID; HPD.[66] Siegel sees me painfully copying the picture in my notebook and has to laugh. "Sometimes I lose the oversight as well. A good exercise to draw it again."

"We lose a lot of energy fighting bureaucracy to get someone placed in a program or alternative housing," Siegel points out the basic problems. "Some apartments are only for psychiatric cases, but they need an official doctor's declaration that they are drug and disease free before a landlord will accept them. We have to get people identity papers, and put them on welfare. When we pick someone up and bring him to the hospital, we sometimes see how much worse some cases are. Completely run down by every disease imaginable. We see the final result of all social evils: disrupted families; a failing shelter system; abused women. Some people will always be vagrants, loners, and losers. That's life. But if people are sliding down the abyss, it is our duty to intervene."

Siegel works the phone to arrange for me to go down with her teams. They work with a police escort, and after countless calls she winds up speaking with subway police spokesman Al O'Leary. I have already spoken to him three times. O'Leary is short. "No way!"

One of the homeless organizations focusing on tunnel people is the BRC, Bowery Residents Committee. For twenty-five years they have been firmly established in the Bowery, New York's traditional neighborhood of vagrants and the homeless. BRC doesn't need to publicize their program. "Through word of mouth, people hear about our programs. They come themselves out of the tunnels, knocking on our door for help," says a proud Eric Roth, the director of the BRC.

"They know that at our place, they won't get arrested, abused or drugged till they are out cold. And contrary to what most people think, homeless are not that transient. They are geographically a pretty stable group. Most of the time, they forage only in a radius of a few city blocks. Outreach is a neighborhood-based endeavor."

The BRC offers a wide variety of programs: rehab for heavy alcoholics, education courses, work programs, a few drop-in centers for emergency cases, apartment buildings for assisted to semi-independent living, re-socialization programs, recreation evenings, and the nearly superfluous outreach program called 'Project Rescue.' Traditionally, the BRC focused on alcoholics, but now the target group is slowly changing to consist mainly of MICA's: a euphemistic but practical acronym for Mentally Ill Chemical Abusers. The newest category is HIV-positive MICA's. "The most difficult group," Roth sighs. "You just don't know which problem to tackle first."

Roth, a big guy with an even bigger beard, is a no-nonsense type. After twenty years' experience he knows what he is talking about and is not sensitive to the newest fads and trends in outreach and social work. Without his cooperation, the classic study *Old Men of the Bowery* would never have been made. Roth receives me in his office, which features a huge aquarium with tropical fish and an enormous mural of the galaxy. On a wall hangs an interesting sculpture of Yin and Yang symbols, Volkswagen hubcaps, and peace signs that would not be out of place in Marcus' cave.

"Outreach is the easiest part of the whole process," Roth says. "Find a homeless person, have a talk with him, give him a sandwich, no problem. Everybody can do that. The question is, what next? Basically, there are two approaches to outreach. At one end of the continuum you see organizations that focus on housing. Everything a homeless person is offered besides housing is considered a bandage and seen as disrespectful." Housing Works and organizations like Pathways represent this line of thought, Roth explains.

"In our philosophy, permanent housing is also the final goal, but we see it as the last stage after a set of programs that have to be run through. These steps can be stopping by our drop-in center and sleeping in our emergency shelter, it also can mean a temporary stay in a half-open institution. If all goes well, the client can move on to a more independent form of living."

"You just cannot put someone who has lived five years on the streets in an apartment," Roth says. "They'll screw up. Some people go crazy if they are suddenly between four walls. Others don't flush the toilets and start to make fires. Rats take over, and in no time it's a mess and they will be kicked out. That's why we start with accompanied living and we give household courses to teach people the simple things of life again."

"The flipside," Roth continues, "Is that this is seen by some as a humiliation. But everybody needs structure. If someone doesn't have a clue about cooking and only lives off of Chinese take-out and pizzas, you have to teach him to cook. You have to explain that at the Chinese restaurant a meal costs five bucks and that for that same money you can get a whole chicken, a pound of vegetables and kilo of rice with which you can prepare a week's worth of food. Then you have to explain that you have to put the chicken in the fridge, if you have already explained how the fridge works, you have to show how to cut the chicken in pieces and fry it. Yes, I can understand that this might be perceived as infantilizing. But they don't know it and they need to learn it somehow."

Roth sighs. "It is unavoidable that outreach workers make a selection of who can be helped on the basis of their intuition and prejudice. If that leads to the creaming of an elite, that's wrong, but let's face it. We don't want people who assault our staff, who threaten others with firearms, who burn things down."

"The three keys to good outreach are endurance, patience, and continuity," Roth says solemnly. "It is not about handing out a sandwich once. It is about giving a sandwich three years in a row, three times a week. We use bait. AC in the summer, central heating in the winter. Food, clothing, and showers to lure them out of the tunnels. You just cannot go down there and say: 'Hey guys, you want housing?' You have to break down a wall of suspicion. And that takes time. There are people that don't accept food, they think you are trying to poison them. Don't force anything. After a year they will notice their fellow homeless are still not poisoned and they will take one. Others refuse to talk to you. Also fine. Maybe at sandwich number one hundred they will say thank you."

I ask if it is possible to join a team to enter the tunnels. Roth has to disappoint me. Because their clients come up themselves, his teams don't have to go down. I cannot get a tour of the Broadway Lafayette station, the most notorious piece of tunnel with the saddest cases.

"If you would have talked in our first conversation about mole people, I would not even have talked to you," Roth says sternly. "It is sad how the media treat the homeless. Or they are sensationalized, or they are romanticized." Roth mentions some of the photo essays that have appeared about the picturesque encampments in the East Village and under the Manhattan Bridge. In the meantime, these camps have been bulldozed away.[67]

"You are cold, you are wet and hungry, you are forced to live in a shack of plywood, you use drugs and alcohol to kill the pain and then you see these aesthetic photos that imply 'This guy is okay.' But these are not okay people. They didn't choose to live down there. They should have jobs, a family. Some of these camps were plagued by fires, fights, murders, terrorized by crack dealers and tuberculosis bacteria. I don't know if that is okay."

Roth is riled up. "You know, at the foot of the Manhattan Bridge you had that big Teepee. I thought it was cute as hell! It was represented as an anarchistic symbol of resistance, a testimony of resilience. But you should have been inside. Democracy, no way. Hierarchy and survival of the fittest, like all over. A stranger just couldn't walk in there and say: 'Hi, folks, I'm homeless, can I live here?' He would be robbed and molested on the spot."

Roth stands in front of his window and looks over Chrystie Street, a backstreet of the Bowery. "If you see how hard some homeless are working...yesterday I saw some of them sawing a fridge in pieces in the smoldering heat, just to earn some money from scrap metal. And it always surprises me how sophisticatedly they have built up their canning business...already sufficient proof that these people don't need to be homeless."

Professor Terry Williams likes to see homelessness in a global perspective. He receives me in his office just after his very busy weekly open hour for students. His course titled Sex in the City has become the hottest at the New School of Social Research. Williams takes his students on field research to dark and kinky S&M clubs like The Vault, and makes them observe transvestites and prostitutes in the Meat Market district just below Chelsea. There is a coming and going of students with wild research plans. A blond exchange student with thick glasses and a baby face— his sweater says *Heidelberger Universität*—will define homosexuality in The Village, conceptually as well as geographically. Last week during field research someone actually pinched his ass, he complains to Williams. "Should I be concerned, professor?"

"Don't worry," Williams says and gives me a wink. "By the way, looks like you have a fantastic entrance." At the hour's end, Williams closes his agenda and gives his time to me.

His tunnel book was finished two years ago, but still isn't out due to contractual complications with the publisher. In his book, Williams presents his thesis of a new underclass, the disposable class. "Every capitalistic system needs a large pool of unemployed people who can be tapped quick and easy," Williams says. "But America did not expect that the surplus would be this big." The tunnel people illustrate this point in a very poignant way, according to Williams. "They are dejected by society and are pushed away to the point where they have become literally invisible. On the other side, these disposable people have not given up the fight. They create in a very inventive way, with the rare resources they have access to, their own environment and sources of income."

Williams goes on. "Society makes it looks like most homeless have themselves to blame for their fate. The concept of individual responsibility is of course fundamental for this country. Imagine, if only 15 percent believed in the American Dream. This country would come to a standstill."

"Some say homelessness is a conscious decision because there are so many programs that can get you off the street. Indeed, you could talk about a series of bad choices, a choice to lose your job, a choice to divorce, to start doing drugs that eventually lead to homelessness. But a civilized society should provide a safety net. And the reluctance to accept help is a cultural and gender dynamic phenomenon. There is a reason there are many more men than women homeless. A man doesn't want help because he might appear vulnerable, weak, and dependent. It's a macho thing."

About thirty organizations and a few federal and city bodies are involved with the problem of homelessness. "It's a multi-million dollar industry," Bernard always says. He is not exaggerating. In New York City alone, the homeless industry has a budget of six hundred million and provides jobs for three thousand people. And these are conservative estimates.[68]

Most of the money is devoured by the DHS, Department of Homeless Services, the New York City agency that, with a budget of half a billion dollars, is responsible for operating all city shelters and welfare hotels. The DHS manages around thirty thousand beds with this money, which means a cost of eighteen thousand dollars a year to shelter any shelter homeless person.[69]

This is a huge amount, and is often quoted by other homeless organizations to advertise their own efficiency. Project Renewal says it will cost them only ten thousand dollars a year to get a homeless person back on track; the Coalition says they only need five thousand dollars to admit a homeless person into one of their drop-in centers.

Why are there so many programs while the number of homeless doesn't seem to go down? Some say it is actually because of this perfect infrastructure that homelessness continues to exist.[70]

Indeed, things are not that rough for New York's homeless who have a wide range of options where they can sleep and eat. Everybody can sleep in a shelter and will be delivered there on request by the police or an outreach team. Then there are the hundreds of churches, soup kitchens, synagogues and mobile teams that hand out meals and food packages around the clock. An organization even publishes the 'Street Sheet'—a waterproof flier giving the addresses and hours of operation of dozens of soup kitchens and shelters in a particular neighborhood.[71]

"All these programs are nice and sweet, but none of them will lead to jobs and housing," says Mike Harris, the Assistant Director of the Coalition. "You undergo rehab, if you are so lucky to find a place on the waiting list with thousands, you take some vocational and job training, but after that you are back on the street again. And everybody needs a place called home…"

Mike Harris is a big black man who, contrary to other Coalition people, is very talkative and helpful. He gets me piles of documents and pounds of information about the homeless problem and the work of the Coalition from another office. "It's ridiculous," he says. "With our budget of ten million we give services that should be the responsibility of the DHS."

Apart from the voicemail experiment, the Coalition has a program with subsidized rent, and they even have a few apartment buildings. They also offer vocational training, organize summer camps for kids of homeless families, and hand out food to thousands in different locations. Every day, the Coalition has walk-in consultations for emergency cases. Mike admits that all these programs are just bandages. As a solution for the huge homeless problem, he sees gigantic construction projects that should provide jobs and housing.

"Damn," Mike says. "Roosevelt had his New Deal during the crisis. The construction of the Bronx Zoo, the Tennessee Valley Project, the Boston subway, they all have created work for tens of thousands of people. It shouldn't be any problem to do something similar now. The money is there, but not the political motivation."

"The problem is that there is no centrally coordinated approach," says Keith Cylar, the vice president of Housing Works. "There is no communication, and everybody does his own thing. The DHS is not constructing houses; other city agencies with construction projects don't have a policy for the homeless. It looks like everybody in this country is pushing the responsibility onto someone else. Homeless are the last item on the budget."

"It sounds interesting to see homelessness in a global perspective," says Sergeant Bryan Henry. "But what can I do with it? I am just here at the corner of 42nd Street and Park Avenue. I am trying to do what I can."

I dropped by the Sergeant's to bring him some photos of our last trip under Grand Central. Henry has just picked up a mole girl seven stories below and has gotten her a sandwich and a coffee.

The girl has been homeless for eight years. She ran away from home at sixteen, and is now addicted to crack. She has already been to rehab ten times without any lasting results. She has an ugly scar running from the corner of her eye to her temple, from a fight with her boyfriend who pulled a knife. She was nearly blinded in one eye. "Oh, Bryan, can you put in the sugar and milk for me," she says like a little spoilt girl that doesn't want to open the sugar and creamer bags herself.

"Stop whining, honey," Henry says sternly. He has made a couple of calls and found an empty bed for her in a rehab center on Staten Island. When she has finished her coffee, she walks out with a big white police officer who will drop her off at the center. She is holding his hand like a sweet little girl. "See you," she waves us a friendly goodbye.

Henry sighs. "A predictable scenario. Three weeks in the clinic, next month back at the station." In the last week, Henry scored a small victory. He managed to unite another homeless girl with her family after a couple of phone calls. "Homeless people are like canaries in a coal mine," Henry ponders. "An indication that something is fundamentally wrong in our society. And the folks you see on the street are only the tip of the iceberg," he continues somberly. "Four times as many people are cramped on top of each other in tiny apartments. Sleeping in the same bed in shifts. Rooms that have been subdivided with sheets and ropes into even smaller cubicles."

When he worked as an NYPD paramedic, Henry confronted the most shocking examples of housing. "And we are still not there," Henry goes on. "Social scientists predict that the generation of crack babies and neglected and abused homeless children that are now growing up will be an extremely violent class. Ruthless killers."[72]

Henry paints apocalyptic visions. "People are already locking themselves in their houses because they don't dare to go out on the streets anymore. In poor neighborhoods, they sleep in their bathtub for fear of stray bullets from gangs; the affluent suburbs transform themselves with barriers, fences, and security officers into impregnable fortresses. The security sector is the fastest growing industry in this country. It looks like we are going back to the Middle Ages. Cities surrounded by heavy walls to keep out the Barbarians."

"Yeah," Henry concludes. "Forgive me for involving Shakespeare, but something is rotten in the State of Denmark."

24. THE ADVENTURES OF FRANKIE, PART 5: FRANKIE TALKS ABOUT HIS FATHER

"It was the gooks that got him on heroin," Frankie says. We are taking a break from canning and are sitting on the edge of a planter eating Big Macs. McDonalds has a special offer, two for a dollar, and we bought six of them. Slowly, Frankie is telling me more about his youth and the big picture starts to emerge. His father returned from the Vietnam War traumatized and hooked on heroin. His mother died in a car crash. Frankie's father met another woman and married her. But she and Frankie hated each other. "Probably the bitch has declared me dead by now," Frankie says and wolfs down his second Big Mac.

Frankie tells me how his father started to drink. One fatal night, he raped his daughter. Frankie blew up. He knocked his father down and put a revolver to his head. "I'm gonna kill you," he said and cocked the gun. His hysterically screaming stepmother prevented him from doing it. That fatal night, now ten years ago, Frankie left his parental home. He never got back in touch. Maybe there was a warrant against him for assault. If that was the case, it is now past the statute of limitations.

"I can go back and laugh in the sheriff's face," Frankie says finishing his third Big Mac. "But why the fuck should I come home?"

We finish our canning route and leave for WeCan on 52nd Street, a big hangar loaded with hundreds of huge bags with cans. Outside, they have a covered area where can men sort out their harvest on big tables. Inside, there is a counter with a cashier where people return their cans, neatly sorted out in flat cardboard boxes that should hold exactly twenty-four cans of the same brand. This way the staff can count in no time and write a check.

Plastic bottles are presented in separate bags. While it is too time-consuming to count the contents exactly, WeCan relies on the honesty of its clients. Frankie loves to cheat.

"Watch me," he whispers with eyes shining. "I only have 350 bottles, but I tell 'em I got 600. Don't say anything, eh?" he adds unnecessarily. Frankie's trick succeeds, and he gives me a naughty wink.

A little later, we sit in the offices of WeCan. With a holier-than-thou face, Frankie fills in a job application form. WeCan doesn't have a very stable work force, so they are always looking for people. It is not a problem that Frankie has a criminal past and has lost his social security card.

"We don't discriminate," a WeCan staff member reassures Frankie. Frankie is now on the waiting list; I promise to write him a reference letter. If he doesn't get his job as a bike carrier, he can always work at WeCan.

We made eighty dollars today, and it is time to go grocery shopping. Bags of chips, three-dozen hot dogs, and big bottles of beer. I buy Frankie a huge pack of dog food. Ever since all his friends moved in, Frankie has started to neglect his dogs and I have noticed how skinny they are becoming. Lady Bug survived the operation from last Christmas, but is skin and bones. Frankie thinks she's got a tapeworm.

Back in the tunnel, the starving animals jump at the food. Frankie has listened to Kathy's advice and made a fence around the roof with chicken wire so the dogs have their own cage. The ten-pound bag of dog food is wolfed down in a few minutes by the slobbering animals.

Inside, it's fun-time again when Frankie unpacks the beer and chips. Maria and Fatima dance to their favorite song, "I Wanna Gangsta Bitch." It is a rap song about a modern-day Bonnie and Clyde who hang out with Mac-10's and Berettas during the day, robbing banks or snuffing crack dealers, and at night make love till the crack of dawn.

Ment is feeding Jazzy orange juice from a baby bottle. He has added just a tiny bit of beer, and Jazzy starts to have difficulties crawling. "August 24th, '95. Jazzy Had Her First Beer," Ment writes on one of the few empty spots on the walls, most of them filled with graffiti and tags of their buddies. Jazzy stumbles through the space and tries to stick her hands in the unprotected fan. Just in time, Fatima jumps on Jazzy and prevents her from losing a few fingers.

"It is not an ideal environment for a baby," Fatima admits when it is quiet for a moment. Frankie and Ment are out to get some more beer and the music has been turned down. Fatima is nervous, because if child protection finds out there is a baby in the tunnel, Jazzy will be immediately taken away. Fatima is thinking of leaving the baby with an aunt in New Jersey until she and Ment have found a good alternative.

Fatima and her baby stayed awhile in Covenant House, a shelter for runaways and homeless teenagers, but they treated her like a little kid and she left within a week. Back home is not an option. She is the oldest of seven kids, and always in trouble with the police for small offenses. Once, she blew up and assaulted a female police officer. She was wrestled down by other officers and was locked up for a few days. When Fatima got little Jazzy, the situation became unbearable. She had arguments with her hysterical mother every day. "The bitch is fucked up," Fatima sums up the situation. Most of the time, the arguments degenerated into fistfights during which mother and daughter were rolling on the floor, pulling each others' hair. "Now, I'm up shit creek," Fatima says. She has a lot of money in the bank, she says, an inheritance from her rich grandma. But her mother has blocked the money because she is still a minor. She is contacting a lawyer now.

Frankie and Ment return screaming with joy. They have been away for an hour, Ment on his rollerblades, Frankie on my bike. They went all over town, and finished a couple of beers as well. Full of enthusiasm, they recount the countless traffic accidents they nearly had.

Frankie takes me upstairs to his bedroom, and shows me a Chinese porn magazine. He points at a girl lying on her back with her legs spread wide open, smiling at the camera. "Believe it or not, Ant, this horny-ass bitch is also an ex of mine," he says proudly. He hides the magazine again, because Maria is not supposed to know. Frankie asks with an excited look if I can make a photo series of Vanessa. She will be back next week. In sexy lingerie, of course. A beaver shot included. Frankie's cheeks start to glow at this naughty idea.

"Yo, everybody," Frankie screams wildly after we have descended the rickety ladder. "Next week, everybody has to leave for one night. Our boy Ant needs to work undisturbed."

25. HOUSING AHEAD

Today is the big day for little Havana. Things have moved quickly, and the Section 8 vouchers that secretary Cisneros promised to the tunnel people are finally materializing, sooner than expected. Dov and Vincent, two staff members from Project Renewal, have visited the tunnel together with people from the Coalition. They spoke with most of the inhabitants, left their names and numbers, and made appointments for the first intake sessions. Little Havana is expected this morning at 9:30 in the downtown offices of Project Renewal. Everybody is excited when I enter the tunnel at eight with coffee and donuts.

"Wow, this time they really gonna help us," Julio say enthusiastically. He has put on his cleanest clothes, shaved himself, and smells of cheap aftershave. Poncho, Getulio, and Hugo also did their best, combing their hair and putting on their whitest T-shirts. Only Estoban did not manage to wash away the dirt that seems to be permanently etched onto his face and arms.

"Oh shit,'" Julio says, disappointed as I hand out the coffee and donuts and he notices there is no beer for him. "You didn't bring breakfast for me?" On our way to the subway, I get him a big can of Bud that he finishes in half a block. Getulio buys tokens and hands them out like a father to his children. We are on location thirty minutes early. Julio manages to bum another Bud from me and drinks it with a straw, happy as a child. Poncho reads the *New York Post* while Hugo asks me about the exact procedures regarding the vouchers.

When Julio has finished his beer, we take a shiny elevator upstairs and enter the fancy waiting room of Project Renewal. Unlike the Coalition's run-down offices, Project Renewal has obviously employed a good interior designer. The receptionist is both polite and charming, and invites us to please sit down. Julio and Estoban feel ill at ease on the expensive leather couches and leaf through the glossy magazines on the coffee table. Getulio and Hugo pace across the shag carpet.

Poncho is now reading the sports section of the *Post*, a story about Yankees pitcher Daryl Strawberry who was caught using coke. "Yeah," Poncho laughs. "He's our favorite crackhead." Poncho hardly uses coke or crack, but loves to provoke. Once, a photographer had entered the tunnel and set up his camera and tripod facing towards Poncho, who was just sitting and watching TV. "If you don't watch out, we steal your equipment and sell it for crack." The guy didn't know how to run fast enough out of the tunnel, Poncho later told me and laughed heartily.

In Castro's Cuba, Poncho was already a happy-go-lucky type. Once, he broke into a cafeteria. He only got a lousy carton of cigarettes and a pack of coffee, but wound up in jail for a few years after being caught. He became quite a successful Marielito, eventually working in the Bronx as an independent truck driver. Poncho says it was New York's parking regulations that caused his downfall. Being quite irresponsible and unconcerned, Poncho totally ignored all the rules and never paid a fine. A pile of accumulating fines combined with late-payment fees forced him to sell all his possessions, including his truck. Poncho wound up in the shelter system and eventually found the tunnel where he constructed a little house.

A smartly designed flier explains the background of Project Renewal. The organization was originally founded in 1967 as the Manhattan Bowery Project. Back in those days, the Project specialized in and catered to heavy alcoholics. Most clients are currently MICA's, Mentally Ill Chemical Abusers.

Project Renewal has the same philosophy as the Bowery Residents Committee: By means of intermediate steps—rehab, vocational and educational programs—they try to restore the self esteem lost during all these years on the street. The final goal is twofold: work and housing. Because of intensive assistance, the success rate is high: the flier says that 90 percent of all clients who follow all the steps of the program end up working and living in a decent place.

A door behind the receptionist opens and Dov Waisman enters. We introduce ourselves and are invited into a conference room, a big space with white and red-checkered tiles. Paintings of tacky snow landscapes adorn the walls. Big letters on colored leaves of paper pinned to the wall spell out 'The Journey Continues.'

Underneath it are balloons that are now withered and sagging. It looks like there must have been a wild church party a few days earlier, with a lotta pep talk, pretzels and, sorry, soft drinks only.

Little Havana takes its place in chairs that form a half-circle around Dov. They look a bit confused about the psychedelic interior. Julio frowns, mesmerized by the red-white chess board pattern of the tiles that surround him.

Dov is a young, friendly, white guy. A checkered shirt that is too big and cheap glasses give him the look of a college student. Five pairs of nervous Latino eyes stare intensely at him. When he gets over his shyness, he comes to the point.

Yes, thanks to the new program of the Secretary, the tunnel people are entitled to alternative housing. Project Renewal has been employed to process the individual cases, and provide assistance and additional programs when needed. The Coalition has the task of facilitating communication between the tunnel people and their aid workers.

To obtain the vouchers, there is actually a lot of red tape involved. The applicant must have identity papers and prove he has an income, be it a legal job or welfare. Also, the applicant must be free of any alcohol or drug addiction. The Havana five get serious faces when they realize the apartments don't come easy. To start with, the issue of identity papers might be difficult. Dov takes up a pile of folders and discusses each case.

Poncho, Getulio, and Hugo are already on welfare. They only need proof from Social Security. That can be arranged in a couple of calls. All three have lost their Social Security cards, but since they are already in the system, it is not difficult to obtain new copies.

The door swings open and a big black man enters. He has gold chains around his neck and two silver teeth shine in his mouth. "Hi, Vincy," Julio calls out happily. The man is Vincent, Project Renewal's other caseworker. Unlike his shy partner, Vincent is the outgoing kind. He himself has been homeless, he tells us, and he realizes it is not easy to get back on track. But it certainly is possible, assures Vincent, and it is worth it.

Then his voice turns serious: "It's ten o'clock in the morning. My nose is telling me that someone has been drinking. And that nose of mine never lies."

Vincent is silent and looks everybody deep in into the eyes. Julio bends his head and looks at the floor. Finally he puts up his finger like a naughty child with a blushing face.

"You come with me for a minute," Vincent orders him. The two disappear and come back fifteen minutes later. Vincent has decided that Julio has to address his alcohol problem and has made him an appointment. Next week Monday, eight AM sharp, he has to be at an alcohol clinic on the Bowery.

With Julio back, Dov gets his file. Julio has more problems. He does not have welfare, and to apply he needs his birth certificate. His mother in the Bronx has it. However, Julio doesn't want to face his mother. She still thinks he is living happily with Debby, and he can't tell her he's homeless and living in a tunnel.

Dov thinks. With a bit of creativity, there might be a way out. Julio exhales in relief.

Dov moves on to Estoban. His case is hopeless. Not only does he speak little English—Hugo has to translate everything—but he has also lost all his papers. Like most Marielitos, he has official permanent resident status, but he's lost his green card. It was stolen out of his pocket when he was sleeping on a park bench. That's why he could never find a legal job, Hugo explains. Estoban looks helplessly around him. He has also lost his Social Security card and has forgotten his number. Dov is stuck, and has no idea how to start getting Estoban's papers back. He leaves the room to make a few phone calls while Estoban paces nervously up and down.

"It's going to be complicated," Dov says when he returns a while later with a concerned look on his face. Estoban starts rapidly talking to Hugo in an angry voice, and prepares himself to leave. We can barely manage to stop him.

"Don't leave him out, man," Julio says indignantly to Dov. He reassures us with a sigh that he will do all he can.

"You know, that's why there are so few people in these programs," Julio says once we all are outside. "When they see all the paperwork, they'd rather stay on the street." Little Havana has mixed feelings; nevertheless, a mood of cautious optimism prevails.

Two days later, Bernard has his appointment with Project Renewal. Dov knows Bernard already from radio and TV, and is honored to meet one of the most famous homeless people of New York face to face. Bernard immediately launches into his eloquent tunnel monologue. Dov is listening with interest, but after fifteen minutes starts to look tired. After a long ontological discourse, Bernard is now discussing the predictions of Nostradamus. Dov, who has studied philosophy at Harvard, is not into mystical vagaries and he comes to the point.

Bernard has prepared himself well and has done all the necessary paper work. He has gone on welfare and has the papers to prove it. Relieved, Dov fills in the applications for the Section 8 vouchers. They will be sent out the same week. Bernard is ahead of everybody in the process, Dov explains, and will be the first one to get his voucher. There is only one small thing: the vouchers were originally meant for tunnel people living in the subway, not the ones that live in the Amtrak train tunnel. But Dov will call DC; he doesn't think it is a problem.

"Tunnel life was beautiful," Bernard says as he bids farewell to Dov and thanks him for everything. "But after eight years, it is time to leave. Only, I would love to spend one last winter on my own down there," Bernard sighs. "To fast and meditate so I can start up top with a clean spirit in a clean body." Dov starts to look concerned again.

Back outside, we have a coffee and Bernard explains his plans. He has little confidence in the Section 8 vouchers. "I only participated to see if they are serious. Call it an experiment." But he is slowly preparing to leave the tunnel. The plan is to seriously start two-for-oneing, and save all the money as a deposit for his move into a new place. Bernard wants to borrow a hundred dollars to start up his canning business. If he promises me not to blow it on crack, I might be able to lend it, I tell him. Bernard swears he will really invest it. Let me think about it, I tell him. I've noticed he's started to slow down on the drugs and is working hard with Pier John.

Then Bernard tells me the good news. Bob is gone. He is back at Pete's Place, the shelter where he stayed before moving into the YMCA in Brooklyn. I can come back to Bernard's bunker. It would actually be a pleasure, because the nuisance I cause rattling my kettles to make my coffee is peanuts compared to the chaos Bob caused. I will move back in a week. My wife is visiting me for a week, and Bernard is curious to meet her. Tomorrow we're all going to the zoo.

Bernard is charmed by my wife Charlotte when I bring her down into the tunnel. She is showered in the sunlight that falls though the grate while she looks around in amazement at the bizarre surroundings. Bernard observes her in the radiant light and winks at me with a sign of approval. With a moist cloth, he wipes off the chairs at the fireplace and serves coffee in mugs that he has cleaned thoroughly.

"Yes," he says proudly as Charlotte strokes a cat that is purring on her lap. "Whatever you might think of tunnel life, it sure is different." He serves coffee and it gets cozy. "People ask me if I ever get bored, if I sometimes go watch a movie. No way, Charlotte. Down here, it's the movies. We had the Frankie and Ment show, the Willy and Sheila show, and last but not least, the Mad, Mad Bob show." Bernard claps his hands with joy. "I only have to sit down at the grill and Yo! pop the corn and let the show begin!"

Bernard is all geared up now, and with his inimitable mixture of slang and eloquent phrases he tells her all about the highs and lows of tunnel life and his former adventures as a coke smuggler and runway model. The dirtiest and sleaziest stories are intertwined with biblical quotes and ontological one-liners: he is obviously doing his best to entertain my wife and succeeding in it. I have already heard most of the stories dozens of times, but Bernard's oratory talents make it a pleasure to hear them again.

As usual, he concludes his discourse with a diatribe about the media. He is now planning to write a short, but powerful and critical essay, about his experiences with journalists. The day before there had been another painful incident with Margaret. She had brought a German film crew to his canning spot. Bernard had told everybody to leave because he wanted to work undisturbed. Margaret had burst into tears. "Why are you doing this to me?" she had sobbed.

"Because your book is finished and I just want peace and this winter I don't want to see no more goddamn press folks," Bernard had bluntly answered. "And why does he get all these special privileges?" she had nastily commented, referring to my long and already extended stay in the tunnels.

"Fuck it," Bernard says. "I told her I was sick of playing mediator. If journalists have problems with each other, they should fight it out themselves. I mean, what do I get out of it?" he rhetorically asks Charlotte. "If she would lower a bag full of dollars through the gate or put a beautiful virgin at the gate..." He shakes his head. "Excuse me, I'm a man, you know. She don' gimme no pussy, she don' gimme no head... In fact, I get nothing out of it."

Bernard gets himself ready to go. He enters his bunker and reappears in his best clothes. He presents Charlotte with two pairs of khaki shorts from Banana Republic. "For you, Charlotte. Margaret didn't want them. I told her she should stop dressing like a scarecrow. The silly thing. She wears, as a matter of principle, only black."

One of the many jobs Bernard has had is as a guide in the Bronx Zoo, so he knows the place like the back of his hand. But that was eight years ago, so we get off at the wrong subway stop and have to walk two miles over the emergency lane of the Bronx-Expressway to finally reach the entrance. Inside, we need a plan, because a lot of things have changed since Bernard worked there. Bernard was a driver on one of the mini trains that take visitors around. He was fired because the animals loved him so much. In fact, the albino Father David's deer was to blame.

Thanks to the visionary missionary called Pere David, explains Bernard, the deer, originally from China, has not disappeared from the face of the earth. There are exactly three-dozen deer left, and while extinct in the wild, they remain in the zoos of London, Beijing, Washington, and New York. And in the whole world there exists only one albino deer. It is in the Bronx. And it was actually this animal that always spontaneously approached Bernard when he had finished working and was daydreaming in front of the deer-park. He didn't know better than to stroke the sweet animal's nose. It is, however, strictly prohibited to touch the animals. "What else was I supposed to do?" he asks Charlotte. She doesn't know. "Should I have kicked his ass?"

We watch the gorilla twins that are attracting crowds; we observe the baboons in their camp and watch them steal each other's bananas with dirty tricks and proudly parade with erect penises. We have to laugh at the dumb and predictable sea lions and take a look at the predator bird show. Specially trained buzzards, falcons, and eagles fall like comets out of the sky and catch the pieces of meat the trainer holds up. "Unbelievable," Bernard mumbles, tidying up his hair after a condor has flown only a few inches over his head. "And people think they are quite something. I tell you, Charlotte, human beings ain't no more than repetitive dickheads."

Ozzy hasn't shown up at his appointment with Dov, and is skeptical regarding the vouchers. "I don't believe it," he says. "First I want to see what happens with Bernard." Ozzy, the neighbor of Joe and Kathy, is a quiet and modest man. With his fashionable chrome glass frames and well-groomed appearance, he has the demeanor of an introspective and respectable schoolteacher. I often meet him in the park when he is doing his daily rounds of jogging. He'd rather not talk with journalists. "I have the impression they make us ridiculous with the term mole people," he says. "And do I get any better from giving interviews? They have a juicy reportage; we are still down here with our problems."

Once, he talked to a journalist. Against his strict request for anonymity, he was mentioned by name in the paper. He was then stopped on the street by former colleagues who had thought that he had just changed jobs and moved away. "Some old friends suspected something when they saw me out on the streets selling books," Ozzy says. Even his brother, who lives in New Jersey and whom he sees once in a while, doesn't know he is homeless. "It is a matter of pride that I don't ask them for help."

Ozzy thinks and counts the years on his fingers. He is fifty-seven years old now. I had estimated him ten years younger, and he is among the oldest of the tunnel dwellers.

"Yes, it has been four, five years that I've lived here." He smiles softly while watching two rats playing tag. "I didn't plan to stay here that long. But life is easy down here. No rent, no bills. You get lazy and complacent."

Ozzy used to sleep in the Rotunda. When the park police swept it clean, Joe invited him to come in the tunnel. The two knew each other from selling books on Broadway. Seven years ago, he was a successful computer programmer. However, Ozzy had a gambling problem. "I could hardly wait till five o'clock. Then I rushed off to the OTB. And for nights, I was playing poker with friends."

To make matters worse, Ozzy had a girlfriend who was addicted to crack. "Once I came back from work and she was lying high on crack somewhere in the corner." Ozzy tells me. "The money that I had set aside for the rent was gone. I told her she had to choose between drugs and me. 'I need crack more than I need you,' she said." Ozzy sighs and rethinks the past. "I was devastated, I went crazy. For three days I walked around dazed, didn't sleep. Then I picked up all my stuff from work and checked into a hotel. Never went back to my office."

In five years, Ozzy can live off of his social security and the pension he built up over the years. Now he is on welfare and can take care of himself without too much trouble.

When he had just become homeless, he tried to get back to a normal life. He was allowed to participate in a housing program, but only under the condition that he spend three, four months in a shelter. "No way I stay in a shelter. Out on the streets it is safer. And where should I have left my suits? They steal like crazy over there." Ozzy shows me the suits from his period as a programmer. They hang on clothes hangers from a beam in his bunker, covered in sleeves to protect them against dirt, humidity, and rats.

Ozzy has tried to go back to work, but his skills are hopelessly outdated. "I sometimes read a computer magazine. It is all gibberish to me." Twice a year he drives with his brother to visit his mother in North Carolina. She just turned ninety-two. "My brother and me have decided that she is getting too old live on her own. Maybe I'll go back to take care of her." Ozzy tells me the labor market is good, some new companies have settled in his old home town. The wages might be lower, but the cost of living is dirt cheap. And his brother can maybe get him a car, so he can look for work.

He smiles. "It is difficult to leave the city behind. New York is addictive. On the other hand, I would not mind going back. Life is more easy-going in the south. People still have manners. We greet each other in the street. That was, for me, the most difficult here in New York. You enter an elevator and say a friendly good morning. New Yorkers look at you as if you are a freak."

26. THE ADVENTURES OF FRANKIE, PART 6: FRANKIE IS MAD WITH HIS FIANCÉE

"Yo, cuz. It's deep," Frankie grumbles in an ominous baritone to Ment. "If a woman comes between two friends, I tell you. That's no good..."

I stopped by at Frankie's to see about the lingerie photo shoot. Vanessa is back in town from her summer camp, but the reunion of the two lovers was not a big success.

Frankie doesn't like to talk about it, but it comes down to the fact that Vanessa thinks that Ment is a bad influence on her boyfriend. Slowly, Frankie was turning in a decent citizen who loved to hang out in front of the TV with a bag of potato chips and a bottle of beer. He was even looking for a steady job, like that of a bike messenger. Ment has awakened Frankie's dormant criminal instincts, and the two of them hang out with a lot of bad friends from back in the day, brooding and scheming evil and stupid plans.

Frankie is now pondering how to find a fitting punishment for Vanessa. Until further notice, the photo session has been temporarily suspended. Fatima is sitting on the couch, nervously chain smoking.

"It is goddamn completely fucked up," Frankie says. The Amtrak cops made another round through the tunnel. They have been doing that quite often lately. They drive around with their blue flashlights and yell "Okay, folks, time to move" through their loud speakers. Most of the time, their efforts to intimidate stop there. Once in a while, they stop and chat a bit with the tunnel dwellers; sometimes they are friendly, sometimes they are nasty. This time, they had driven past Little Havana. They had shone a flashlight on Julio and Poncho who were just watching TV, but left them alone.

They had stopped at Kathy's and talked a bit with her and inquired about Joe's health. Frankie talked to the cops from his roof. "Why all these pampers in the tunnel, do you guys have a baby?" they barked at him.

Indeed, the diapers on the garbage piles around their bunker look quite conspicuous. Inside, Fatima was trembling with fear. Frankie kept talking to them. He knew they could not enter his place without a warrant. After only fifteen minutes, the cops left.

"Somebody must have snitched on us," Frankie says. I reassure them that I did not say a word to anybody. I didn't even tell the gossipy Bernard, to whom I mostly tell everything. But a lot of people on the South End know about the baby, someone might have slipped a word to the police. Or maybe a jogger saw Maria and Fatima trying to carry the baby stroller secretly into the tunnel. Something needs to happen, Frankie says concerned. "We don't want no heat in the tunnel."

27. THE CASE OF BOB

Bernard is in the best of moods when I move back into the tunnel a week later. "Welcome back, Tut," he says while making a fire. "Finally a normal person to talk to." I put my luggage back in Bob's bunker and assess the damage after a few weeks of Bob. It isn't too bad. A few more piss bottles have been added to the collection, while my stock of clean underwear has disappeared. For the rest, Bob has only sat on his favorite couch at the coffee table.

Bernard serves coffee and is in a chatty mood. The radio plays "Let It Be." "Fuck this Yoko. The bitch broke up the band," sneers Bernard. "And when a man allows a woman to come between him and his friends, he ain't nothing but a faggot! Hah, that John Lennon," Bernard shakes his head. "He needed to proclaim that they were more popular than Jesus. And look what happened to him. Five, six years in rehab, trying to get his act together. And finally he is ready to go back in the studio, and he is gunned down by some idiot on his doorstep. Yes, yes, Mister Lennon…" Bernard says with derision.

"Sitting in the Dakotas in a nine-room apartment. One room was totally white, the piano, the carpet, the walls, everything completely white. Fuck it. What has he done for the poor people in New York? Nothing. Once he gave a lousy hundred-thousand dollars at a charity ball of the police club. They bought bulletproof vests with it. The rest of the time he was jetting up and down to India. He could have helped a lot of the poor people over here with that money. And Paul fucking McCartney, the same shit," he continues contemptuously. "Together with Tina Turner and Michael Jackson 'We Are The World' singing with their choir-boy faces. Five hundred million worth of income on stage, trying to be cute. It's gonna be a big party in Hell…"

The God of Bernard is stern, but righteous. Sometimes he punishes immediately, sometimes only after a few years, sometime only in the afterlife, but in the end, nobody can escape his wrath. Bernard is deeply religious. I noticed lately that he always prays before dinner, very discreetly, his hands on his lap under the table, his eyes cast down for a moment.

Bernard has received a religious education in the South. Additional inspiration he got from one of his favorite books, *The Aquarian Gospel of Jesus the Christ*, an obscure new-age work filled with mystical and obscure references. Bernard is helped by promptings from God on a regular basis. For example, it's thanks to God Bernard now has a huge pile of beautiful firewood. The wood was finished, Bernard explains. He walked up top and said: "Okay God, where's the wood?"

"Two streets to the south, then turn left for another block and a half," a voice said. And there were two hundred pounds of first grade pinewood waiting for him in a trash container.

In the same way, Bernard found the bunkers. When he had first become homeless, he was sleeping under a bridge in the park. During a desperate night, he prayed to God. The next morning, he found a big survival knife. "It was the first sign of God," he says. "Then I knew all would be all right." The knife was near an entrance in the tunnels, used by gay men to have secret sex in the dark. Out of curiosity, Bernard crept through the opening and entered the tunnel. Then he heard a voice; "Go half a mile north." And there, Bernard found what is now his camp.

"He will never leave me alone," he says. "All I need comes to me automatically."

Bernard tells about the Purgatory. "On a cold winter night we were all sitting here around the grill fantasizing about Judgment Day. God is sitting on a throne and the sky is one gigantic video screen. And everybody knocking on heaven's gate has a video clip with all his sins. 'Play the tape!' God tells them. Everybody has to do it. Nobody is exempt. Also the guys that beat to death baby seals."

Bernard had just seen a documentary about it. "Two of these sweet, cute eyes are looking innocently at you, and then Bang! Splash! Blood all over the fucking place. At least they throw the bodies in the sea, so the sharks can enjoy a good meal; if not, it would be even more scandalous. Low-ass motherfuckers. Their clips will be shown five hundred times and they will be forced to watch it all over again time after time. And Bob," Bernard laughs. "God doesn't even want to judge him. A special eternal flame will be prepared for him." Then Bernard gets serious. "What a miserable human, that Bob," he says shaking his head. "Whatever it was that broke him, he should get over it and get on with his life."

Bernard tells about the day Bob's heart broke and he left home to wander the wide world. An afterthought in a family where his two brothers were seventeen and twenty-one years older, Bob once heard a fierce argument between his parents in which they both blamed each other for Bob's birth. A terrible mistake, Bob overheard his parents calling him. The next day, he ran away from home. "It's sad. His philosophy of life is 'Fuck them before they fuck you.' Behind everything he does, there is some hidden agenda. He's a pathetic liar."

Bernard tells me more of Bob's tricks. "For an entire year, he had been working honestly at WeCan. Everybody trusted him. One time, Guy Polhemus, the boss, asked him to cash a check for a few hundred bucks. A few other homeless also gave him their checks for canning. Bob jumped in a cab and never came back. Went on a six-day speed binge. Another day, I would do a paint job for a super. Bob comes later, and offers him a sharper price. The super gives Bob an advance to get paint and brushes. And gone is Bob. One time he had learnt a song. 'Have you got an eeny-weeny eetsy-peetsy tiny-winy little piece of crack.' With dance steps," Bernard sighs. "I was just smoking when he danced inside my space. 'Bob,' I said. 'Asshole. Fuck off. How long have you been studying on that one?'"

Bernard sighs. "Unbelievable. Bob thinks he is such a genius. But people give him some bucks just to get him out of their face. At the end, Terry Williams would just give him a ten so he would be gone. One time Bob came complaining to me. 'Nobody likes me,' he mourned. I told him: 'Think deeply, Bob! Did you ever give someone a reason to like you?'"

Bernard throws spaghetti in a pan and opens a can of Bolognese sauce. From his bunker, he gets a big bag of pistachio nuts. "Saved out of the hands of Tony," he says, presenting me a small dish as a starter. "He had found them on the street and wanted to feed them to the squirrels in the park 'Gimme the nuts, you moron,' I could just say in time. These dirty animals are better fed than most people in New York," Bernard has to laugh about the incident. "Yes, Dune, that's the way things go down here."

From the trash around the garbage pile he pulls out a camping table and sets it up on the little paths next to the tracks. I get a good bottle of wine out of my bunker, somehow left untouched by Bob. "A Californian Cabernet Sauvignon," Bernard reads the label. "A bit dry," he remarks and gets a bottle of sweet missionary wine out of his bunker. I can hardly hide my horror when he mixes the two wines. "Ah, you see Dune, a real smooth-drinking wine," he says when he leans happily backward and sips from the awful mix.

Above all, Bernard is a typical American. Everything needs to be smooth, creamy, full, and flavored. He never drinks a normal ice tea, no, it has to be strawberry-flavored ice tea, just as he prefers his coffee with hazelnut or swiss-almond flavor. It is a disturbing trend in America: Cherry Flavored Coke and Pineapple Flavored Chocolate Milk. I would venture that when we have come full circle, and coffee tastes like chocolate and vice versa, they will introduce original coffee flavored coffee on the market.

Bernard serves dinner. "Yeah, Wild Bob. One time, he made a brilliant remark. 'Modern man is not complete without chaos.' If only he could apply it to himself," Bernard laughs out loud. Then he turns quiet and thinks for a while, sucking up strings of spaghetti. He has a weak spot for his old friend and is genuinely concerned about him. But sometimes he gives up all hope.

"I told Bob, 'Cut the crap. One day you'll really need money. If you want to go back to Chicago, to your brothers, who can you turn to? Who still wants to give you any money?' But Bob doesn't give a shit. His dream is to die with a pack of cigarettes in the pocket of his shirt, a thermos of fresh coffee on the table, and a pipe of crack in his mouth."

A few cats crouch around the table. One even jumps on it and starts to lick Bernard's plate. He kicks the animals away. "Go back to work, you dirty cats. Better sharpen your claws and move your asses. Everything that crawls around between the Northern Gate and the South End, grab it by its neck. It's no goddamn amusement park here." With cries of terror, the cats disappear in the darkness. Bernard takes another sip of his wine cocktail. "Yeah, Bob. Death is creeping up on him. Time is running out. And he knows it. If it's not a heart attack, it will be AIDS. Or he will be gunned down by someone he once deceived. And me, they will kill me as well, as a witness."

According to Bernard, he knows Bob is HIV-positive because he once found a flier for organizations that cater to homeless people with AIDS. And Larry, a temporary roommate of Bob, once found three "big-ass dongs" while cleaning up the bunkers. As big as cucumbers, Bernard describes them graphically. Once, Bob had something vague going on with Jeff. That's why Tony and Bob never got along. "Bunch of idiots," Bernard mumbles. "All of us could have been rich down here if we had worked together. We could have done two-for-oneing, stashed the cans for

Pier John, we could have started a complete business. But they never trusted me. Cheap bastards and petty crooks, that's what they are."

Bernard sighs in exasperation. "Bob told me that the director of Pete's Place cried when he left for the YMCA. 'You see, they'll miss me.' I told him, 'Bob, they cry because they will miss your money. That SSI check now goes straight to the Y.' Bob gets off when people care about him. What the fuck. It's human nature to care. It's an instinct, nothing else. Why pat someone on the back for being natural?"

"Bob is one of the most honest people on this planet," extols the Reverend William 'Bill' Robinson, Bob's spiritual counselor. "He is an extremely sensitive, smart man. Never was he ashamed of his addiction. And if we look deep into our souls, we are all addicted to something. Money, Fame, Power. But we refuse to acknowledge that."

Father Bill worked in Pete's Place when Bob arose from the tunnel and washed up there.

"His life is a saga. Out of the darkness, into the full light," declared Father Bill to the *New York Times*. The paper thought the resurrection of Bob intriguing enough to devote a main article to it. Now the amicable pastor is affiliated with Saint George's Church in Brooklyn. Over there, we discuss Bob's journey from the tunnel to Pete's Place, to the room he got at the YMCA, his descent into the tunnels and now again, his second voyage upwards to Pete's Place.

"The most beautiful thing Bob ever accomplished was leaving the security of the tunnels. It was dark and cold over there, but at least, everything was safe and secure," Father Bill proclaims with a solemn voice. "A home is not a place where you just spend the night, it is the place where people know you and value you. Bob needs the positive signals of other people. That is why it did not work out at the YMCA. Bob had there a cold, impersonal room, a cell where you could not even write on the walls."

The juxtaposition of light versus darkness is Father Bill's favorite metaphor. "When you live in the darkness, things can be fuzzy. You cannot discern beautiful things. Only in the light can you see beauty with clarity. Seeing is a gift. But it's a two edged sword. In the light, you also see all the cracks. How much of the truth can you bear? Bob saw, but sight has a burden."

"The soul of a homeless man," the Reverend sermonizes, "is just like anyone else. We are all lone sojourners, on our way to the House of God. Only if we are united with him, we will attain our completeness. Every good Christian should know this. Homeless illustrate this incompleteness in a very graphic, visible way. It shocks people. That's why they are pushed out of sight in most places. Homeless don't have pretentious existentialist theories. They live them in their daily lives. They are a lot more honest than most people. And I am asking myself," Father Bill muses, "if this is the real essence of our help to the homeless. Is there real compassion, or is it just 'Gee, it would be nice if we didn't have to look at them.'"

"You see, I always told everybody. It is only after the first hit that I get unreliable." Bob is all smiles and his sky blue eyes twinkle. I visit him at Pete's Place and have just reported back to him that according to Father Bill, he is one of the most honest people on this earth.

"Actually, I didn't do that many scams. Okay, I admit," Bob confesses, "that once in a while I ripped someone off. But sometimes the opportunity was too good. And when the dollars look me deep in the eyes, it is hard to say no. But most of our money, we made ourselves. Also for food." Bob straightens his back. A proud man is speaking. "Bernard and me, we never begged, we never went to soup kitchens. In fact, we were the elite of the tunnel."

Pete's Place, a basement in a church, is a small drop-in center affiliated with the Partnership for the Homeless, an organization like the BRC and Project Renewal. At first sight, Pete's place looks like a pleasant spot with a TV-room, billiard space, a library and quiet reading corners. Then I notice that all the visitors sit on worn-down couches like zombies, staring blankly in front of them. Others pace restlessly up and down between the bookshelves with ripped paperbacks and the very tiny billiard table. At night, the visitors sleep on the benches in the church.

When I present myself at the reception desk, Bob is always in front of the TV. His face lights up when the lady at the desk screams his name and he sees me. Except for all the programs and workshops (this evening there will be a lecture on 'Faith Sharing and Life Experience'), these visits are the highlights of Bob's existence. Once I did not show up as promised: Bob told me he had been upset all day. "They kill him over there," Bernard told me. "With his heart problem, he is forced to sit there all day in front of the TV. Canning and some fresh air would do him good."

I bring Bob a few photos where he's collecting cans with Bernard. Bob hugs me, grabs the pictures out my hands and shows them to the director of the center. "You see, Anita, here is the proof. I have been working all that time honestly with Bernard."

Anita is not convinced. She took it very seriously when Bob temporarily regressed to his drug-filled tunnel life, Bob explains as we are drinking a coffee on the sidewalk. "Never talk about drugs here," he says. "In fact, the less people know, the better. Bernard and I made a deal to never mention it to the press." Now Bob says he has totally stopped doing drugs. At the YMCA in Brooklyn, the temptation was too great. "There was a 24/7 crack spot around the corner." Next week, his SSI payments will be restored and he will pay off all his debts. Bob is optimistic. "Don't tell Bernard anything. I want to surprise him when I have my money."

This is the third time Bob has told me that his suspended SSI will be paid out soon. Most of the time, there are incomprehensible and vague stories where there doesn't seem to be any logic. But it is in fact complicated. The money is held at the YMCA and once it is released over there, it will go to Pete's Place, where they will give him a sort of allowance. Of course this is when he's actually receiving SSI, because many times it has been cut off for reasons Bob fails to explain.

It was a cold winter morning in February, 1994, when Bob left the tunnel. Stalactites of ice hung suspended from the grate, a chilly wind blew through the darkness. "I woke up, my clothes were damp and cold, I had a pain in my chest. The coffee was finished and there were no more cigarettes. Nobody had money, because we had smoked it all. We couldn't even make a fire because there was no wood. And on top of everything, Bernard was in a terrible mood. It was all too much. I just walked out of the tunnels, all seventy blocks to here. Right through a snowstorm. I arrived as an ice cube. With a beard of two years."

From outreach workers who had talked to him for years, he had heard that at Pete's Place there would always be a warm bed ready for him. Bob took a hot shower and crept under the blankets.

After Bob ran away as a teenager, he never saw his parents again. He didn't show up to the funerals of his Polish father and his Irish mother. He doesn't have any contact with his two brothers, a priest and a cop who must now be in their seventies. He once wrote a letter to the monastery where his brother was, but never heard anything back. When he was twenty, Bob married an Irish girl. They broke up after six months. "She drove me crazy. Told me what to do and even worse, what not to do. She wanted to go back to Ireland. Fuck it, I said. I never saw her again."

San Bernardino, Sacramento, San Francisco, and San Diego are some of the cool-sounding places where Bob worked as a cook. He also had odd jobs as a truck driver, and worked at a slaughterhouse and a cattle ranch. Bob was the archetypical hobo. "The good life. I was all over the country." He stayed either in cheap hotels, or rehab clinics. "They knew me by my first name," Bob says. He lost track of the number of rehab programs he underwent.

"I think I never really wanted to kick off. Tried to be high all the time. Non-stop. Running away from problems." Because Bob preferred to work as a cook in hospitals and dietary centers, he could get his hands on diet pills and amphetamines, codeine and cocaine if he was lucky. "It was all the same to me. As long as I got speedy."

In the '80s, Bob tried his luck in New York. "Yeah," he says proudly. "The fastest egg man in Manhattan. Could break and clutch twelve dozen eggs in three minutes, while at the same time smoking and drinking coffee."

When Bob was working as a cook in a soup kitchen on the West Side, he met Bernard who was volunteering in the kitchen. "Every night he stole huge amounts of food for his fellow tunnel dwellers," Bob remembers. "I immediately took a liking to him."

Back in the tunnel I check on how far everyone has gotten with their vouchers. Tony is not interested. He's already spent years on the waiting list for the housing he is entitled to as an ex-con. Besides, he doesn't think the eviction will happen. He's even working on big plans to turn the tunnel into a huge storage space for cans when Bernard has gone. If things go wrong, he can maybe rent a small room in his sister's apartment building.

Marcus doesn't have time to bother with alternative housing, because a girlfriend is staying over and he's fully occupied with her. The hippie girl he met at the Rainbow People has exhibitionistic tendencies: after two cans of beer, she pulls off all her clothes and starts to run around naked in between the trees. "You can't do that here. *Ici, c'est la grande ville,*" Marcus tells me and shakes his head. She has been hanging out now for a day and a half in Central Park, at a gathering of New York Deadheads. They are holding a memorial for Jerry Garcia, who has just died.

"Unbelievable, that Marcus," Bernard sighs. "He is living on another planet. He really has to get his ass in gear, before one day he will find his cave all bricked up."

Kathy and Joe passively wait for the things to happen, just like Ozzy. Frankie doesn't want to have anything to do with the Coalition. He still has never forgiven the fact that a year ago they gave him chocolate chip cookies that were old and stale. And last week, he spent the whole afternoon waiting for the Coalition.

"That's why I say, 'Fuck them!'" Frankie says angrily. When they finally came and knocked on his door, he told them to come back another time, because he had to go out canning. In Little Havana, they have given up all hope.

Hugo tells me that Poncho had called Dov to ask how things were proceeding. Dov had told him that indeed there might be some problems, because the vouchers were originally meant for subway tunnel people. Disappointed, Poncho had thrown the receiver down on the hook. "Getulio and Poncho are devastated," Hugo says.

"You see that they are just liars," a drunk Julio is screaming. He had visited the alcohol clinic. By the reception, he had already turned around and left. "You should have seen the light inside," he says. "They had these lights at the ceiling that emitted some kind of weird light. To make you crazy."

Hugo has problems with his welfare that had become workfare. He had to pick up garbage in the park during the burning heat. After two days, he stopped showing up. Now he has a job as a delivery boy for a laundry. He makes twice as much money, but that doesn't help get the vouchers. You need to prove a legal income, but his new income is off the books.

"Yeah," Julio yells, waving a can of beer. "We don't like to be told what to do. That's why we're down here."

Later I call Dov. He is nervous. At the moment he is busy talking to DC, so the vouchers will also be valid for the Amtrak tunnels. "Please, tell the people they need to be patient. We are doing our best."

28. THE ADVENTURES OF FRANKIE, PART 7: STUPID PLANS

"The girls are pissed off," Frankie says when Maria and Fatima walk away angrily with the baby stroller. We are in Riverside Park on a Friday night. Tonight is boys' night. Frankie and Ment will hang out with their crew in the city. The girls are angry because they can't join them. "Fuck it," Ment hisses and puts his rollerblades on. "Damn right you are, 'cuz," Frankie adds. He is leaning on Maria's bike, a tandem, and lights a cigarette.

There are more things wrong. Fatima is pregnant again. Ment is the father. It is not the right time for a baby. They are considering an abortion. But that costs a lot of money, Ment explains.

"We want to go to a good clinic. Not to some kind of butcher."
They need six hundred bucks. By any means necessary. Frankie
already has a plan.

We go looking for their friends. Ment leads on his rollerblades;
Frankie follows him on the tandem. I am on my racing bike.
Frankie rides like a maniac. Like a wild bull, he charges with his
bike in between two rows of cabs on Broadway, preferably against
traffic. Screaming pedestrians jump away. "Watch it, suckers!"
Frankie screams at them. With his fists, he hits cabs on the roof
when they are blocking his way and yells, "Fuck you, asshole!"
Every five minutes, Frankie and Ment stop to make some phone
calls. They leave messages on beepers and answering machines.
The crew has to be hanging out somewhere, where exactly they
don't know. That's why we have to check out all possible meeting places.

At a park basketball court, somewhere in Midtown, we take
a break. "We call this The Yard," Frankie says. "Here we always
hang out with the crew. We play ball, smoke buddha, you know,
all those magical things us young people like to do." Frankie has
to grin at his own words. "And sometimes we just walk around.
Cruising up and down the Avenues, drinking forty ounces. All
night long. We get two, we pay one." They can secretly slide the
second huge beer bottle down into their baggy pants. "Yeah,
two-for-one, that's our stylo."

The crew doesn't show up at the Yard. We ride back to Riverside Park on 72nd Street, back to Rockefeller Center on 48th. Ment
places a few other calls. Finally, we find the crew hanging out
drinking beer in front of a grocery in Hell's Kitchen. Ment and
Frankie shake hands and get a couple of 40s. Their friends are
white guys in their twenties, looking like grungy skinheads.

Frankie presents his master plan. They will rob Vanessa's
mother. Hit two birds with one stone. They need money for the
abortion, and on top of that, it will be the perfect punishment for
Vanessa. Because not only has Vanessa tried to break up Frankie
and Ment, she's not exactly a saint either. Frankie takes me apart
for a moment. "She has laid the whole crew already," he whispers. "And I tell you, Ant, that's no good."

The plan is to take a shower at Vanessa's place. When she is not watching, Frankie will sneak into her mom's bedroom. He has already been nosing around there, and knows there is a little safe with money under her bed. "With a big-ass wad of bills. All tens and twenties," he stresses. It simply can't go wrong. Because he is under the shower, he has a watertight alibi. He just hasn't realized that he will leave a trail of water drops from the shower to the broken safe. The crew is shaking their heads. "You are crazy," the oldest one says. "You guys are the only homeless among Vanessa's friends. First thing Five-O's gonna check out is the Freedom Tunnel."[73]

29. ADVANCED CANNING I:
BIG SHOT TONY

"Happy to see you. Finally someone I can trust," Tony says, relieved when I show up. He pulls out a ten-dollar bill and sends me to get coffee and cigarettes. He's already lost twenty dollars by asking the same of two other homeless buddies who just took off and never came back. Tony is two-for-oneing at Sloan's supermarket on 96th Street, and I help him so I can witness the miraculous multiplication of his dollars. "You see," Tony says when I return and give him back all his change, "here I am every night a winner." Tony says he's given up horse betting. For the past week, he has been every evening in front of the supermarket doing business.

He not only buys up cans, but also the bonus points on Marlboro packs that he can sell for double the price to some other guy on the Upper East Side. In fact, he buys everything offered by the sad parade of crack-addicted homeless people who hang out in the neighborhood and stop by at Tony's. One has a plastic bag holding twenty crushed cans. Tony is strict.

"Straighten those cans out," he barks at the client. He points at a Ballantine Ale can. "Yo, man. This is a dead can." Even the two-for-oners in Harlem refuse those. Other clients offer cuckoo clocks, sneakers, and decaying porn mags—with beaver shots in washed-out magenta colors—that they might sell for twenty cents.

Tony is playing the successful businessman, waving a big wad of singles and handing out quarters and dimes to his clients. With the eye of a connoisseur, he looks at a disposable camera, tries in vain to sell it to me, and finally offers the client a dollar fifty—half a hit of crack.

Tony has even employed an assistant, who is just arriving. He's a young white guy with a big beard who doesn't looks like he has any serious drug or drinking problems. The man is not homeless but lives on welfare in a cheap SRO hotel.

He helps Tony for ten bucks a night. His task is sorting out the cans and putting them in different bags: two bags with cans that have to go to WeCan—one for beer cans, one for soda cans—a third bag for plastics, and the last bag with cans that the assistant will put in the machine tonight at Sloane's. This is a time-consuming job; the machine processes only three cans a minute and Tony can't be bothered with that. "You see," he says, "I have to watch everybody constantly. They try to rip me off, I have to make sure the cans are sorted correctly and I have to keep the sidewalk clean."

In fact, Tony does not touch a single can. He doesn't want to soil his hands, because he has to count his wad of crispy dollar bills all the time. I watch Tony until he also puts me to work. "When you have nothing to do, sort this bag out," he commands. Tony is obviously very pleased that he can show all his black clients that he has two white guys working for him, who obey all his commands without questioning his authority. Unlike the clean cans I collect with Frankie and Bernard in the early morning, the cans offered to Tony are collected by the scum of can men who don't mind digging deep in every public waste basket in their nightly quest in search of a hit. Some cans smell of puke, others have traces of dog shit or moldy Chinese food.

"Fuckin' dirty-ass cans," I say when the greasy cans slip out of my hands.

"You expected them to be spic and span?" a black girl with a sweet, childish face says. She must have had polio as a kid, because she walks with spastic movements and her torso is bent over at a ninety-degree angle, so I can see her tiny décolleté under a much-too-big T-shirt.

With a magnificent gesture, Tony pulls a handful of quarters and dimes out of his pocket and pays the poor girl one dollar for her forty cans. "One hundred for you, honey," he says affably and winks at the girl who immediately hands the money over to her friend, a big black guy who smells of alcohol.

Tony in the meantime has ordered me to count a new bag of cans. When I am finished, I talk to another black couple, Bobby and Lisa. He is a big guy with a shopping cart filled with cans, she is a little girl that hops behind him with a baby stroller. I've seen them working a few times while canning with Bernard. Bobby and Lisa know I am the reporter from the tunnel, and have heard from Julio that once in a while I give a modest fee to the tunnel people for their help.

Wouldn't I be interested in making a story about them? For only thirty bucks a day, I can follow them around in their daily life. I am too busy in the tunnel, I explain, and have to disappoint them. Bobby tries to convince me I could score very well with their unique life story. He gives me a short synopsis. Bobby lived in a hotel and fell in love with Lisa, who was wandering on the streets. She moved in with him. Another hotel occupant made sexual overtures; Bobby beat the guy up, sending him to the hospital. Bobby and Lisa were kicked out of the hotel. Now every night they sleep in a tender embrace on the steps of a church on the corner of Central Park West and 96th Street. "A true homeless love story," Bobby stresses, "Hard to find." I thank them for their touching story and promise them that if I meet a film crew looking for a story, I will send them over.

In the meantime, Tony is totally absorbed in his new role as successful entrepreneur. He has just bought a portable TV for seven dollars, and the pile of bags with empty cans around him is getting bigger all the time. Too much to drag by hand to the tunnel, that's why he pays Lisa four bucks to get his shopping cart that is parked outside a tunnel entrance. "You see," Tony says proudly while waving his dwindling wad of dollar bills. "The money is going fast."

It disappears quickly, I remark carefully, but will he make any money back? Tony laughs confidently. "Wait and see. Tomorrow I will double my capital." When I have counted and sorted out another bag of cans, I go get coffee for us at the Dunkin' Donuts. An unwashed can man walks up to me while I am paying at the counter. "You are mister Anthony?" he asks politely. I nod. "Tony requested me to ask you to come back as soon as possible," the messenger relays. Together we rush back with the coffee.

"I am running out of money," Tony says. "Go to the bank and withdraw twenty dollars. In singles. Tomorrow you will get it back."

When I return with the money, Tony is busy talking to a few black kids in a shiny dark BMW that is blocked by another car in front of the supermarket. They have big golden chains around their necks, black lights illuminate their car. Rap music turned all the way up makes the car tremble. Tony can fix it. The store manager owns the car that blocks the rapper's BMW. Tony will get him.

"Get the manager," Tony says to the messenger and gives him seventy-five cents. Tony beams with pride when the manager appears and drives his car away. The kids pull away with screeching tires while Tony waves them a friendly goodbye.

It is now 10:30 PM and Bernard shows up, walking unsteadily on his feet. Today I leant him the hundred dollars for his canning business, but obviously, he has first treated himself to a couple of hits. "Tonight I am not in the mood to work," he apologizes with a soft voice. Tomorrow he will start seriously with Pier John. He leans against a parking meter and watches Tony telling the highlights in his career as a street scavenger to a breathless audience of Bobby, Lisa and some other can people.

Once, someone came running out of a cab, all gasping and panting. Tony emphasizes his story with dramatic gestures. He had a big suitcase with the JFK airport tags still on. Tony paid twenty bucks for the stolen suitcase, without even having inspected the contents. The man took off and Tony opened the suitcase. He found two Colt 45s. Within a few minutes, he had sold the guns for three hundred dollars. Tony doesn't mention that he probably lost that money the next day betting on the horses.

"You're a crazy motherfucker," Bobby shakes his head, full of admiration. "Yes," Tony confirms confidently and straightens out his big, red suspenders. The store manager has listened to the story with a broad smile and gives me a wink. Tony now pays two other can people a dollar each to clean up the mess on the pavement, empty bags and boxes left behind by his clients. "Unbelievable. What a theater..." Bernard sighs as he watches Tony doing his thing. "He thinks he is some big shot. But it's only chaos."

Bernard explains why Tony's approach is wrong. "It's so simple," he says. "You let them throw the cans in your shopping cart, and put on every corner one empty bag. And while you are counting the cans, you put them in the right bags. The golden rule for a two-for-oner," Bernard says. "You sort when you count. And ready you are. And never get personal with your clients. Not because you look down on them, but because it doesn't bring you anywhere. You buy their cans, you give them their money, and bye-bye, see you! Most friendships here are only based on who is getting high with who, who buys the next hit. If the money's gone, the friendship is over."

Bernard knows most people hanging out in front of the supermarket. "All of them losers and hardcore crackheads," he says with disdain. Tony is ready to leave, and the supermarket is about to close, when Jeff walks up. Tony introduces him to the other can people as his son. Jeff bums ten bucks, and disappears into the night. "The kid is taxing Tony heavily," Bernard mutters and shakes his head. Jeff is back again from his rehab upstate, but upon arrival in New York immediately took up his bad habits. "Everybody that returns from a rehab in the city hits the stem again in a few days," Bernard says. "Jeff is no exception. Only six feet under will he say bye bye to crack."

Jeff still spends some time with Tony in the tunnel now and then, but most of the time he stays over with another sugar daddy—a dirty old man who lives in a hotel on Broadway, according to Bernard. This man tried to have Tony put in jail for the rest of his life by making Jeff file false declarations with the police. Jeff declared that Tony had tied him up, forced him to smoke crack, and raped him. At first, Tony was really concerned and had shown Bernard the court papers to ask him for advice. It never made the courts, because the story was so obviously a set up. The prosecutor refused to handle it.

When I help Tony to bring back all his cans in the tunnel, he confirms the story. If Tony were not on life-long probation, he would have strangled his rival a long time ago. He has forgiven Jeff. "Sometimes the kid doesn't know what he is doing," he says. Even so, Tony decided to lower Jeff's stipend. Now he only gets ten dollars a day, instead of the twenty-five he used to extract from Tony.

The next day, I accompany Tony to get estimates for printing his T-shirts. Tony knows I lent Bernard money to invest in his canning business, and now I cannot refuse to help Tony set up his T-shirt business. Coincidentally, the unkempt moviemaker gave me the idea. A week ago, I was sitting on a park bench working on my field notes, when suddenly the moviemaker joined me. He asked me to tell Bernard to stop by to watch the footage. And I did not have to sleep in the tunnel, he added, I could also stay over at his place. This time, some green snot was hanging from his nose. I politely turned down his dubious offer.

Then he started to talk about the progress of his documentary on the street scavengers of Manhattan. A while ago, he had met an artist who, while waiting for his breakthrough, was dealing in old junk he found on the streets. The artist had mentioned designs that had to be printed on fabric. Together, they had looked up some addresses from printers in the Yellow Pages. Unfortunately, it never worked out.

It took me awhile before I realized the artist could only have been Tony. Indeed, Tony confirms that his financial cooperation with the cineaste did not yield any results. That is why he is so glad I am taking his plans seriously. His parole officer is also pleased to see Tony staying on the right side of law and working hard to become a decent citizen. When the T-shirts are ready, his parole officer has promised to buy at least a dozen to hand out at the Parole Board offices.

One printer already gave an estimate for a lithograph of his designs: one hundred dollars for a design in two colors, thirty for each additional color. Now we just have to find cheap T-shirts in the garment district around 28th Street. Tony knows a lot of Korean wholesale retailers where he always buys his umbrellas—when rainstorms are hitting the city—or party hats and horns for New Years Eve. He usually manages to make a threefold profit on these items.

On our way downtown, we cash in the cans from last night. The final profit of playing the King of Cans for one night is two dollars. I don't ask for the money I lent him because then he would have made a loss. But Tony is not disappointed. He still has his starting capital, and tomorrow is another day.

His shopping cart is even more merrily decorated with flags and teddy bears, and when we walk through Times Square he waves at the tourists who try to take pictures of him from open decked buses. "Yes, honey, you can snap my picture," he yells at a Japanese girl who shyly points her camcorder at him. Tony is in the best of moods today and nobody can spoil it.

We stop at a newsstand to buy the latest edition of *Fortune* magazine. The manager of Sloane's has told Tony he has a big photo inside. Bill Gates is on the cover, but we can't find Tony's photo. Maybe it was last week's issue, he says resigned. When I later ask the manager from Sloane's about it, he bursts out laughing and admits he fooled us.

Sitting on the sidewalk, we drink a cup of coffee and Tony complains about Bernard. Just as Bernard refuses to believe Tony has stopped gambling, Tony doubts Bernard's solemn declaration that he has slowed down his crack use.

"Two weeks ago, Bernard got his first welfare check. Two hundred bucks. And what do you think: next morning he is bumming a cigarette off me. Blew all his money in one night." Tony shakes his head. He uses nearly the same words as Bernard does when he is gossiping about Tony's gambling habits. "But on the other hand," Tony says wisely, "the Bible says 'whoever is without sin, let him throw the first stone.'"

Tony finishes his coffee and we go on. A small boy being pushed in a wheelchair by his parents stares fascinated at Tony's decorated shopping cart. Tony looks back with compassion, and he gives the boy one of his teddy bears.

He dreams on about his T-shirt business. "You need only one spark to light the fire," he says burning with optimism. Once he's become a fortunate business man, he's going to buy a huge estate for neglected orphans. With big playgrounds, swimming pools and a petting zoo.

Tony already knows an advisor to help him purchase his property. Once he found the wallet of a realtor on the street. No cash inside, just thirty credit cards. "More than Donald Trump will ever have," Tony assures me. Tony brought back the wallet to the rightful owner. He got a hundred-dollar reward, and the assurance he could always count on the services of the broker when needed.

Once he's filthy rich, Tony will be driven around in a limo through the streets of Manhattan. But he will never forget where he came from. "Stop there at that garbage can, driver," Tony imagines. "I see an empty can."

Once in the garment district, we visit a few wholesalers. Soon Tony realizes he is taken more seriously when he parks his shopping cart around the corner, and not in front of the store. But it is sad. One store only sells T-shirts that have already been printed, others only have a few dozen plain shirts in stock.

"We're talking thousands!" he yells at the seller and indignantly leaves the store. At the end of the day, even after visiting a lot of stores, we have not found a good bargain. The cheapest we can get, once we've included the printing process, will come out seven dollars a shirt. No way will Tony be able to compete with the stores who sell their tasteless T-shirts for three bucks apiece to tourists.

30. ADVANCED CANNING II:
PIER JOHN

Pier John operates his two-for-one business on 94th Street close to the park, right in front of the cheap hotel where he lives. Every summer evening, at 11 PM on the dot when the supermarkets close, he starts working. When I arrive just after eleven, he has already set up shop: one big shopping cart, on every corner an empty bag, just as Bernard had explained. Next to it are a few empty cases for bottles. There are two chairs behind the cart: Pier John sits on one of them, reading his newspaper and sipping coffee at his ease. The other one is for Bernard who will arrive any moment.

Pier John is a heavy-set man, and with his beard and glasses he looks a bit like a black Santa Claus. He is also a careful, discreet man who has a lot of experience with street people and is bound to never do or say impulsive things. He is even more discreet about his actual earnings. "That will only give the IRS bad ideas," he told the *New York Times* once, when they devoted an article to him in 1989.

Pier John tells me about Chris Jeffers, a fellow two-for-oner who let himself be portrayed as a successful business man in the *Times*. The former homeless man even posed in suit and tie in between bags of empty cans for CNN and NBC's *60 Minutes*. "These cans were, by the way, not his own, but from WeCan," Pier John says with a grin. Jeffers bragged he made at least seventy thousand dollars a year. In no time the IRS was knocking on his door.

Jeffers went broke. Where he is now, nobody knows. "He became some kind of phantom," Pier John says. "Some say he is a broker on Wall Street, others say he is just hanging out there, begging with a paper cup."

Jeffers started out wrong right from the beginning, Pier John says. He had rented a little van, but always parked it in a rather inconsiderate way at the park. He never cleaned up his mess. He allowed his clients to hang around, resulting in drug and alcohol abuse and a lot of noisy quarrels. People in the hood started to complain. Also, he managed to invoke the wrath of the cops. Each day he got parking fines. When the innocent van owner wanted to renew his expired driving license, he had to pay fifteen thousand dollars in fines first. Jeffers got wind that the owner wanted to kill him. Jeffers just left the van on a street corner and went underground. Local criminals stole all four wheels from the vehicle.

Pier John is careful. "Nobody knows my real name. You know, there are a lot of Johns in the city," he says with a mysterious smile. "And we always clean our mess. If clients start to make problems and scream, I tell them to go somewhere else. I will never fight with them. You can only do this business if you don't have the neighbors against you."

He points at all the AC units hanging out of most windows on the street. "You see, these things are buzzing here all summer. Nobody hears me working out here."

Pier John used to have a good job at an accountant's office. A quarrel at work got out of hand and became a nasty shouting match. Pier John left his job. He gambled away all his savings and in the end was kicked out of the house by his wife.

First a bit embarrassed and ashamed, later full of confidence and 100 percent dedicated, he picked up canning. "It was a good therapy for me. I was too busy to think about gambling." Once a successful can man, he started to devote himself to two-for-oneing.

At the moment, he is one of the most successful can brokers in the city. With the money he makes and the welfare check, he can make a decent living and even make a substantial contribution to the maintenance and education of his two daughters, both living with their mother.

Twice a year, Pier John does something in return for his clients: on New Year's Eve, he gets a few bottles of vodka and treats everybody to a shot. On Labor Day, he always organizes a picnic in Riverside Park. "You are a greedy pig if you never give something back to your clients," he explains these nice gestures.

The picnic was last week. Pier John bought sesame-seed buns, Swiss cheese, and chorizo sausage, as well as a few cases of soda.

"If they want beer, they should get it themselves," he said strictly, while putting out all the goodies with Bernard on a big blanket. Bobby and Lisa were there along with all of Little Havana, and the polio girl also came for a bite. There were lively discussions about which supermarkets and two-for-oners accepted what kind of cans, when, and how many.

Coincidentally, Do-Gooder Galindez passed by while on a summer stroll with a very beautiful girl. Galindez had heard about the alternative housing program and congratulated Bernard. "How do you feel?" Galindez had asked amicably. "I feel nothing 'cause I still got nothing," Bernard rudely answered, focusing instead on the big breasts of Galindez's girlfriend, charming her with his tunnel monologue. "Did you see her wink me?" Bernard asked me when Galindez had left. "The poor girl misses a lot with that faggot."

It is getting to be midnight when Bernard arrives. A short while later, the first clients also show up. Bernard and Pier John love to chat like two old spinsters, but they also work remarkably smoothly as a team. Bernard counts and puts the cans in the right bag; Pier John watches and pays the client. In only a few moments, every client is helped with no unnecessary fuss, leaving satisfied and happy with their earnings. "Watch us, Duke," Bernard proudly says when he returns to his chair, "Tony could learn something from this."

Pier John used to work under the bridge at 96th Street. It was always dark there and a bit sketchy, that's why he decided to work in front of his hotel. The day after Pier John left, Walter was killed underneath that bridge.

"Walter was an obnoxious motherfucker," Pier John says. "He got an inheritance of twelve thousand dollars and didn't know how to spend the money fast enough."

"Yeah," Bernard adds. "In a month's time he had blown everything. Coke, chicks, booze, limos. He wanted to have it all, but time was running out on him."

"Yeah," says Pier John, sipping his coffee. "He was a fucking piece of shit."

31. ADVANCED CANNING III:
WECAN

"Our director Guy Polhemus started with the best of intentions," says Bennet Wellikson, the administrator of WeCan. "Unfortunately, we spend most of our time and energy in prolonged legal battles. We are nearly bankrupt." For the third time, Polhemus has not showed up for our appointment, so the talkative administrator explains all the ins and outs of the recycling business in general, and WeCan in particular.

Apart from the legal and financial complications, deceit, theft and dishonesty are rife in the world of cans. Basically, WeCan's biggest problem is its cash flow. Wholesalers, distributors, and breweries refuse to take back the cans from WeCan and pay for them. Legally, they have to do this, but unredeemed cans are a gold mine. That is why the brewers find all kind of loopholes and tricks to circumvent their obligations. Wellikson estimates that in this way, Manhattan's Coca Cola Company makes extra profits of fifty million a year.

"It is a mega-million mafia," Wellikson says. "To evade the duties, large quantities of soda are smuggled across state lines. Some supermarket chains even cooperate with the breweries." One of WeCan's biggest creditors is Anheuser-Busch, the brewer of Budweiser. Miller Brewing Company, the importer of Heineken, is another nasty client.

From the outset of WeCan, there were problems with Bud. After three months, the bags of empty Buds kept piling up, filling the modest storage space of WeCan to choking point. The distributor of Anheuser-Busch in Queens refused to take back this growing mountain of cans.

Polhemus, however, had to pay the homeless for their cans, and had to advance thousands of dollars out of his own pocket. It took a *New York Times* article about WeCan's story, exposing the scandalous behavior of the nation's biggest brewer, to force Anheuser-Busch to accept the millions of cans. Anheuser-Busch did not show up to reclaim the cans, leaving the transport to WeCan.

The Coalition for the Homeless had to provide a truck to bring all the cans to the brewer on the other side of the East River.

"To annoy us, they counted all the cans at a painstakingly slow pace, one by one. It took them a week to count them all," Wellikson remembers. "Then we had to wait another few months for the check. This way, WeCan went nearly broke a few times. Most of the time, however, payments came in just in time, or a subsidy, donation or grant saved WeCan from bankruptcy.

"In the summer it is always the same thing," explains Wellikson. "Every idiot puts some water, sugar, and colorants in a can, comes up with a crazy name and introduces with a lot of noise a new drink on the market. And we get stuck with the Snapples, Suckels, or Prickels cans that we can't get rid off because these businesses no longer exist when the summer is over."

In the first years, WeCan had secured the cooperation of hundreds of companies that would save up all the cans in their cafeterias. WeCan had purchased a truck and picked up the cans on regular days. It never became profitable, Wellikson explains. Not only did it take too much time to navigate the congested streets of Manhattan, WeCan's workers, mostly homeless and can people, were not the most reliable and showed great creativity in scamming WeCan."

Wellikson has to smile. "Along the routes, they had made deals with friends to catch the bags that they were throwing out of the truck. Sometimes the trucks arrived empty. Or they tipped buddies who said they were from WeCan and picked up the bags themselves and shared the profits."

WeCan is once again going through a difficult period. Wellikson sighs. The bank has been threatening to suspend credit, while WeCan will hear at any moment the outcome of their lawsuit against the distributor of Pepsi Cola. "If you call us in three months and the phone line is disconnected, then you know we are really broke," Wellikson says dramatically.

Last summer, WeCan employed a consultant to analyze its business structure. After intensive and very expensive research, the recommendation was that WeCan should pay their clients only four cents a can. "And of course we cannot do that. Our clients are people that have already been screwed most of their lives."

Guy Polhemus has a dark, concerned look on his face as he poses behind his desk for a photo. On his desktop rests a small pyramid built from empty cans, behind him on his wall is a huge map of the world. "Yes, a journey around the world in a sailing boat, that is what I need," he says. "Eight years of work, and still hassle and bullshit. I only deal with bureaucrats, lawyers and brewers. I hardly have time to stay in touch with the homeless. A shame, because we have wonderful personalities amongst our clients."

Polhemus knows most canning people personally. I convey to him the kind regards of Wild Bob, and his face brightens up with a smile. "Yeah, Buffalo Bob, that's what I used to call him. What a guy…" Polhemus confirms that Bob worked for a year as a decent and reliable worker before suddenly losing it and running away with a lot of cash. "That's typical Bob," says Polhemus forgivingly about the unfortunate events. "One year he works perfectly, then something goes wrong and suddenly he's flipping out." Bob was first employed as a security guard. He lived on WeCan's premises in a little van between the bags of empty cans. "Nobody dared to come close when Bob was in his van," Polhemus laughs. "He had long hair and a huge beard. Just like a werewolf. Kids ran away screaming when Bob walked down the street." Several times Bob and Bernard invited Polhemus into the tunnel for coffee and to see the murals done by Chris Pape. "They have it way too good down there. They will never leave voluntarily," Polhemus remarks.

Polhemus came to New York in the late '70s to try out his luck as a copywriter. During a drunken night with colleagues, Polhemus made a bet about the Super Bowl. He lost, and as agreed had to work as a volunteer in the soup kitchen of a church in Lower Manhattan. Polhemus was at the entrance, handing out meal tickets and manning the coat check. "The homeless carried huge bags with cans I had to watch," Polhemus tells me. "It was a zoo.

After dinner there were always fights over who had which bag. The pastor got crazy and told me that he could not can't handle it any longer in his church and that we had to find a solution."

The homeless explained to Polhemus how difficult it was to redeem cans at the supermarket, notwithstanding their legal obligation to accept 240 cans per person per day. Polhemus could not believe that the supermarkets would tread on the few rights the homeless still had left. When Polhemus accompanied a few homeless people and saw with his own eyes the arrogant way supermarkets behaved, the idea for WeCan was born.

"It immediately became a total hit among the homeless," Polhemus smiles. "Word was on the street and within two days our place was packed." Since its opening at the end of 1987, WeCan has paid out twelve million dollars to can people, and created fifty full and part-time jobs. "We give people part of their pride and dignity back. We never pay cash, but a check they have to cash around the corner. That makes them feel like they got a paycheck. And we are no baby sitters. If our clients want to get high or drunk, it's their problem. If they want help for their addiction, if they looking for continuing education or possibilities for alternative housing, then we can help them and refer them to the organizations we cooperate with. Unfortunately we cannot offer any services ourselves. Most of our money is spent on lawsuits."

32. LORD OF THE TUNNEL AGAIN

After his bad start, Bernard has now seriously started two-for-oneing. We hardly see each other, because he works the night through. Five times a week, he helps Pier John. They start at midnight and work till six. In the morning the huge numbers of empties are put into a rented station wagon: crates in the back, bags tied on the top. Then they drive to WeCan, where they work another few hours to redeem the cans. At 9 AM, the working day is finished and Bernard has earned forty dollars.

Not a huge amount, but the two get along very well and Bernard sees his job with an experienced two-for-oner as a form of internship. Saturday and Sunday evenings, he works on his own on the sidewalk in front of Sloan's. "The manager was impressed how organized and clean I worked compared with Tony," Bernard says proudly. Slowly Bernard starts to save money. It helps that he's slowed down on the crack. There are even days he doesn't touch the stem.

Bernard is in a good mood while he tells me about his plans one morning over a bowl of hot oatmeal. He gives his money to his father in Harlem who is saving it for him and has promised a big bonus when his son has saved up his first thousand. Bernard is thinking about buying a small van he can use to drive all Pier John's empties to WeCan, because the station wagon costs twenty dollars a trip. Sometimes Pier John has so many cans they have to make two trips. Bernard calculates that if he gets a van for fifteen hundred, he can make the money back in two months.

In another development, the movie people from Hollywood have contacted him and sent a first draft of the script. Bernard is now trying to get an advance, so he can furnish his apartment. When everything is over, he plans a long trip through Europe.

Behind us we hear rustling. In the dark space near the toilet facilities we see big white underpants floating in mid-air. They slowly rise and then disappear.

Slowly someone emerges from the black hole. It is Burk, who joins us at the fire while tying up his pants. Bernard offers him a bowl of oatmeal. Burk is leaning forward, the bowl on his lap, and uttering unintelligible sounds. Bernard has to turn the radio down to understand something.

"Downtown I met Batman. And Buddha coughed in my face."

Bernard and I exchange puzzled looks.

"The bowl is hot," he suddenly says. Irritated, Bernard gives him an old newspaper that he can put under his oatmeal. Burk is quiet for a while, rocking a bit on his chair, and then asks Bernard if he gets his welfare next week. Slowly he spoons up his oatmeal, and when the bowl is half empty, he trudges away without saying anything.

"Unbelievable," Bernard sighs. "The guys walks fifteen blocks down to take a shit, in front of my kitchen of all places. He can't even say thank you for breakfast." Bernard tells me that Burk spent a long period in a clinic where they tried out all kind of drugs on him, turning him into a retarded child. Heavy crack use caused the additional mental damage. "But the motherfucker is not completely crazy. Knows exactly when I get my welfare check. And then he is knocking on my door for a hit. But what the fuck do I care. I have more important things on my mind." He kicks away a cat and pours the coffee.

"Watch this, Turn," he says, and goes into his place, to emerge a bit later with a big envelope. "The notorious movie script. They sent it yesterday from LA."

Lord Of The Tunnel is the obvious title for the film. It is a heavily dramatized version of Bernard's tunnel life. In the opening scene we see Bernard in a white, sterile room with a big spotlight focused on him. He is being subjected to a psychological evaluation. This scene slowly fades out and turns into flashbacks of Bernard's life. We see him as a handsome young man posing on trendy fashion shows and photo shoots. We see Bernard the family man, who lives together with a beautiful black Broadway actress, raising a cute little baby.

Next scene. Bernard snorts coke and gets bad friends. The beautiful wife kicks him out of the house. Fast forward. Bernard is waiting for her at the artist exit at a Broadway theater. She ignores him with a haughty attitude and jumps in a cab. Bernard is heartbroken. A judge rules he is no longer allowed to see his child. The poor Bernard wanders the lonely, rainy streets of Manhattan. A gang of thugs beat him up and rob him of his last possessions. He wakes up in a puddle of blood under a bridge. As a beaten man, he wants to crawl into a hole in the ground, and he enters a huge, subterranean space. He gets lost in a labyrinth of tunnels and finally, completely exhausted, he bumps into Chris Pape. Illuminated by torches, Pape is spray painting graffiti on the tunnel walls. Pape fixes up the injured Bernard. Once healed and strong, Bernard decides to call the tunnel his new home. Pretty soon new people come to live in the tunnel and an eclectic, dynamic community comes into being. In dark caves, we see poets recite their poems in front of an audience of shabbily dressed homeless people. Intellectuals discuss the meaning of life with junkies and dropouts, blind violin players make music, and in every empty space, artists make huge reproductions of Dali, Goya, and el Greco. Nurses run a clinic where simple afflictions are treated with love and care; a crew of chefs prepares culinary masterpieces over an open fire.

Next scene. We see Bernard as the uncrowned king sitting on his throne.

Strict but righteous, he declares the rules of the tunnels. No drug use in public spaces. No screaming. No dying in the tunnels: anyone who feels it is his last day is kindly requested to go up top and check in at a hospital.

A small palace coup by the traitors Hector and Shorty is effectively smothered by Bernard. They are evicted and banned for life from the tunnels, the worst possible punishment for tunnel people. The crucial scene. Bernard's brother shows up in the tunnel and offers him money to leave. He pulls out a briefcase with dollar bills, fifteen thousand dollars total. "For no money in this world will I give up the truly veritable life," Bernard tells his flabbergasted brother. Furious, he disappears.

The bad brother can't stand losing and is scheming dirty plans. We see him take his briefcase of cash to the psych clinic from the opening scene. The clinic is in financial difficulties and could use a cash influx. The last scene is the same as the beginning. The bribed director tries to have Bernard declared mentally ill, but his intelligent answers to all questions confuse his interrogators.

In the end, he has a brilliant monologue, which makes the director burst into tears. She asks herself if perhaps she is the one who is crazy, with Bernard the only normal human left in this world. Fade out from Bernard, back in the tunnel and preparing a delicious stew above the fire, recounting laughingly his strange adventures up top to his fellow tunnel dwellers.

"Yes, of course it's Hollywood," Bernard admits. He has to seriously sit down with the movie people and discuss how to make the script more realistic and credible. But Denzel Washington was already approached as the leading actor and he was immediately interested.

In total, Bernard will receive 150,000 dollars for the exclusive film rights to his life. A lawyer he still knows from before his tunnel life has advised him on the contract. When the deal is done, he wants to retreat to his family's estate. His great grandparents, former slaves, received at their liberation thirty acres of wetland in South Carolina. The property has been divided between his cousins and is partially rented out to Campbell's Soup Company that is using it to grow vegetables for soup. Bernard wants to buy up all the parcels, and spend his days as a recluse in the middle of magnificent nature. "And then everybody can drop dead. Then I only want to see raccoons, alligators, and catfish."

33. THE ADVENTURES OF FRANKIE, PART 8: FRANKIE MAKES MASHED POTATOES

"Ant, you should come over tonight and have dinner with us," Frankie invites me cordially when I give him a copy of the reference letter I personally handed to Guy Polhemus from WeCan. I recommended Frankie as a "reliable, honest, hard working young man." I actually meant it, because except for some stupid tricks, Frankie are Ment are guys with hearts of gold. When I definitively go back to Europe, I have promised Frankie my bike, so that he can get a steady job as a bike messenger and stay out of trouble. Frankie's place is crowded and messy when I show up at dinnertime.

Frankie's place is crowded and messy when I show up at dinnertime. Obviously nobody is still obeying the no-shoe rule. The white carpet is smudged with mud and other stains. Jazzy tips over an ashtray, throws a cup of orange juice on the couch, gets slapped by Maria, and starts to cry. A dirty diaper is stinking in the corner. One new improvement is the screen that protects the fan, so the baby can no longer poke her tiny fingers in between the blades.

Ment is injured from a small accident with a friend who has an off-road motor bike in the tunnel. Ment wanted to try it out and fell down. Now his back is scraped open, and his hand is a bloody mess. Concerned, Fatima is stroking his head and cleaning his back with a cotton swab drenched in hydrogen peroxide. Ment is biting his lips with the pain. His hand is soaking in a bowl with a reddish-brown iodine solution.

Once his damaged skin is soaked loose, it has to be cut away so the small pebbles and grains of sand and little pebbles under his skin can be removed. My tiny Swiss army knife with its scissors, tweezers, and toothpick is used as the operation equipment. Fatima and I start to remove the little pebbles but Ment screams and orders us to stop. He'd rather do it himself. He puts a handkerchief between his teeth and, his face distorted by pain, starts to wiggle loose the pebbles with the toothpick. In the meantime, Frankie is busy cooking. He can hardly watch the bloody operation and focuses on the meatballs cooking in a big frying pan. "I told you so, watch out with that motorcycle," he says in a whining voice.

"Fuck you," growls Ment. Frankie shrugs his shoulders and proceeds to make mashed potatoes. He is boiling water in a huge pot and adds instant mashed-potato powder. He mixes the substances with a big ladle and adds a bit of the water from the green beans and gravy from the meatballs, so the stuff gets a grayish color. Frankie tastes it. "Too dry," he mumbles and throws in half a pack of margarine. Now it is too greasy, so Frankie adds a bit more potato powder. His hand slips, however, and the substance becomes too stiff again. He throws in a cup of water and lets Ment try it.

Blobs of mashed potatoes fall on the floor and Ment accidentally tips over the bowl that holds the iodine. A big reddish brown stains starts to expand across the white carpet, turning purple where the iodine enters into a chemical reaction with the starch in the potatoes. "More butter," says Ment. Frankie throws in the remaining half pack of margarine. Fatima in the meantime tries to clean the carpet with Ment's T-shirt.

The Coalition might pay a visit at any moment, and they are not supposed to know there is a baby in the house. Every time the dogs barks, Maria is sent upstairs with the baby and Frankie takes a look to see if someone is coming. Maria swears at Frankie, because the tiny sleeping attic is suffocatingly hot.

Ment has succeeded in operating on himself satisfactorily. The loose pieces of skin are gone and the wound is clean. He patches himself up with a dirty handkerchief as a bandage. If infection or other complications set in, he can always go to the hospital under a false name.

Frankie serves dinner on plates that are way too small. In every serving of mashed potatoes, he makes a little hole and dumps the over-cooked and crushed string beans into it. Then he pours the gravy on top and throws a meatball on everybody's plates. The dirty-brown substance sloshes around.

Since Ment has trouble eating with his injured hand, half of his food falls off his plate. A meatball rolls between the sheets of the bed on which he is sitting. We eat our food in silence, balancing plates overflowing with murky liquid on our laps. The carpet starts to look like a Pollock painting. Frankie wolfs down his meal, burps loudly, and looks around.

"Yo. Damn it," he grumbles. "It's a goddamn filthy pig sty here. Look at the floor, look at that pile of dirty plates." Accusingly, he looks at Maria, who is responsible for doing the dishes. "Time we have a house meeting and we divide some house-hold chores." Outside, the dogs start to bark. "Damn it," Frankie swears. "Upstairs, you guys."

"Fuck it," Maria swears back, and disappears into attic after throwing a sneaker that lands in the pan with mashed potatoes.

"Don't let them in," Frankie calls to Ment who is taking a look. "These creeps only want to sniff around here."

Moments later, a fat black guy with a big beer bottle pokes his nose around the corner. It's Chuck, a house friend who stops by quite often.

"I'm sorry, my nigger. Tonight is not the right night," Frankie tells him. "We are expecting these slimes from the Coalition."

Chuck feels the tension and discreetly pulls out.

"Bunch of assholes," Frankie mutters. "They promised to bring my birth certificate last week." I suggest he pick it up himself. Frankie never thought about that. He doesn't even have the phone number and address of the Coalition. Maria and the baby come down. It is getting late. Nobody expects the Coalition anymore.

"I need these assholes like I need a hole in the head," Frankie raves on. "I have been homeless for ten years. Never got more out of them than some lousy-ass sandwich." We open a few beers and play music. Slowly, the dark clouds above Frankie's house are passing by. Fatima took a new pregnancy test: This time it was negative. And after consultation with his friends, Frankie's deserted his stupid plan to rob Vanessa's mother. He has even come to terms with his terminated relationship with Vanessa. "The bitch sure was a good fuck for three months."

Maria grasps her head in exasperation. "Oh Frankie, you are terrible."

34. BURGLARY IN THE TUNNEL

Bernard and I inspect the damage made by the burglar. The door of Bob's bunker is in two pieces, the upper part dangling on the chain, it still has the lock to which only we have the key. It must have been Bob, thinks Bernard, searching for a crumb of crack in the shag carpet. Yesterday, Bernard bumped into him on the block where he was canning. When Bob said out of nowhere that he had not been in the tunnel, Bernard already smelled a rat.

Inside, nothing has been taken, nothing even moved. We find only a piece of paper on Bob's favorite coffee table: a form for Bob to re-apply for his SSI benefits. Bernard and I exchange a glance of mutual understanding. Perpetrator and motivation have been established.

Bernard gives the windows and doors a second inspection. One sheet of plywood has been carefully pushed away. This is the way Bob must have crawled in, on his desperate quest for a hit. Judging by the splinters, the door must have been smashed from the inside.

"Aha," Bernard says. "Now I understand everything. The idiot panicked and wanted to get out as fast as possible. Duke, I always told you, I should have been a detective." Bernard says it with no trace of irony.

Bernard has also had a burglar. His drawers have been rudely opened and the smart denim shirt I gave him has disappeared. It is not likely that it was the Kool-Aid Kid. After doing some time in prison, he has been spotted again in the tunnel. Sometimes, he rummages through Bernard's place in search for food, but he never leaves a mess. Maybe Bob was responsible, but there's no way to prove it.

The Kool-Aid Kid and Bernard are getting along better, sometimes he treats Bernard to prime quality crack. "That's his way to pay for all the stolen eggs," Bernard told me last time, his tone reconciliatory. "Somehow, he has good manners."

The Kid is on the run from a gang in Brooklyn, we now know, because of a drug deal that went wrong. His brother has already been killed, executed point blank, and the Kid is next on the hit list. That's why he is always armed with a small nine millimeter. At the moment, the Kid makes his living by dealing crack. Bernard once saw the Kid working on 33rd Street, right around the corner from the police precinct.

I repair Bob's door and step on a dead rat. Lately, there has been a nasty smell of rotting dead bodies around my bunker. A little further down, one of Tony's cats is slowly disintegrating after being hit by a train. Bernard and Tony fight every day over who has to bury the remains. Soon, that will no longer be necessary because rats have been nibbling away at the dead cat.

Tony's other cats sometimes catch a baby rat, but since Tony spoils his cats too much with hearty snacks, they only eat the heads. Maybe baby rat heads are delicacies for cats. Tony picks up the decapitated baby rats and slings them away by their tails. Most of the time, they land in front of my door.

Tony is two-for-oneing at Sloan's. I want to comment on the dead baby rats, but Tony is too busy talking to a girl that wants to sell him a few bottles. The girl has only been homeless a few weeks and doesn't understand a thing about the canning business. She has never heard of WeCan and she always arrives too late on garbage days, so she is only left with the glass bottles that are too heavy for most can people. She even doesn't know the expression "dead can."

Tony patiently explains everything to her in a hoarse voice. I take over when his voice has totally broken down into a squeaky whisper. When we have finished discussing cans, we start to talk about the tunnel. The girl has heard a lot about it from other homeless people. They even have a baby there, she says softly.

A bit shocked and surprised, I ask her where she got that information. Scared, she looks at me like she has just given away a deep dark secret. I go get some coffee to put her at ease, and continue the interrogation. She heard it from a guy that used to live in the tunnel, and some time ago visited his old friends there. Buddy is his name.

Now I understand. Buddy the snitch, kicked out personally by Frankie. I promise to be discreet and the girl tells me the whole story.

According to her, Buddy had visited Frankie and Ment and had seen the baby. For days, he had been nagging other homeless people about how irresponsible it was to have a baby down there. Finally, tormented by doubt but convinced he was doing the right thing, Buddy reported it to the police. Full of remorse over betraying his old friends, Buddy had cried a few times the following week. Mystery solved and it was obvious. Buddy the slimy creep. The girl sees me getting angry and excuses herself. It's time for her to get her daily shot of heroin.

"See you, honey," Tony whispers to the girl. He lost his voice at the horse races. He had put the last of his money on his favorite horse. Tony cheered the animal with hysterical screams, but it let him down just before the finish. He lost his money and his voice at the very same moment.

"Didn't you stop betting?" I ask.

Tony shrugs his shoulders. "That's life," he croaks with great difficulty and proceeds to sort out his cans. To save money, he has fired his assistant.

35. IN THE LION'S DEN

"We could have kicked out everybody by force a long time ago," Captain Doris Combs says. "The fact that we have not done so proves we are sincere and honest."

I have penetrated the lion's den and am facing Captain Combs, the feared Amtrak police chief, in her office three stories down in Penn Station. Captain Combs is a big, strong, black woman with steely, piercing eyes.

"I guess you heard a lot of bad things about me," she grins.

"Well, people say a lot things…" I answer evasively.

"Yeah, don't tell me," she smiles wryly. "I am indeed a tough one. I come from a dirt-poor family," she explains. "As a kid, I learned how to fight."

Combs is in the company of Richard Rubel, Amtrak's Community Relations Officer. He is a friendly white man who is very interested in my tunnel adventures. Rubel has a background in social work and has been appointed to set out an effective yet humane policy to approach the problem of the homeless living in the Amtrak tunnels. Amtrak learned a lesson from the ongoing lawsuit over the physical harassment of the homeless at Penn Station. "Repression is not the answer," Combs says. "We try to offer the homeless a variety of social services. But the problem is that most homeless are completely isolated. They feel rejected and decline all assistance."

"The newest trend is the idea that we have to see the homeless as clients. We have to sell our services to them, instead of forcing them to go into a mass shelter." Rubel adds. "They are individual consumers who all need a unique combination of assistance programs." Amtrak is using the expertise of MTA/Connections for their new approach.

One thing is for sure: the tunnel people will have to leave. The problems are getting out of hand. There are accidents when people are hit by trains, and Amtrak is slapped with big fines by the Fire Department for all track and tunnel fires. And if there should be some serious train accident, the blocked and clogged emergency exits will be a living nightmare.

"We are working in phases," the captain says. "Currently, we are renovating parts of the tunnel. At the same time, we do outreach. Mind you, in coordination with the Coalition and Project Renewal. When the people are gone, we remove all livable constructions, secure the tunnel and close the gates, so no new people will settle down." Combs and Rubel know most tunnel dwellers by name.

"Joe is the most stubborn of the whole bunch," says Combs. "He refuses all help. He even wrote a letter in which he threatened to sue us in case we evict him." Of course I want to see the letter. "If you show us your pictures, I will show you the letter," Combs says slyly.

I mention Bernard. "How did he ever get these keys?" I ask as innocently as possible.

"Just like you don't know that," the captain says rudely. Her cozy mood has disappeared. To talk about nicer things, I mention the movie script and that Denzel Washington will be playing Bernard. Combs brightens up.

"Really? And am I in the script? Then I want to be played by Whitney Houston." Her laugh echoes through the basement of Penn Station.

36. HOPELESS LITTLE HAVANA

There is a new rumor circulating in the tunnel that the Coalition will stop by. Twice, it has been a false alarm but this time even Bernard knows about the visit.

In the meantime, Dov has sorted out the misunderstanding with DC. In a noble gesture, the Secretary has decided that the vouchers will also be valid for the Amtrak tunnel people. I am at little Havana, watching TV and waiting for things to happen. Julio is still mourning the loss of his favorite cat Pelusa. He found her dead a few days ago, one of the many that according to Julio were poisoned by evil tunnel dwellers. A little farther down the tunnel, he has made a wooden cross, and placed a votive candle and a little statue of a cat to mark the place Pelusa is buried. Julio cheers a bit up when I give him photos of the deceased.

At the mouth of the tunnel we see three silhouettes emerging against the red of the setting sun. First they stop at the house of José, the fat Puerto Rican. Then they approach little Havana. I recognize Marc and Margaret, the third man is Mike Harris from the Coalition. Mike Harris has been appointed as the trouble-shooter, because handing out the vouchers has proven to be a painstakingly slow process. He's replacing Bob Kelty, who was way too soft and sweet and has been given a job in California. Mike prefers the no-nonsense approach.

He is carrying a big pile of files and takes everybody's case apart. "Here is your birth certificate," he tells Julio. "And now go like hell and apply for welfare."

"Wow, thanks man!" Julio calls out happily. "Wanna beer, man?"

"I don't drink during work," Mike answers brusquely.

"And what have you been freaking," he sternly says to Poncho. "We are still waiting for your proof of income." Poncho grumbles he is working on it and will stop by tomorrow to drop it off. "OK. Cool. Next one," Mike says and takes the files of Estoban, Getulio and Hugo.

I hop on my bike to warn Frankie that the Coalition is coming. But there is nothing to be afraid of, since Fatima has already left Jazzy temporarily with her aunt in New Jersey. We wait down-stairs for the visitors.

When they arrive, Mike gives Frankie his birth certificate. Pleased, Frankie goes upstairs. Tomorrow, he's going to immedi-ately start looking for a job as a bike messenger. Then he will also stop by at the Coalition and Project Renewal to finish the last of the paperwork. Ment refuses every sort of assistance. "Frankie takes everything as long as it's free," he says scornfully to Mike. "But I will stay in the tunnel. I already came down here as a kid. Nobody can kick me out. Worst case, I brick myself in, and re-inforce the doors with steel." Ment has already started renovat-ing an empty bunker. He wants to live there with Fatima. Mike shakes his head. "Listen, my friend. We have to sit down and

have a man-to-man talk. You are mixing up fantasy with reality."
Ment shrugs his shoulders and goes upstairs. Kathy is listening
and sighs deeply. "Me and Joe are ready. Once the paperwork is
OK, we are gone."

The delegation proceeds to Bernard's. Mike doesn't need to
take care of his case because he actually has all his paperwork
finished, he's just curious to see how Bernard lives.

From a distance we can already see a big fire burning at the grill.
Bernard presents everybody with chairs and makes a pot of tea.
He is extremely polite and friendly, even towards Margaret, about
whom he was ranting and raving for half an hour yesterday.

"Mike, at this level, complacency is the greatest danger,"
Bernard starts as he serves the tea. I already know the story and
go upstairs to get Tony, who by this time must be finished two-
for-oneing at Sloan's. When we come back, Margaret is crying
softly, and Bernard has wrapped his arm around her. A young
cat from Tony's litter just died. The cute furry kitten walked up
to the grill, its breath started to rattle, and after some spastic
wiggling it simply passed away. Bernard lifts the cat up. Blood is
dripping from its mouth.

"Next patient," Bernard calls out rudely. "Tony, that litter of
yours, they are all degenerated animals. Spontaneously they just
drop dead, one by one."

Together with Margaret and Tony, we bury the cat close to
the toilet facilities. "He is lying," Tony says indignantly. "He just
stepped on it with his big feet. It was pure murder."

In my last week in the tunnel, I slowly turn into a messenger
and do-gooder myself. I ride up and down to the Coalition and
Project Renewal, getting from Mike and Dov what is needed for
the vouchers and telling everybody what papers and forms they
still need to obtain, fill in, and return.

I go with Estoban to a Catholic relief organization that helps
Cuban refugees with legal problems, and I push Julio to apply
for welfare. One evening, I am at the South End discussing everybody's case. On TV we see the Croatian troops march through
the Krajina, causing an exodus of desperate Serbian refugees.
Hugo is slouched on a chair.

"Oh, man, I think I fucked up," he groans. By not showing up to workfare where he had to pick up litter in the park, he lost his welfare. It will take at least a few months to go through the whole process again. He doesn't dare call Dov to break the bad news. "We had to clean the park during the heat wave," Hugo says. "It is not an excuse, but I can't stand heat. It was also the same week when we heard the vouchers were maybe not for us. I just gave up all hope."

Hugo looks like a mess. He missed his weekly shower at a friend's SRO hotel—he can only go on Sundays when there is no one at the desk. Now he has a small prickly beard, grayish skin, and smelly clothes. "I hardly dare to walk the streets."

He also lost his job as delivery boy for the laundry. The boss lost his patience when Hugo not only wanted to get paid daily, but even started to ask for advances. Slowly, Hugo is sliding down into his old drug habits. He will never admit he uses crack, but it is easy to see. More and more often, he starts asking to borrow just five dollars. After he returns from canning, I watch him go into his little house, then reappear ten minutes later to sit in front of the TV with glassy eyes.

Julio, in the meantime, has really started to hit the bottle. The only sober moments he has are the few minutes in the morning when he staggers hung over to the icebox to get his first beer. "He expects to find Debby at the bottom of the bottle," Frankie had told me pointedly.

Today wasn't Julio's day. He rubs his painful jaw: yesterday he got hit by a bookseller on Broadway. Later on he will take revenge. He gets up to get another beer. Little Havana's only light fixture, a strong bare bulb on the ground, projects giant shadows of him onto the tunnel walls.

"Fuck it," Julio says. He was busy all day trying to get on welfare. Together with Poncho he went to the Social Security office. "Dirty fucked up mother fucking assholes. Spent half a day in the waiting room. And then they gave me two pounds of forms to fill in," Julio blusters. "Goddammit. Old forms that are no longer valid." Julio gets up to show me the paperwork. He can't find it, and only after fifteen minutes of stumbling around with a flashlight does he locate the papers between a pile of moldy books on the ground. Angrily, he points me at the small letters. *Form 2-b model* 1993 it says.

"You see, they are just deceiving us," he accuses. "Just shut the fuck up for a moment," Poncho calls out. "There is nothing wrong with these papers." Poncho is getting tired of Julio; all he wants after a hard day's work collecting cans is just to watch the O.J. Simpson case on TV.

Julio is getting ready to have some serious talk with the bookseller up top. He puts a big knife in the inside pocket of his leather coat. I join him and suggest he put the knife in my backpack. He might stumble and hurt himself. Grumbling, he hands over the knife and pulls an even bigger one from his back pocket. Luckily the case with the bookseller is resolved very quickly. It is a huge guy who apologizes for hurting Julio. "But you were pretty shit-faced and annoying," he adds. "OK, let's forget it," Julio says and shakes his hand. After all, he is an important customer who buys many of his books. Julio hasn't eaten anything, so we have a burger and fries at a bar.

"Wow, thanks man," he says smiling when the waitress brings him a juicy burger and a pint of beer. "Goddamn long time ago I was in a pub." Julio gets sentimental and talks about his daughter. It's the first time he's talked about her. By now she must be six. Julio hasn't seen her in five years.

"Boy, she is a cute girl! Damn, I would have loved to be a good father." Tears are filling his eyes. The kid dates from the time that Julio was living upstate. He lived with his girlfriend and her family in a trailer park. One fatal night there was a party. Booze, snacks, and coke. His mother in law entered just as Julio was snorting a line. "Finish the party and tomorrow you're gone," was the only thing she said.

Julio looks sadly down at his glass of beer. It must be difficult trying to get back into the system and reorganize his life. About the same time, Julio continues, there was another party. It was a pretty wild, somewhere in the woods, with whiskey, beer, speed, acid and guns. It got out of hand. Two guys started to fight and they shot a third one. Everybody was arrested. The white killers blamed Julio. He was allowed out on bail; his father paid. Julio ran away and disappeared. Still, he is a wanted man. "I swear to god, I am innocent. But it was their word against mine. Two white boys against a Puerto Rican. Who will ever believe me?"

"Oh, Dov, my man, it's crazy," Bernard complains like an old woman to Dov at Project Renewal. "It is a mad house here. Yesterday the BBC came, Margaret left another six messages and tomorrow National Joe will be here for a few days." Bernard means *National Geographic*, but Joe sounds cooler. "And this morning I still had to collect my cans," he continues. Bernard interrupts his litany, "Duke, you have an extra quarter?" and puts it in the pay phone.

"Yeah, Dov, I am still here. Next week three Japanese, then Channel Four, Duke is finishing his book and maybe later someone from the Deutsche Rundfunk."

"Duke, quickly, another dime." I pull one out of my pockets.

"Yes, Dov, I still hear you. In short, my peace and quiet has gone up in smoke."

Bernard is quiet for a moment. Dov has finally found the opportunity to say something back. "Okay, understood. Yes, thanks so much for all your efforts. See you tomorrow morning." He turns to me smiling. "It's all done. Tomorrow the last paperwork and then I will get my voucher. I never thought they were serious."

"Bernard, you are the vanguard of the tunnel people," Dov says solemnly the next morning. With a firm handshake, he gives Bernard the form with which he can obtain his Section 8 voucher at the New York Department of Housing. "Man," Bernard says, "This is between us, but I will be surprised if other people finish the process. Watch my words." Dov nods, concerned.

We take off to the Coalition, ignore the upset receptionist, and walk straight to the office of Mike Harris. Proudly, Bernard shows him the form. Mike's office looks like a crisis center. He is on a cordless phone, doing business with City Hall and DC while he orders assistants walking in and out to fax proof of incomes and birth certificates, restart suspended welfare procedures, and print out lost Social Security cards.

"It looks like they don't care down there," Mike sighs in a quiet moment. "They expect us to bring the keys of their new apartments on a silver platter." An assistant whispers something in Mike's ear.

Bad news. While waiting for the voucher that could come in any moment, José was temporarily staying at the YMCA. The next day, he moved back to his tunnel shack because he could not conform to the house rules. "Damn it," Mike curses. "And when they finally are settled in their apartments, they expect us to come over to change a broken light bulb." Mike's initial optimism in the housing project has gone. The red tape is bad enough, but the uncooperative attitude of the tunnel people is highly discouraging. "Mike," Bernard says resigned, "you can lead a horse to the water, but you can't make it drink."

"Bunch of ungrateful dogs," Bernard says as we walk back. "They don't realize this is the first and last time they'll get such an exceptional chance." Bernard has in the meantime tipped off a homeless friend. It is a man who has been sleeping in the park for years. Bernard has told Mike the man lived all that time as a recluse in the tunnel.

"He will be worth it," Bernard says. "But the others, they will eventually choose chaos."

Joe and Kathy are cooking dinner. Plastic bottles burn in an empty oil drum that serves as a makeshift stove. Joe throws a chunk of margarine into a dented frying pan sitting on top of the drum. Sooty flames shoot up into the air. Joe is bitter about the Coalition and Project Renewal. "Hey man, they came down here to offer us help. Why should I go to them? The assholes still haven't brought my birth certificate."

"Come on, Joe," I say. "You have to do a bit of work yourself as well. Bernard got his voucher yesterday."

"Yeah, of course, the mayor," he answers sarcastically. "They gave it to him because he is black."

"Come on, Joe," I try another time.

"Damn it," Joe says, angry. "I don't want to talk about it anymore." He goes back into his bunker and slams the door shut behind him.

Winter

January 1996

37. THE TUNNEL EMPTIES

A blizzard has hit New York. It is so bad it will later become known as the notorious Blizzard of '96. Heavy snowstorms paralyze the city for a week. The tunnel people survive. In fact, not much has changed since last summer. I called Dov and Mike once in a while from Europe. They told me that everything was working out, albeit at a slow pace. Marc and Margaret also informed me about new developments: basically, there haven't been any over the last four months.

I crawl into the tunnel through an emergency exit where some bars have been sawed away. It's cold, dark, and damp. Packs of snow are below the grates, melting water is dripping from the walls. Carefully, I knock on Bernard's door. He is expecting me. I left a message on his voicemail that I would stop by today.

"Git yer ass in here!" he calls out happily. He gets out of bed and lights a few candles. It looks as though time has come to a standstill. Bernard is still underground and his place is still the same old mess. Bob has returned definitively to the tunnel. He has lost his SSI benefits. He is no longer welcome at the YMCA or at Pete's Place. And Tony is still down in his bunker.

Bernard hasn't used his voucher: he could only get a place in the Bronx or Brooklyn, but he wanted to stay on the Upper West Side.

At one point, his voucher expired. It has been extended, but now Bernard is having trouble with his welfare, that is to say, he's actually lost his benefits. He was on workfare and had to shovel snow during the blizzard. There were twenty inches of snow.

"The idiots," Bernard says. "They can't expect someone who doesn't have a decent warm home to work in the freezing cold?" Bernard and Bob did not leave the tunnel for four days. A thick layer of snow had covered the grates, so they had hardly seen any daylight. They had, however, stocked up with plenty of water, food, and firewood so they could survive without problems. Bernard will talk with Dov next week to sort things out. He is now completely fed up with the tunnel. Most of all, it is Bob who's driving him crazy.

"It's an unbelievable chaos. Bob is sent by God to drive me out of the tunnel," he says dramatically. Slowly, Bernard is making preparations to leave. Pedro and Harvey have saved some nice furniture from the garbage and set it aside for him. Bernard is also cleaning up his place and throwing away old stuff. He gives me an expensive Shetland wool sweater, fancy Italian suede shoes, and a backpack he won't be able to use. Then, Bernard starts in on the usual tirade about Margaret. "Damn it. She is still yelling every day through the grate and whining I have to see Dov."

"She is just concerned about you," I say. Margaret had told me on the phone that Bernard's voucher could expire any moment and wouldn't be extended for a third time. She had asked me specifically to remind Bernard, because she realized she was getting on his nerves. "Fuck it," Bernard curses. "Her book is finished but the tunnel remains an obsession." He shows the publication. It has beautiful photos of him, but he is not happy with the final result.

"She did not put the best photos in it," he says indignantly. "I offered to help her with the final edit, but she is a stubborn bat."

I continue towards the South End. The house of Frankie and Ment has disappeared. Its smashed wooden walls lie on the ground in front of the bunkers belonging to Joe and Kathy.

"They ran into trouble with a Puerto Rican gang." According to Joe, Ment had burglarized the leader's home and stolen twenty-five thousand dollars. The victim soon realized who the perpetrators were, and paid a visit to the tunnel with his gang. Frankie and Ment drew the right conclusions and disappeared. Where they are, Joe does not know. Kathy and Joe finally got their vouchers this week. They are looking for an apartment. Project Renewal has given them a list of landlords and housing corporations that will accept the vouchers. One complication is that Joe slipped on the icy railroad tracks a week ago and has sprained his ankle. At the hospital they bandaged his foot, but he still needs to walk on crutches for three weeks.

Julio's case is also closed. He got welfare and workfare: he is cleaning bathing facilities for seventy hours a month. He used to take showers there himself. He also says he's seriously cut down on his alcohol intake. He proudly shows me a flask half-filled with vodka. "I've already had it for two days." Next week, Julio will start looking for an apartment. It will be difficult, because he still has to keep on canning because he needs the money for clean clothes and subway tokens. He already blew all the welfare money he got the week before.

José got housing. He now has a room in an SRO hotel around 140th Street. But he has heart trouble and the hospital that treats him is at 72nd Street, too far to take a daily trip. That's why José has decided to keep his tunnel shack as a second home. Six days a week, he stays over in the tunnel. Estoban has crept away under his blankets. He still hasn't gotten his identity papers.

Margaret told me he visited the organization that helps Cuban refugees a few times, but he was discouraged and scared away by the long line of clients. And Estoban can't afford time-consuming bureaucratic procedures, because he needs to work every day to get his daily amount of cans.

Hugo looks like a zombie, with an unkempt beard of months, ripped clothes, and a wild skittish expression in his eyes. He got his voucher three months ago, but he didn't do anything with it. It expired and was not extended. His welfare has also been suspended. He never dared to call Project Renewal. Cans and crack are all that remain. In a soft voice, he gives evasive answers to my questions and stares at the ground the whole time.

"It was a promising case," Dov says. "But Hugo turned out to be the biggest disappointment." Margaret and Marc tried to mediate, but that did not help. Hugo has withdrawn into himself like a shy bird. "The moment he got the voucher, he threw himself off the cliff," Marc says. "The challenge must have been too overwhelming."

The good news is that Sergeant Bryan Henry of the Metro North Police in Grand Central has been promoted to Captain. The bad news is that Captain Combs has been demoted to Sergeant. The lawsuit against Amtrak has finished her. Streetwatch, a home-less advocacy group, had taken footage that featured Captain Combs harassing homeless people with her billy club. She is now working on a small train station close to her home in Dela-ware. "She is happy over there," PR man Richard Rubel says dip-lomatically. "Sergeant Combs now can devote more time to her family since she doesn't have to travel every day up and down to New York." Enthusiastically, Rubel tells me about the station's new approach towards the homeless. Under Combs' rule, the po-lice focused mostly on the way homeless looked. Now the police are only focusing on their behavior. A homeless person can be ejected from the station only if they break the law.

"For a small troubled group of hardcore service-resistant in-dividuals, we have the law," Rubel says firmly, "But we prefer a soft approach." Since their positive cooperation in the tunnels, Amtrak is using Project Renewal to help improve the situation at its stations. They also stay in regular touch with the Coalition, and even allow Streetwatch to monitor the situation. "The beau-ty of our new program," Rubel exults, "is that experienced and qualified outreach workers can get the homeless straight in touch with service providing organizations."

Rubel shows me confidential papers. It is Amtrak's three mil-lion dollar budget to clean up the tunnels, now definitively ap-proved by the Board of Directors. Three hundred thousand has been set apart to remove all garbage and demolish shacks, bun-kers, and other constructions. One hundred and fifty thousand has been set apart to put up new fences. One million is for po-lice protection during the clean-up operation. The operation will start next spring. Amtrak expect that most tunnel dwellers will be in alternative housing by then.

"The lawsuit of the Coalition was a first-rate public relations di-saster." Captain Bryan Henry explains Amtrak's new approach. "Homelessness is not illegal and even bums have human rights. You can't billy club them out of the stations. You just don't do that…"

I congratulate Bryan Henry on his promotion and mention

the demotion of Sergeant Combs. Henry tries to hide his smile behind his hand, but soon bursts out laughing. A colleague has to calm him down. The last time I heard a police captain laugh so loud, it was when Captains Combs told me she wanted her movie role played by Whitney Houston.

"Listen," Henry says, now serious again. "Not only Amtrak, but also the government wants to bring the tunnels under control. The World Trade Center, Oklahoma City, everybody is scared of new terrorist attacks."

Unlike last summer, Mike Harris from the Coalition is once again optimistic about the process. Five tunnel people have already left. Frankie and Ment are the first ones. To make it less complicated, José is counted in as well. Four and five are the twins. They got their vouchers and found a place in the Bronx.

The twins are identical black brothers, originally from Georgia. They lived in a little shack near Julio, but I hardly got to know them because they were always outside working together. They were not particularly smart or educated, but since they did not have severe drinking or drug problems, and were confident in the housing procedure, it went smoothly. Mike tells me that all the others either have vouchers or will get them any moment. A few will be moving this weekend; the coalition has temporarily stored their personal belongings. "A few tunnel people have an understandable fear of starting a new life," Mike says, "But most are smart and intelligent people. We are confident they will manage above ground." Things got slowed down because of DC, Mike says. Most federal institutions were not functioning for weeks due to a budget conflict between Clinton and Congress. Money flow came to a stand still and all government workers were sent home for a month. Also, it looked like budget cuts would stop the voucher program.

"It's simple," Mike says confidently. "Our aim is no more people in the tunnel. Whatever will happen, we will accomplish our mission."

38. THE ADVENTURES OF FRANKIE, PART 9:
OUT OF THE TUNNEL

"Me and Ment, we don't talk no more," Frankie says. "And next time I see him, I'll put a gun in his face. To pay back what he pulled on me all these years. I tell you, Ant, it took me five years to get at that point."

Frankie is, as he calls it, 'stayin' out down low.' He went underground temporarily at a friend's place on the 27th story of a depressing apartment building in Hell's Kitchen. I visit him there in a small room he is sharing with a friend. In the meantime, Frankie has his voucher, and next week he'll look for a place in Brooklyn.

What exactly happened remains unclear. Marc partially confirmed Joe's story, but also told me other details. Taking revenge, the ripped-off gang smashed the interior of Frankie's home. Frankie fled the tunnel and could take shelter at a friend's place. Ment stayed with Fatima and the baby who had been taken back from the aunt in New Jersey.

But they didn't have much choice. Not only was the Puerto Rican gang still a threat, Ment was also wanted by the police. Still on probation, Ment never kept his appointments with his parole officer.

The three of them took the Greyhound bus to Oregon, where Ment has a cousin. Marc paid for the tickets. Now Ment is working on one of the boats, fishing off the coast of Canada and Alaska for cod and salmon. It's hard but well paid work. To keep other people from living in their place, Frankie and Ment tore it down together.

Frankie tells me another version. There was a fight about money. "Ment had already borrowed two hundred bucks to score some smack. He's a filthy junkie. Then he had to borrow another fifty to fuck Fatima in peace in some motel. I refused. Ment smashed the TV. Damn it, a brand new wide screen I had found on the street."

"A perfect couple together," Frankie sneers. "Fatima is a whore. Never worked in her life. And Ment will spend half his life in jail." After two earlier convictions, assault and armed robbery, Ment only needs to pull one stupid thing and he'll be behind bars for at least twenty years, thanks to the new three strikes legislation.

The fight gave Frankie the final motive to finish with tunnel life. "I don't even come to the neighborhood any more," he says bitterly. "I don't want to see those bums anymore. But I still have to settle a score with Joe. And Greg, I still owe him a bullet."

Greg was a black man who lived in a tent halfway to the South End. He moved out to go into rehab, but got on crack again and moved back into the tunnel. When Greg freaked out, he always tore the electricity cables, so Frankie was plunged into darkness.

"Damn," Frankie continues. "If I see people canning now...I can't imagine that I used to do that, too. Now I take a shower when I want, I put on clean clothes, and the girls, they see it..." Frankie grins. He says he now has five girlfriends at once. He kicked Maria out, but Vanessa returned.

Once living in Brooklyn, he's going to get off welfare and look for work. "I want to be a productive citizen," Frankie declares solemnly. "You know, have a job, pay taxes, raise kids. I tell you, no mo' of that gangsta shit."

39. MURDER FOR THE GARBAGE

Tony's got his grayish, wrinkled winter skin back. He is still addicted to gambling and has no plans to leave the tunnel. "Tony thinks the tunnel is forever," Bernard says.

Jeff still stops by once in a while. The last time he came, he set fire to Tony's storage space under the emergency stairs. Scorched toasted teddy bears and ashes of charred porn magazines are now rotting in a mud puddle formed by melting snow.

When I see Tony at the grill, he is talking some unintelligible macho talk about cooking up heroin and nine millimeters. It seems like his mental capacities have deserted him. Then he leaves to watch TV at his sister. His merrily decorated shopping cart has been taken by the park police and put outside with the garbage.

Marcus is packing to spend the winter with the Rainbow People in Florida. He's already taken the necessary precautions in case he doesn't find his cave upon his return. Most of his valuable books are stored with friends. He doesn't care much about his other belongings.

"The refugees from Bosnia and Rwanda also lost everything, and they also go on with their life," Marcus says stoically. "It's all in the mind, *tu sais*."

The Coalition and Project Renewal came knocking on his cave a few times to offer vouchers, but Marcus does not like 'free government handouts.' "They were really pushing me. I don't understand. I asked them if they got a commission on every accepted voucher."

Burk is still wandering around the tunnels in a dazed state of mind. Margaret, who knows him from back when you could still have a reasonable talk with him, tried to take him to the Coalition and talk him into a voucher.

"Margaret is crazy," Bernard tells me. "Burk is a ticking time bomb. You can't put him in front of Mary Brosnahan in an office. He will pull out a knife and scream 'you white bitch!'"

Burk is not exactly a choirboy, Bernard knows. He spent twelve years behind bars for an extremely violent rape. A while ago, he gave Bernard a pile of porn magazines. With a razor blade, he had made deep cuts in all the faces and breasts.

"He's a sick-ass motherfucker," Bernard says, shaking his head.

Bernard and Bob have invited me for a farewell dinner, and I make my last tour through the tunnel. At the South End, I bump into Poncho and Getulio. Poncho, who is already a pretty upbeat character, is now even more radiant and cheerful. "We got that place, man!" he yells and hugs me. Even the melancholic and sad Getulio now has a faint smile on his face. With clean clothes, washed face, nice fur hat and an umbrella under his arm, he looks like a distinguished gentleman. Together they went to Brooklyn and found a spacious apartment. They will move in a few days. They're now on their way to arrange a van to move their belongings.

It is impossible to talk to Julio. He has been on his monthly booze binge, drinking vodka for two days straight and he screams insults at me. He wants to eat a hamburger with me up top; I tell him I don't go out with drunken people. "Asshole," he yells, while he is trying to put on a shoe. He bumps his head against the wall and falls back in bed. He has a wild and scary expression in his eyes and looks like he has aged ten years. He reminds me of the old, wrinkled alcoholic bums you find on every street corner of big Latin American cities. "In the summer we gonna watch the bands in Central Park," he shouts, slurring from under his blankets when I leave.

Bernard is busy cooking when I arrive. Bob is washing the dishes and setting up the camping table next to the tracks. He proudly shows me the groceries he's just bought: batteries, coffee, spaghetti sauce, candles and a pack of herbal tea for Bernard. "First we cover our asses," Bob explains. "Then we see if we have the extra money for a hit."

Bob and Bernard say they don't use crack anymore. They prefer to smoke base, a bit more expensive, but less diluted. It produces a longer-lasting high without the pathetic thirst for another hit. Most of the time, they get some after dinner and smoke it, each in their own place, before going to bed. "Tune, by now you know the whole tunnel," Bernard says while Bob is pouring him a cup of tea, "But tell me, nobody does it like us."

"Yeah," Bob says. "We stuck it out till the end." Tomorrow they'll go to Project Renewal. Dov is planning to move tunnel dwellers who haven't found an apartment yet into the Holland House, a newly renovated Hotel on 42nd Street with large rooms that even boast a small kitchenette. Bernard won't even mind that he'll still be among the tunnel dwellers. "As long as I don't have to sleep in the same bed as them," he says. This is the twentieth time Bernard says he is definitively moving out of the tunnel. It is also the twentieth time I believe him.

Bernard stirs in the pasta sauce and tells me about his plans. They are very vague. He hasn't heard back from the Hollywood people. But sooner or later they will get back in touch with him. Now he is in business with the shabby moviemaker. Bernard visited him at home, and he had opened the door wearing only boxer shorts. After Bernard requested him to get dressed properly, they watched his footage.

According to Bernard, it was good stuff. Not just the footage of himself, but also of other canning people, newspaper thieves, booksellers and all kinds of other hustlers from all over Manhattan. Bernard offered to help remix the footage at his brother's studio, the documentary maker from Atlanta.

After that, Bernard doesn't know. First he wants to do a computer course, Margaret has offered him the chance to do this at her university. Or maybe he will put his memoirs onto paper. Or maybe not. He doesn't know, but he is not worried. "I am at my best when everything is against me," he says. "Something will come up." One thing is sure: Bernard now feels it's time to close this period in his life as a tunnel dweller.

"In my time it was still feasible. But America ain't seen nothing yet," he says prophetically. "This will be the lifestyle of the future. There's gonna be murder for the garbage…"

When Bernard has drained the pasta onto the rails, he serves dinner. Cannelloni with tomato sauce and grilled hot dogs is on the menu. In another pan, he has toasted pieces of French bread and covered them with creamy butter. Bob pulls out a grater and a chunk of Gruyère cheese. The three of us pray quietly before dinner. In the distance a train is approaching. The conductor hoots in friendship. We wave back.

Epilogue

September 2009

40. THIRTEEN YEARS LATER

Luxurious apartment buildings with tacky names such as Trump Place and Heritage Tower look down on the South End. A new bike path lines the park and the Hudson, leading all the way down to Lower Manhattan. The tunnel entrance has been hermetically sealed off. On a grass field where tunnel people once parked their shopping carts, young urban professionals now flirt with each other at the dog run.

Ment still knows how to get into the tunnel. A few blocks up, hidden under the brush, is a rabbit hole that gives direct access. Marc, Bernard, Ment, and I go down and enter the darkness. We slide down a steep slope of sand and debris and come down at the place where Greg once pitched his tent, not far from Julio's former house. Light falls through the grate and soon our eyes get used to the dimness.

The tunnel is eerily empty and smells mushy. Old tracks have been removed and a strong fence has been erected along the tracks that remain. All livable constructions have been demolished and most garbage and filth has been dragged away. To judge by the fresh graffiti, the tunnel is still the stomping ground for taggers in the hood.

Bernard looks around in amazement. "Wow, I wouldn't have missed this. Thanks for inviting me to come along."

Marc muses about time going by, "Like stepping back in a time capsule." Neither have been back in the tunnel for thirteen years. Ment still goes down on a regular basis and shows us his latest tag, a few meters wide.

The tunnel is supposed to be deserted, but within a few minutes we have our first encounter with some of the remaining inhabitants. A bare-chested, dark skinned man slowly appears from a dark cavern in the wall. He looks like a ghost and I hold my breath. Bernard recognizes him. "Hey, Burk, it's me," Bernard tries to put him at ease. Vaguely, Burk stammers a few words and returns into the dark like a lost soul. According to Bernard, Burk was hospitalized for a few months in a mental institution, but as soon as he got out, he went back into the tunnel. "Coo coo for cocoa puffs," Ment says and proceeds to explain the expression to me.

The other remaining tunnel habitant[74] we meet is JR, who now lives in an alcove that can only be reached with a ladder. JR used to live in the loading dock on the Hudson, where Ment and I once climbed. We call his name a few times, and after a while a bald head appears around the corner. Ment manages to persuade the man to climb down. JR is an old man, with a bloody crust on his head and a nasty tumor swelling in his neck. "The Amtrak police leaves us alone," he explains and allows me to climb up and peak into his bedroom. It is stuffed with an incredible collection of junk from the street, too much for the eye to even register. It reminds me of a wild conceptual installation made by some freak artist I once saw in a hip museum. "I like the quietness here," JR says, and he climbs back in his den.

Deeper in the tunnel, we stumble upon the place where the bunkers of Joe, Kathy, and Ozzy once stood. They are now torn down. Piles of reinforced concrete are all that is left. Marc, Ment and I look at the heaps of debris. Bernard wanders off and disappears around the large, slow bend in the tunnel. Probably to check out his former camp.

41. TRACKING DOWN THE TUNNEL PEOPLE 1:
BOB, MENT, BERNARD, FRANKIE, JOE
AND KATHY, JULIO, TONY, MARCUS

Bob is the easiest to track down. Project Renewal managed to place him in the Holland House, a run-down hotel on 42nd Street, now turned into a shiny SRO hotel for low income and homeless people. After leaving the tunnel, I stayed in touch with Bob for the first few years and took him out for lunch whenever I was in New York. But over the last decade, I neglected my social duties. It is therefore with a little apprehension that I dial his number in the Holland house that I still have written down in my old notebooks. I am afraid Bob has passed away; he must be approaching seventy now and has not exactly led a healthy life. A man with a tired voice picks up the phone. It is Bob. He still remembers me. We set up a lunch meeting a week later.

Bob has become an old man. He'd always had grayish hair and a wrinkled face, but now his movements and speech also have become slow and sluggish. A pair of enormous, horn rimmed glasses are new. Thanks to miracles and medical science, he is still alive. Doctors have performed two quadruple bypass operations. "God must be smiling on me," Bob says. "I have the best cardiac surgeon and vascular doctor in town."

Since Bob left the tunnel, he has been in the Holland House. He says he is off drugs and has cut down on smoking. In the Holland House, he even had a small job, organizing the monthly tag sale. I invite Bob out for lunch, and he takes me to a corner deli and orders fried egg sandwiches. We sit down at some park benches surrounded by the mid-town lunch crowd while homeless people scavenge around us. Bob's life is not that exciting any more. He had to give up his job at the thrift store because he cannot lift weights of more than five pounds. Some days he spends the whole day just watching TV in his room. "After the operation, I got depressed," Bob tells me. "Had trouble breathing and panic attacks. At that point, I thought, just dig a hole and throw me in it. The breathing problems were temporary, the doctors told me. Now I am okay."

Bob has never seen his family again. His brothers and parents must be dead now. "No family, no kids. When I am dead, it's finished," Bob shrugs. Occasionally Bernard stops by. Margaret shows up at least every few months and always takes him out for lunch around Christmas. "I don't have many friends," Bob admits. "But I like it that way."

Ment sends me a text message: "Sorry, ten minutes late." He shows up at the corner of 7th Avenue and 50th Street a few moments later, a few blocks from the small basement room he rents. He is now forty years old, with a rugged, red face from outdoor work. For years, Ment worked on construction sites in

Manhattan and the fishing boats off the coast of Alaska. They were hard but good paying jobs.

Getting a hold of Ment was easy. Marc has been in touch with him all these years and gave me phone numbers and emails for both Ment and Frankie. Frankie now lives in North Carolina and is married to a girl—according to Marc an "awful woman." According to Ment a "psycho bitch."

"We are no longer friends," Ment says. "I went down to Carolina and spent thousands renovating his house. He treated me like shit. We had a fallout. I told him 'bye bye and gimme a call when you divorce the bitch.' Yeah," Ment sneers, "I think he will stay with her. Sometimes it's cheaper to keep'r."

Ment has two kids with Fatima; she lives in Yonkers with Jazzy who is now fourteen. They are divorced, but he still sees his kids regularly and pays whatever he can for child support. At the moment, Ment is romantically involved with a twenty-seven-year-old student. The girl is married, but trying to divorce her husband. A very messy situation. In two weeks, Ment's going off again to Alaska on a two-month fishing trip. Other that that, he says he is still involved in shady business. He doesn't want to talk too much about it, and it is hard to figure out how much is bravado, how much is truth.

Kathy opens the door. Ment and I have been knocking on it for several minutes. We're standing in front of her railroad apartment in East Harlem, in a predominantly Hispanic neighborhood. Kathy is taken by surprise when she sees me and we set up a lunch meeting for later in the week. I am relieved when she opens the door a few days later; I still remember the dozens of times I knocked in vain on their bunker door in the tunnel.

Kathy has gained considerable weight and her skins looks unhealthy. She still smokes; her teeth are grayish and she has a nasty cough. Joe can't join us because he's lying sick in bed. "He is sixty-five now, but he still looks pretty young for his age," Kathy assures me. In a Dominican restaurant around the corner, we have a nice chat over chicken with rice and beans. Kathy is very friendly, inquires about my family and has to laugh every time I give her some details on the more dramatic and stupid episodes in my life.

Her life has become nice and quiet, she says. They are happy they left the tunnel behind. But sometimes she misses her old, uncomplicated life. Currently she is fighting the landlord to have her bathroom fixed. All the hassle makes her sometimes long for the simplicity of the tunnel. Kathy is pretty well updated about the former tunnel people. Her sister has children and they live on the Upper West Side and Kathy works taking care of her kids. That not only keeps her busy all day, but on the streets near Riverside she hears all the latest news. She knows that Greg is holding down a job and doing fine. She does not know Ozzy's whereabouts. The sad news is that Tony recently died of a heart attack. He'd moved into an apartment, but "he started to hang out with the wrong people," she says. "Doing drugs and all sort of other bad things."

Kathy is proud of their drug free existence. "We were the only ones in the tunnel that didn't drink or do drugs," she smiles. "Even now. We still pay our bills on time, we don't bother anybody." In their building a lot of people are doing drugs, she says. "They get into trouble, then they go into rehab and the government pays everything for them."

Kathy and Joe are still in regular contact with Ment. In fact, when they were kicked out of their first apartment, Ment, Fatima and the kids moved in with Kathy and Joe. They stayed for three months. "It was a zoo. They never paid one cent to the household." Kathy complains. The cable bill was running sky high. "I am disappointed," mourns Kathy. "Whenever Ment needs us, he shows up. When he has money, suddenly you don't see him any more." Still, she has a weak spot for him. "He is always running into problems. I don't like what's going on now with that twenty-seven-year-old girl. Tell him to stay away from her. It smells like trouble…"

At the exit of the Broadway 96th Street subway exit, I am waiting for Bernard. Suddenly, my arm is gripped by a big, strong guy who booms in a heavy voice: "Could you please come with us for a few moments!" For a flash I think I am being kidnapped, then I realize I am not in a war zone and I look into Bernard's laughing face. Still the same old joker. He no longer has his Rasta hair, but he still has his big smile and shining eyes. It was easy to reach him; Bob gave me the number of Bernard's cell phone—a heavy old school Nokia—and within a few days we meet up for lunch. We walk down Broadway, and in no time, just like in the good old days, we wind up discussing women and the trouble they cause. Bernard laughs. "The most powerful men were brought down by women. Empires and kingdoms crumbled because of pussy." At a nice place with white tablecloths, we sit down and have lunch and a Stella Artois. "Next time bring some Chimay from Belgium," requests Bernard, sipping his Stella.

Bernard updates me on his life. He has become a family man, moved in with his father in Harlem to take care of him now that the latter is legally blind. On the weekends, he goes down to Baltimore to see one of his sons, who now has a daughter. In fact, Bernard has become a grandfather twice over. For the future, he foresees that he also will have to take care of his ailing mother in Florida. His family is obviously glad that he finally left the tunnel. "I knew I could leave any moment," Bernard boasts. "It was a good period of my life. But I still miss the solitude. Now I am confronted with so much bullshit up top." Once he got back into the system, an old student loan emerged. "Once you pop up on the screen, they got you." Now he works at the Parks Department maintaining Central Park. He works the 'grave yard shift' as he calls it, from 10 PM until 6 AM in the morning. "At least I don't have to put up with all the chatter of these dingbats," he says of his female colleagues. "At night I am alone with the raccoons and the squirrels."

Bernard stopped doing drugs. "Once in a while a beer and a little reefer, that's it. People always made such a big deal about us doing drugs down there. But hey man, for us, it was just a way of socializing. The guys on Wall Street snorting coke, they are the ones that really get high. What we got was just some aggravation."

For a while, Bernard worked in a soup kitchen on the Upper West Side where he heard all the news about the former tunnel people. He knows that Julio is dead. He started to drink really heavily, at one point he was even drinking rubbing alcohol. "A few months ago they found him here, unconscious on a traffic island in the middle of Broadway," Bernard explains. "They brought him to the hospital where he was declared dead. His liver was gone."

Contrary to what Kathy says, Tony is still alive and kicking. We meet him on the corner of 73rd Street and Broadway, where he is selling books on a cold winter morning. Tony still looks good for his old age—he should be over sixty-five by now. He is living in a small room in East New York, a seedy area far out in Brooklyn. It is a long train ride to Manhattan, but Tony is not complaining— the rent is only three hundred dollars a month.

However, José, the old Porto Rican, died. "As soon as they put him in an apartment, he put on weight. He had nothing to do. At the end he was 230 pounds," according to Bernard. Margaret, who still visited José once in a while, managed to organize a decent funeral.

Marcus has also passed away. Some of the hippies that always hang out at the Strawberry Fields Memorial in the Park told Bernard. "Marcus had an infection in his leg but he did not get treatment," Bernard says knowingly. "It got ugly and eventually developed into gangrene."

Regarding Bob, Bernard is frankly surprised that he is still alive. "Bob told me once 'When I die, throw a pack of Pall Malls, no filter, in my casket. And don't forget the lighter.' After two open-heart operations, that idiot is still smoking. He told me he did not want to live beyond sixty-five," Bernard laughs. "He is now sixty-seven years. God won't let him cheat. Bob won't go easy."

42. TRACKING DOWN THE TUNNEL PEOPLE 2: PONCHO, GETULIO, HUGO, LEE, DEE, HENRY, RALPH, GREG, TITO, ESTOBAN, JOSÉ

Poncho wound up getting a nice place in the Bronx. The last time I saw him was two years after he had left the tunnels. At that time, he was smiling and happy as usual and had found a good paying job in construction work. He told me that Getulio was also picking up the pieces and doing fine.

It is unknown what happened to Estoban and Hugo. Hugo most probably is roaming the streets. Marc saw him once. He looked awful and was still heavily using crack. Marc stayed in touch with most of the people in the South End that were featured in *Dark Days*. I hardly covered "his" people in the South End, although I knew them by name.

Lee killed himself. "He sat down on the tracks in a Buddah pose," Marc explains. "I pulled him off. He told me he just wanted to die. The next day he did it again. And he succeeded."

Dee, a tough-talking black woman who lived in a remote shack near little Havana, wound up in jail for selling drugs. Henry, her neighbor, migrated to Utah and was reportedly united with his family. Ralph—the white man with a drooping moustache who became Marc's *de facto* production assistant— turned into a success story. So did Greg, the man who lived in the tent. Ralph is currently working as a hotel manager in upstate New York. He also owns a cleaning company. Greg became a superintendent in the Bronx, and did such a good job that he ended up taking care of five buildings: a super super, you could say. Tito, a Hispanic man I once briefly met, currently works for a rehab center and tours the country showing Marc's documentary and lecturing high school kids about the dangers of drugs, as illustrated by his life as a former crack-addicted, homeless person.

Estoban was last seen by Bernard in 2008, as unwashed and dirty as ever. He must have been close to seventy years old. He has probably died by now.

"It was sad," Margaret tells me over coffee in Union Square Park. Margaret's book *The Tunnel* was very successful, and somehow she became Godmother to all the tunnel people. "Estoban was the most difficult case because he had lost all his identity papers. Dov put an incredible amount of time into him, but the red tape drove Estoban mad," Margaret recounts. "They went together to all these places, to the social security office, to the immigration office, to the welfare office. Every time there was something wrong. Once they said his photo did not look like him, another time he needed yet another piece of paper. It got to the point that Estoban lost all hope." At the end, Dov and Estoban thought they had everything together and they went together to the immigration bureau. There they heard the application was still not complete. "Something snapped in Estoban," Margaret tells. "He tore up all his paperwork in front of the officer and stormed out. Of course, Dov could not start the procedure again."

José was found dead in his apartment in the Bronx. "It was all the way up in Grand Concourse," Margaret explains. "He hardly knew anybody there. All he had left was eating." José had no known relatives so nobody could officially identify his body—he had lost touch with his children from a marriage twenty years earlier. José had nearly met the same fate as all the other unidentified dead—an unceremonious burial in an unmarked grave in Potter's Field. City detective Floyd Coore put extra energy in the case. He found Margaret's phone number in José's notebook and alerted her. With financial support from the Coalition, Margaret tried to organize a decent funeral for José. After the *New York Times* devoted an article to the quest for a final resting place for the former tunnel dweller, readers donated generously to the Coalition.[75] A funeral parlor in Queens offered its services free of charge and a pastor donated a plot at the exclusive Kensico cemetery. Now José rests in Valhalla, NY, on a quiet hillside among illustrious names such as Tommy Dorsey, Sergei Rachmaninoff, and Ayn Rand.

43. AN ACCEPTABLE RATE

According to Stephanie Cowles at Project Renewal, "the mortality rate is actually pretty astonishing. We have calculated that out of thirty tunnel people, four, perhaps even more, died within twelve years of moving out. That is a death rate close to 15 percent, however, not uncommon in the homeless population. These people have every illness imaginable. For years, they have gone without a doctor; they have not seen a dentist."

Cowles had coordinated the tunnel project and supervised Dov Waisman. "Poor Dov," Cowles looks back with a smile. "He was fresh out of college, law and philosophy at Harvard, and then they gave him this impossible job. But he gave all he had."

Cowles is reasonably positive about the results of the housing program. "We are realistic and have learnt from experience. It's considered an acceptable rate when 20 percent of former homeless who receive housing are back on the streets within a year." An organization such as Pathways has comparable statistics. Cowles points out that there is a difference in success rate between homeless people from the streets versus the shelters. The street homeless fare much better. "They have more adaptive skills than the shelter homeless who seem to have developed a more dependent attitude." In outreach lingo, these skills are called "ADLs": Activities of Daily Living, such as getting food, setting up some form of housing, cooking a meal. Of course, most tunnel people had created a relatively sophisticated environment when compared with street or shelter people.

"We are happy we could clear the people out of a dangerous situation," Cowles concludes about the tunnel. "But we are disappointed we could not give them more assistance once they were in housing. Some of them needed a complete support team: a case manager, a doctor, a nurse, an occupational therapist."

Public relations man Richard Rubel is quite lyrical when I call him at the Amtrak offices where he still works. He is very happy about the way the whole process worked out, from providing housing to the tunnel dwellers, to the final cleaning up and closing off operation. "In fact, it was a beautiful ending. But I have to say: without the personal contacts of Marc and Margaret, we could not have succeeded."

Dov moved back to Los Angeles where he is originally from, and is now a law school Professor. "It frankly does not surprise me that some died, but it is really heartening to hear that most of them are still in their housing and doing fine," Dov tells me over the phone. "The biggest challenge was getting them to decide if they wanted to live in an apartment or if they wanted to continue staying in the streets." Dov explains they had found a place for Dee, the tough-talking black woman, on Staten Island. "'I am not gonna take it,' was her first reaction. Three days later, I got a call from her. She was ready to accept it. Other people were skeptical about the process. Some, like Bernard, were very attached to the independence they had in the tunnels. For him, the tunnel had become part of his identity."

That the tunnel people were not exactly model citizens was another big hurdle. "What do you do with people that have serious afflictions that got them on the streets in the first place?" Dov asks rhetorically. "We had to do a follow up. But what can you do if they don't show up at the detox program, if they start doing drugs again? You can't take the key from their apartments away."

Dov confirms Margaret's story about Estoban. "Getting all his legal papers was a nightmare. Waiting at the INS, at that time the Immigration and Naturalization Services, and being told off again, he ripped up the only identity paper he had. That was the end of the story." Dov is sad to hear Hugo did not make it. "His English was perfect and he helped me a lot translating for the other Hispanics. I can remember visiting him for the first time in his new apartment in East Harlem, and he saying in his mellow, laid back way 'Hey man, thanks man....'"

44. 'TIS WHAT IT IS

Marc, Ment and I sit down on a few cinder blocks at Bernard's destroyed camp. Back then, we would have lit a cigarette, but all of us have stopped smoking. *The Third of May* is still intact but slowly decaying, as are most of the other pieces done by Chris Pape. Next to Pape's piece with Bob's and Bernard's portraits, he has spray painted the following words: "In December 1995 The Forgotten Men of the Tunnel Received City Housing. They've Just Begun to Move. Freedom 1995." The phone rings. It is Bernard. He tells me he left the tunnel at an open gate a few block up at Marcus' old cave. Bernard had to go home to make breakfast for his father. We were worried that he had left us because he was overwhelmed by emotion. I ask Bernard if it was not too hard for him to see his camp torn down. Bernard laughs. "Don't worry, it was not a shock for me. I was down there when they demolished it. Hey, man, what can I say? 'Tis what it is. That's all I can say."

APPENDIX: A LETTER FROM JOE

AMTRACK POLICE
PENN STATION
NEW YORK, NEW YORK

AMTRACK, POLICE
        MY NAME IS JOE. I HAVE
BEEN LiViNG IN THIS TuNNEL SiNCE
FEB 1973. I AM AT 80ST + 81ST
BEHiND THE WALL OF COLumNS.
I MAKE MY LiViNG By dOiNG BOOKS
+ MAGS + COLLECTiNG CANS. I dONT
PANHANDLE, I dONT COLLECT ANY
CHECKS OR RECiEVE WELFARE.
 WHAT I MAKE FEEDS My GiRL +
ME + MY dOG + CATS. BACK iN 1990
AMTRACK (BOSSES) CAME DOWN
HERE AND SAID EVERYBODY THAT
IS BEHiND THE WALL dOES NOT
HAVE TO BE KiCKED OUT OF HERE.
SO I AM NOT LEAViNG MY HOME
IF YOU KiCK ME OUT OF HERE YOU
WiLL BE GOiNG AGAiNST YOUR WORD
+ YOU WiLL BE CAUSiNG ANOTHER
HOMELESS PERSONS TO THE STREETS.
I AM NOT HOMELESS OVER 22 YEARS iN
THIS TUNNEL.

(PAGE) OVER

281

IF By CHANCE I AM OUT WORKING
+ SOMETHING HAPPENS TO my HOME
SUCH AS

     BREAKING INTO my HOME
OR A SUDDEN FIRE SHOULD
    DESTROY my Home + Possessions
OR my Dog + CATs INSIDE + OUTSIDE
ARE missing OR DESTROYED
I wiLL HOLD you RESPONSIBLE
I wiLL TAKE WHOEVER TO COURT
I wiLL SUE — I wiLL wiN !!
I HAVE NO OTHER PLACE
To go To, THis is my HOME

       THANK You
       M - JoE
P.S

  20 PRECIENT goT THE SAME
LETTER SO HAS:
AMTRACK HEADQUARTER PHILa
COALTION FOR HomeLESS
PROJECT REACHOUT
DEPT OF HighWays + TuNNELS

ENDNOTES

1 Detective Thomas Frye from the 24th precinct on the Upper West Side arrested Shorty and Hector. Bob and Bernard were witnesses at the court session and were compensated—as usual—for lunch and travel costs. Detective Frye told me that Hector was released on bail, paid for by the Coalition for the Homeless. Hector wanted to flee, but was arrested again at the Port Authority Bus Station where he was trying to board a Greyhound bus to Texas. It appeared that he was also wanted for murder and rape in San Francisco. Bernard told me that it was Shorty who was released on bail. According to him, Shorty was the illegitimate child of a senior executive at the Coalition. Mike Harris from the Coalition for the Homeless told me the bail story was nonsense. Shorty was sentenced to five years; Hector got a sentence of ten to twenty years.

2 See Chapter 31: Advanced Canning III: WeCan

3 Michael Kauffman, "A Middleman's Ventures in the Can Trade," *New York Times*, September 23, 1992.

4 Center for Constitutional Rights, "*StreetWatch v. National Railroad Passenger Corp,*" http://www.ccrjustice.org/ourcases/past-cases/streetwatch-v.-national-railroad-passenger-corp.-%28amtrak%29. The case *StreetWatch vs. Amtrak* (officially called *StreetWatch v. National Railroad Passenger Corp*) was filed in 1994. StreetWatch was a project of the Coalition that focused on the physical abuse of the homeless by authorities, be it police of private security guards. The lawsuit was brought against the Amtrak police alleging that they were ejecting people they considered to be "undesirable" from Penn Station, and in some cases, harassing, arresting, and brutalizing them. Amtrak lost the case, and ordered by an injunction to stop expelling individuals from the station based purely on their appearance. Amtrak also had to pay certain homeless defendants between five thousand and seven thousand dollars each. The *New York Times* also pub-

lished an article on the case: "Amtrak is Ordered Not to Eject The Homeless from Penn Station," by Richard Perez, February 22, 1995.

5 Employment, work and jobs are relative concepts. One could argue that all the hustles in the informal economy also constitute a form of (self) employment. While in the tunnel, no one I spoke to had a steady nine-to-five job, but nearly everyone worked in the informal book or can sectors. Some people received welfare, and collected cans on top of that. Others had irregular part-time jobs such as courier, messenger, delivery boy, sandwich man, or flier distributor.

A table on page 18 of *Over the Edge: The Growth of Homeless in the 1980s*, by Martha R. Burt, mentions that 5 percent of homeless single males had a steady job. Burt defines a 'steady job' as working for at least three months for the same employer. The same table says that 39 percent of the subgroup *homeless males with children* had a job. She found that this subgroup, however, constituted only 1 percent of the total homeless population.

6 Statistics from Burt show a sudden growth in the number of homeless women and children between 1984 and 1988. By 1990, homeless woman and children made up 9 percent and 1 percent of the total homeless population respectively. It looks like the number of homeless families is steadily increasing. In a recent report from 2009, the Coalition for the Homeless says that 25 percent of the current shelter population now consists of families. In the most recent HUD survey, the Annual Homeless Assessment Report to Congress of 2008, the number of persons living in families of the total homeless population is said to be 37 percent.

7 The Coalition obtained this number from a study carried out by Rosenheck for the Department of Veterans Affairs Medical Center in Connecticut. "The Proportion of Veterans among Homeless Men" was published in the *American Journal of Public Health* in 1994.

This study found the percentage of veterans among homeless males to be 41 percent, not much higher than the percentage of veterans among the total male population at that time at 34 percent. Rosenheck explains the difference is caused by a relatively large group of white males aged between twenty and thirty-four. Veterans in this age group are five times more likely to be homeless than their peers who have not been in the army. In comparison with other veterans, this age group saw very little war and/or combat. This group also had a significantly lower social economic status, given that people from lower social economic strata more often choose a career in the army. Rosenheck argued that homelessness within this group was inherent to belonging to a vulnerable social stratum, instead of caused by their status as veterans.

A recent study by HUD, the 2008 Annual Homeless Assessment Report, says that 11.6 percent of the homeless population are veterans, slightly higher than the percentage of veterans in the general population, which is 10.5 percent. The report, however, warns that these numbers should be closely watched as there will be a great influx of veterans from the recent wars in Afghanistan and Iraq.

8   Burt, *Over the Edge*, 22; Metraux et al. (2007), 9-3. In the tunnel, more than half of the residents had a 'shady' past, had been convicted of a crime and served time. Some of these crimes included murder, rape, robbery, theft, and drug-related offenses. In a recent study of Metraux and Culhane, it was found that 23 percent of the New York shelter population had been incarcerated in the previous two years. One must realize, however, that jails are full of those who have been convicted for non-violent drug offenses, from the possession of small quantities of weed to selling large quantities of coke and crack. The draconic Rockefeller laws in New York State, where possession of 2 ounces of cannabis originally carried the same minimum fifteen-year sentence as second-degree murder, are responsible for the high incarceration rates. In 1994, out of the twenty-three thousand people in New York State sent to prison, 45 percent were convicted for

non-violent drug offenses. See the interesting article in the *New York Magazine*, "Drugs are Bad, the Drug War is Worse," February 5, 1996.

9 My own observation in the tunnels. One man, Henry, had joined the army, but was discharged even before graduating boot camp because of drug use. He does not call himself a veteran, although technically he could. Nurses and administrators who have been working in the army are also called veterans after they have left the service.

In the '90s, most people were tempted to think of veterans as the men who fought in Vietnam. Most of these "Viet vets," however, received good benefits and were rarely homeless. The principal exception in the tunnel was Joe, who refused all government support. Photographer Margaret Morton told me that some homeless people copied war stories from real veterans. "He stole my Vietnam story," she once heard a homeless man complain.

Rosenheck's 1994 study for the Department of Veterans Affairs Medical Center gives interesting numbers. Only 7 percent of those between the ages of twenty and thirty-four saw actual combat; 79 percent served after Vietnam. Of the veterans between ages forty-five and fifty-four (of an age to serve after the Korean war but before Vietnam) only 17 percent saw combat. Of the two age groups thirty-five to forty-four and fifty-five years and older, 40 percent saw combat in Vietnam, Korea or the Second World War. Rosenheck's study is based on numbers of 1987. When I published *Tunnel People* in 1996, veterans of the invasions of Panama and Grenada, the interventions in Haiti, Somalia, Bosnia, and the soldiers in the First Gulf War (that all took place in the early '90s) were not included. Current in-depth studies that include the post-9/11 Afghanistan and Iraq wars are not yet available.

10 My personal observations of a group of roughly ten to twelve homeless people, who could be found with great regularity holding paper cups at the given spots such as subway exits, restaurants, banks. Bernard knew all of them not only by name,

but also the full details of their crack use. Most of these individuals claimed they needed the money to buy food. On the Upper West Side however, nobody needed to go hungry. There are some twenty different places—churches, community centers, soup kitchens—that provide free meals and food packages.

11   Burt, *Over the Edge*,16.

12   Rossi, *Down and Out in America*, 117-141. In a recent study form the HUD, (AHAR 2008, 29) the percentage of blacks in the sheltered homeless population is given as 42 percent, not as big as Rossi's number, but still roughly four times as much as the portion of blacks in the general population. Being a vulnerable population edging on the lower social economic strata of society, blacks are also heavily overrepresented in the HIV-positive population and are the majority among the incarcerated.

13   Jencks, *The Homeless*, 46.

14   Toth, *The Mole People*, 5.

15   Jencks, *The Homeless*, 47. "It inspires incredulity amongst the worldly and it leads the credulous to underestimate how much help the long-term homeless really need."
Burt, *Over the Edge*, 81. "... this strategy [to arouse sympathy and support] may dwindle when middle-class Americans come face to face with the facts."

16   Goodman, *New York Times*, February 1992.

17   Dugger, *New York Times*, February 1992. The survey was commissioned by the specially appointed Mayoral Commission On Homelessness. Participation was on a voluntary basis. In earlier surveys, when people were asked directly if they used drugs, only 18 percent admitted they did so. The commission recommended, among other things, smaller shelters and additional rehabilitation programs.

18   Jencks, *The Homeless*, 47.

19   Skid Row originated from the word Skid Road — the road where seasonal workers and loggers skidded tree logs in the Pacific North West. In the winter, when snowfall hampered operations, most loggers were out of work and hung around the skid road, hoping to find a job. Now Skid Row has entered mainstream language and is used by street people as well as sociologists to indicate a rundown neighborhood frequented by vagrants and the homeless. In New York, it has traditionally been in the Bowery.

20   Robinson, whom I met with at Saint George's Church in Brooklyn, used to work at Pete's Place, a small church operating in downtown Manhattan. He became Bob's spiritual counselor when he left the tunnel, and stayed to stay in touch with him. See chapter 27: The Case of Bob. O'Flaherty mentions the American versus the British tradition of defining homelessness. In the U.S., he explains, homelessness has the notion of being uprooted, and implicates a detachment from social and family networks. In the English tradition, there is more emphasis on the legal right to occupy a residential space. In the last view, squatters are officially homeless.

21   Rossi, *Down and Out in America*, 10 and Jencks, *The Homeless*, 3.

22   Jencks, *The Homeless*, 4. Welfare hotels are, in fact, small shelters for families with children who cannot safely stay in shelters for single males. The rooms are paid for by the Welfare Department and, in New York, the Department of Homeless Services. Advocacy groups and most researchers consider the welfare hotel populations as homeless.

23   Cohen and Sokolovsky, *Old Men of the Bowery*, 61. In 1986, the governor of New York estimated that there were half a million "couch people" in his state.

24 Burt, *Over the Edge*, 139 and Jencks, *The Homeless*, 16.

25 Jencks, *The Homeless*, 12-16.

26 The 2008 Annual Homeless Assessment Report gives the following numbers for 2008: About 664,000 people were homeless—sheltered and unsheltered—on a single night in January 2008. About 1.6 million people were homeless in emergency shelters or transitional housing at some point during the year between October 1, 2007 and September 30, 2008. (HUD [2009], 30)

27 Barak, *Gimme Shelter*, ix. Snyder, and his organization the Community for Creative Non-Violence, were among the first who brought the problem of homelessness into the spotlight in a radical way. Tactics included sit-ins, pray-ins and prolonged hunger strikes on the steps of the Capitol. Disillusioned by the results of his movement and plagued by other problems, Snyder committed suicide in 1990.

28 Jencks, *The Homeless*, 2. Snyder admitted in a TV-interview, that if the HUD-number (one tenth of his estimate) was accepted, "it would take some of the power away... some of our potential impact... and some of the resources we might have access to, because we're not talking about something that's measured in the millions."

29 Rossi, *Down and Out in America*, 45-81; and Jencks, *The Homeless*, 1-20.

30 Burt, *Over the Edge*, 140.

31 Burt, *Over the Edge*, 140, Barret, *The 1990 Census Shelters and Street Enumeration*, 191 and *2007 Annual Homeless Assessment Report to Congress*, 4. The 2007 AHAR also mentions the results from censuses and surveys from the late '80s and early '90s. An entire chapter is devoted to methodology of counting and sampling. Sheltered and an estimate of the unsheltered homeless are included in the total counts.

32 About 7,000 homeless in shelters and 5,000 families (18,000 people) in welfare hotels. See the statistical report, historical data on the NYC DHS website.

33 The estimate of 40,000 to 120,000 is from Captain Bryan Henry of the Metro North Police. In their annual report of 1994, the Coalition mentions a number of 75,000. Keith Cylar from *Housing Works* gave a figure between 200,000 and 300,000.

34 Annual report, *Coalition for the Homeless* (1994), 12.

35 Cohen and Sokolovsky, *Old Men of the Bowery*, 38.

36 Ibid., 40. Also see the third chapter of *The Homeless in History*, in Beard, *On Being Homeless: Historical Perspectives*, which gives an excellent historical overview.

37 Matthew 25: 34, 35. "Come, you who are blessed by my Father; take your inheritance, the kingdom prepared for you since the creation of the world. For I was hungry and you gave me something to eat, I was thirsty and you gave me something to drink, I was a stranger and you invited me in." I Peter 4: 9 "Offer hospitality to one another without grumbling."

38 Cohen and Sokolovsky, *Old Men of the Bowery*, 41.

39 See Max Weber, *The Protestant Ethic and the Spirit of Capitalism* (1922).

40 The American Civil War, the sudden influx of migrants in the middle of the 19th century, the financial crash of Black September in 1873, devastating drought in the Midwest in the 1930s, and the Great Depression are examples of crises that led to high rates of homelessness. Cohen and Sokolovsky cover these events in depth. In the same way, the banking and foreclosure crisis of 2008 has resulted in a growing number of homeless people and the emergence of new Hoovervilles. The term

'hooverville' was coined during the reign of President Hoover in the Great Depression for shanty towns built by the homeless and unemployed.

41   Anderson, *The Hobo*, 198.

42   Anderson, *The Hobo*, 171-184. The IWW had at its heyday in 1923 more than one hundred thousand members. It encountered heavy government repression and some of its leaders were killed. Today, although shrunk to less than one thousand members, the organization is still active (for example, with organizing Starbucks baristas.) The IBWA no longer exists. Today, the acronym stands for International Bottled Water Association.

43   Cohen and Sokolovsky, *Old Men of the Bowery*, 55. More realistic estimates give a number between two and five million homeless people. The economic recovery in 1936 and the War reduced the homeless army to a few ten-thousands.

44   Quoted in Cohen and Sokolovsky, *Old Men of the Bowery*, 55.

45   Jencks wrote two articles in the *New York Review of Books* in March and April 1994 that served as excellent synopses of his books.

46   Rossi, *Down and Out in America*, 154.

47   Tranquilizers such as Librium and Valium, neuroleptica and anti-psychotics like Haldol, Leponex (Clorapine) and Largactil (Thorazine).

48   *Madness and Civilization* by French author and structuralist Michel Foucault laid the ground for this movement.

49   Jencks, *The Homeless*, 37.

50   Ibid., 52-55.

51   Hopper, *Economies of Makeshift*, 197.

52   Hacker, *Two Nations*, 94.

53   Jencks, *The Homeless*, 55

54   Williams, *Crackhouse*, 13. The Iran-Contra affair, in which allegedly cocaine was smuggled into the USA to finance the Nicaraguan Contra rebels, gave further fuel to conspiracy theories. In "Dark Alliance," an article series originally published in 1996 in the *San Jose Mercury News*, journalist Gary Webb even ascertained that the Reagan administration protected inner-city drug dealers from prosecution. In a national report, Webb's allegations were denied. Webb himself died of two gunshots to the head in 2004. It was ruled as a suicide. Major papers, such as the *Los Angeles Times* and the *Chicago Tribune* have defended Webb's articles.

55   Bernard told me the closest crack dealer was one block and a half from the tunnel. To "score a dime bag of weed" he had to walk at least fifteen blocks. For an interesting exposé on the crack culture and economy, see Levitt and Dubner, *Freakonomics*, Chapter 3: Why Do Drug Dealers Still Live with Their Moms?

56   Hacker, *Two Nations*, 46.

57   Nancy McKenzie, *The AIDS Reader*, 179.

58   Coalition for the Homeless, Annual Report (1994), 5.

59   See the chapters "Budget Cuts and Rent Control" and "Do Shelters Cause Homelessness?" in Jencks, *The Homeless*. The advocacy group WRAP takes a strong position on cutbacks on housing subsidies. In an article in the *Journal of Urban Economics*, Cragg and O'Flaherty point to an increase in the shelter popula-

tions in New York in the '80s because shelter people could jump the queue for the waiting list for cheap, subsidized apartments.

60 Coalition for the Homeless, Annual Report (1994), 2.

61 Jencks, *The Homeless*, 71.

62 In the summer of 1987, I stayed for a week as a low budget tourist in the Sunshine Hotel. The rooms were small, dirty and noisy, but at least one had privacy and an undisturbed night of sleep. See also Hopper *Reckoning with Homelessness*, especially the chapter "Streets, Shelters and Flops."

63 Rossi, *Down and Out in America*, 103. Most tunnel people to whom I spoke had the same opinion.

64 Another organization that was responsible for the clean up of Grand Central Station and its immediate surroundings was the Grand Central Partnership, a Business Improvement District. Their approach was controversial: The Partnership recruited homeless people from a local shelter and paid them 1 dollar an hour for repair and cleaning jobs. Some of them even forcefully removed fellow homeless people from the areas around ATMs. Grand Central Partnership called this 'an outreach and job training program;' the Coalition called it exploitation and started a lawsuit: *Archie et. al. versus The Grand Central Partnership*. Archie was one of the homeless who was abused. In the end, a federal court ruled that the Grand Central Partnership had violated minimum wage laws. See also James Traub's article "Street Fight," *New Yorker*, September 4, 1995.

65 MTA/Connections cooperates with Project Reachout, Project Renewal, Volunteers of America, Project H.E.L.P., Bowery Residents Committee and Lenox Hill.

66 DHS: Department of Homeless Services; BRC: Bowery Residents Committee; HUD: Department of Housing and Urban

Development; HHC: Health and Hospital Corporation; BID: Business Improvement District; HPD: Housing, Preservation and Development.

67 In 1990 and 1991 most of these encampments were destroyed. The authorities said it was because of drugs spilling over into the neighborhood; homeless advocacy groups pointed to the planned visit of South African President Nelson Mandela who was not supposed to see shanty towns in New York.

The forced evacuation of hundreds of homeless people camping in the East Village's Tompkins Square turned into a battle between police, squatters and left wing activists. Squatters saw the clean-up operation as the beginning of the gentrification of their neighborhood. See the *New York Times* article by Thomas Morgan, "A Shanty Town Grows in the Shadow of Skyscrapers," 1991.

68 In 1995, the DHS had a budget of half a billion dollars, and employed 2,500 people, DHS spokesperson Olga Escobar told me in an interview. On top of that, the dozen or so homeless advocacy groups each have a budget of a few million, and employ hundreds of people. (For example, in 1995 the Coalition had a budget of four million, Project Renewal ten million, MTA/Connections one million.)

Not included are the federal programs of the HUD (the Department of Housing and Urban Development) whose section eight voucher program costs nine million dollars, for example, and all subsidies and contributions of New York city bodies such as HPD (Housing, Preservation and Development), and the HRA (Human Resources Agency).

69 According to the Coalition, it costs the city thirty-six thousand dollars a year for each homeless family staying in a welfare hotel.

70 Jencks, *The Homeless*. See the chapter "Do Shelters Cause Homelessness?" He argues that for people on the edge of homelessness ("couch people" and families cramped together in over-

crowded apartments) the option of homelessness has become less of a deterrent since shelters and soup kitchens take the hard edge of homelessness. There are also cases of people who have moved into shelters and welfare hotels to get on the waiting list of the few, cheap apartments the city has available for emergency situations.

71 Most neighborhoods have their own *Street Sheet*. The one for the Lower East Side provides twenty-three addresses for shelters, soup kitchens, rehab clinics, AIDS groups, clothing distribution points, and centers that give free legal advice.

72 Recent research concludes that the effects of cocaine/crack on unborn babies are less harmful than originally feared. Brain abnormalities or developmental problems in infants and toddlers could not be attributed to cocaine use of the mother. Marijuana, alcohol, and nicotine do actually more damage. (Frank, 2001)

FAIR magazine points out that the "crack baby" theory might have racist origins: most crack-addicted mothers are inner city black woman. While the effects of nicotine and alcohol during pregnancy are proven, one never hears about "liquor kids" or "smoke babies." (Jackson, 1998)

73 "The Freedom Tunnel" is the street name given by people from the graffiti scene to the Amtrak Tunnel. It might be a reference to Chris Pape AKA "Freedom," who used the tunnel walls as his canvases; it might be a reference to the sense of freedom from conforming to society and freedom from paying rent, according to a Wikipedia entry.

74 In January 2010, Bernard worked as a tunnel guide for two journalists from *Le Figaro* magazine and toured them around for several days. They found more than seven people still living there, albeit under extremely squalid circumstances. I took another walk with Bernard through the tunnel and was pointed out several very well hidden dwellings. The saddest case was a

man laying on a mattress behind "Julio's wall" amongst piles of broken glass bottles. The last remaining people seem to be tolerated by the authorities.

75 Nina Bernstein, "Waiting for a Final Resting Place; Friends Seek Proper Burial for a Former Tunnel Dweller" and "In Death, Pauper Finds Generosity," *New York Times*, June 11 and 16, 1999.

WORKS CITED

Associated Press. "Homeless Advocates Protest Radio Show." *New York Times*, November 20, 1994.

Anderson, Nels. *The Hobo: The Sociology of the Homeless Man*. Chicago: University of Chicago Press, 1975 (originally published in 1923).

Barak, Gregg. *Gimme Shelter*. New York: Praeger Publishers, 1991.

Barret, Diane et al. *The 1990 Census Shelters and Street Enumeration*. United States Bureau of the Census, Washington, DC, 1991.

Barley, Nigel. *The Innocent Anthropologist. Notes from a Mud Hut*. London: Penguin Books, 1983.

Baudrillard, Jean. *America*. Translated by Chris Turner. New York: Verso, 1988.

Beard, Rick, ed. *On Being Homeless: Historical Perspectives*. New York: Museum of the City of New York, 1987.

Bernstein, Nina. "Waiting for a Final Resting Place; Friends Seek Proper Burial for a Former Tunnel Dweller." *New York Times*, June 11, 1999.

Bernstein, Nina. "In Death, a Pauper Finds Generosity." *New York Times*, June 16, 1999.

Bijbel, Willibrordvertaling. *Boxtel*. Netherlands: Katholieke Bijbelstichting, 1977.

Bragg, Rick. "Fleeing the World Underneath." *New York Times*, March 28, 1994.

Brown, David. "'Crack Baby' Theory Doubted; Study: Effect of Mother's Drug Use Less Severe Than Thought." *The Washington Post*, March 28, 2001.

Bovenkerk, Frank. *Binnenstebuiten en ondersteboven. De antropologie van de industriële samenleving*, edited by Lodewijk Brunt. Assen/Amsterdam: Van Gorcum, 1976.

Burt, Martha. *Over the Edge: The Growth of Homelessness in the 1980s*. New York: Russel Sage Foundation, 1992.

Coalition for the Homeless, *Homelessness in New York*. New York: Annual Report, 1994.

Coalition for the Homeless, *NYC Homeless Shelter Population Reaches All-Time High*. New York: Report, October 2009.

Coalition for the Homeless, *Homeless Families with Children*. New York: Report, July 2009.

Cohen, Carl and Jay Sokolovsky. *Old Men of the Bowery: Strategies for Survival Among the Homeless*. New York: The Guilford Press, 1989.

Cragg, Michael and Brendan O'Flaherty. "Do Shelter Conditions Determine Shelter Population? The Case of the Dinkins Deluge." *Journal of Urban Economics*, 46 (1999): 377-415.

Dehavenon, Anne Lou. *Out in the Cold: The Social Exclusion of New York City's Homeless Families in 1995*. New York: Action Research Project on Hunger, Homelessness and Family Health, 1995.

De Tunnel. Directed by Dree Andrea. International Documentary Festival, Amsterdam, 1994.

NYC Department of Homeless Service. "Historic Data. Charts and Graphs Trending Shelter Census Since 1980." http://www.nyc.gov/dhs.

Duggan, Dennis. "His Life Was Like a Box of Grenades." *New York Newsday*, March 30, 1995.

Dugger, Celia. "New York Report Finds Drug Abuse Rife in Shelters." *New York Times*, February 16, 1992.

Dugger, Celia. "Threat Only When on Crack, Homeless Man Foils System." *New York Times*, September 3, 1992.

Ellison, Ralph. *The Invisible Man*. New York: Vintage Books International, 1990 (originally published 1950).

Frank, Deborah. "Growth, Development, and Behavior in Early Childhood Following Prenatal Cocaine Exposure." *Journal of the American Medical Association* 285 no. 12 (March 28, 2001).

Goodman, Walter. "TV Journalists Urge to Prettify the News." *New York Times*, February 19, 1992.

Graft, H. F. *The Adventure of the American People. A History of the United States*. New York: Rand McNally & Co, 1960.

Guez, Sabine, "L'envers d'une ville: New York underground." *Les Inrockuptibles*, Paris, March 1995.

Guez, Sabine. 'Les hommes taupes.' TV-documentary. TV2. Paris: March 1995.

Hacker, Andrew. *Two Nations. Black and White, Separate, Hostile, Unequal.* New York: Ballantine Books, 1993.

Henneberger, M. "U.S. to Offer Housing Vouchers to Lure Homeless from the Subways." *New York Times,* November 18, 1994.

Holdt, Jacob. *American Pictures.* Copenhagen: American Pictures Foundation, 1985.

Hopper, Kim, e.a. "Economies of Makeshift: Deindustrialization and Homelessness in New York City." *Urban Anthropology* 14, nos. 1-3 (1985).

Hopper, Kim and Ellen Baxter. *Private Lives/Public Spaces. Homeless Adults on the Streets of New York City.* New York: Community Service Society/Institute for Social Welfare Research, 1981.

Hopper, Kim, Reckoning with Homelessness, Ithaca & London: Cornell University Press 2003.

HUD. *The 2007 Annual Homeless Assessment Report to Congress (AHAR 2007).* Washington DC, 2008.

HUD. *The 2008 Annual Homeless Assessment Report to Congress (AHAR 2008).* Washington DC, 2009.

Horowitz, Craig. "Drugs Are Bad, The Drug War Is Worse: The No-Win War." *New York Magazine,* February 5, 1996.

Jackson, Janine. "The Myth of the 'Crack Baby.' Despite Research, Media Won't Give Up Idea Of 'Bio-Underclass'." *FAIR,* September/October 1998.

Jencks, Christopher. *The Homeless.* Cambridge, MA: Harvard University Press, 1994.

Jencks, Christopher. *Rethinking Social Policy. Race, Poverty and the Underclass.* Cambridge, MA: Harvard University Press, 1992.

Jencks, Christopher. "The Homeless, Housing the Homeless." *New York Review of Books,* March 12 and April 21, 1994.

Kleinfeld, N.R. "Police Reach Out to the Homeless, But Often Find Efforts Rejected." *New York Times,* November 16, 1994.

Liebow, Elliot. *Tell Them Who I Am. The Lives of Homeless Women.* New York: The Free Press, 1993.

Levitt, Steven D., and Stephen J. Dubner. *Freakonomics: A Rogue Economist Explores the Hidden Side of Everything.* New York: Morrow-Harper, 2005.

Kaufman, Michael. "A Middleman's Venture in the Can Trade." *New York Times,* September 23, 1992.

Kaufman, Michael. "Walking the Beat in the Subway's Nether World." *New York Times,* November 14, 1992.

Krauss, Clifford. "Special Unit Ushers Homeless from Subways." *New York Times,* September 4, 1994.

Main, Thomas. "Hard Lessons on Homelessness." *City Journal,* Summer 1993.

Main, Thomas. *Achieving Quantum Change in Urban Bureaucracy: The Case of New York City's Department of Homeless Services.* Expected publication 2010.

McCann, Collum. "'People Say We Eat Rats, but Food is the Least Damn Problem in New York. It's Peace of Mind That's Elusive.' Bernard Isaacs, Manhattan Tunnel Dweller." *Observer Magazine,* July 1995.

McKenzie, Nancy, ed. *The AIDS Reader. Social, Political and Ethical Issues.* New York: Meridian, 1991.

McNamara, Alix and Anthony Richards. "The Rail World." *Manhattan Spirit,* New York, July 27, 1995.

Metraux, Stephen and Dennis Culhane. "Recent Incarceration History Among a Sheltered Homeless Population." *Crime and Delinquency* 52, no. 3 (July 2006).

Metraux, Stephen, Roman Caterina, and Richard Cho. "Incarceration and Homelessness." *Toward Understanding Homelessness: The 2007 National Symposium on Homelessness Research.* Edited by Deborah Dennis, Gretchen Locke and Jill Khadduri. Washington DC: U.S. Department of Housing & Urban Development, 2008.

Morgan, Thomas. "A Shantytown Society Grows in the Shadow of Skyscrapers." *New York Times,* October 20, 1991.

Morton, Margaret. "Homes for the Invisible." *New York Times,* October 7, 1995.

Morton, Margaret. *The Tunnel: The Architecture of Despair.* New Haven, London: Yale University Press, 1995.

O'Flaherty, Brendan. *Making Room: The Economics of Homelessness*. Cambridge, MA: Harvard University Press, 1996.

O'Flaherty, Brendan. *City Economics*. Cambridge, MA: Harvard University Press, 2005.

Orwell, George. *Down and Out in Paris and London*. London: Penguin Books, 1989 (originally published in 1933).

Perez-Pena, Richard. "Amtrak Is Ordered Not to Eject the Homeless from Penn Station." *New York Times*, February 22, 1995.

Reinarman, Craig and Harry Levine. "Crack in the Rearview Mirror: Deconstructing Drug War Mythology." *Social Justice* 31, nos. 1-2 (2004).

Richards, Eugene. *Cocaine True, Cocaine Blues*. New York: Aperture Foundation, 1994.

Rimer, Sara. "Can Picker: $35 a Shift, No Benefits, No Bosses." *New York Times*, September 6, 1989.

Riis, Jacob. *How the Other Half Lives*. New York: Dover Publications, 1971 (originally published in 1890).

Rosenheck, Robert, et al. "The Proportion of Veterans among Homeless Men." *American Journal of Public Health* 84 (1994): 466-499.

Rossi, Peter. *Down and Out in America. The Origins of Homelessness*. Chicago: University of Chicago Press, 1989.

Spradley, James. *You Owe Yourself a Drink: An Ethnography of Urban Nomads*. Boston: Little Brown and Company, 1970.

Tierny, John. "In Tunnel, 'Mole People' Fight to Save Home." *New York Times*, June 13, 1990.

Tierny, John. "After Sixteen Years, Squatter Leaves Tunnel." *New York Times*, March 13, 1991.

Tierny, John. "Mole Returns to His Hole Without a Movie Deal but With Love." *New York Times*, November 30, 1991.

Toth, Jennifer. *The Mole People. Life in the Tunnels Beneath New York City*. Chicago: Chicago Review Press, 1993.

Toro, Paul. "Toward an International Understanding of Homelessness." *Journal of Social Issues* 63, no. 3 (2007).

Traub, James. "Street Fight." *The New Yorker*, September 4, 1995.

Tsemberis, Sam, Leyla Gulcur, and Maria Nakae. "Housing First: Consumer Choice and Harm Reduction for Homeless Individuals With a Dual Diagnosis." *American Journal of Public Health* 94, no. 4 (April 2004).

Voeten, Teun. "Newyorkse stadsnomaden. Ethnograaf Terry Williams: 'De onzichtbaren een menselijk gezicht geven.'" *Markant*, July 2, 1993.

Williams, Terry. *The Cocaine Kids: The Inside Story of a Teenage Drug Ring*. New York: Addison-Wesley, 1989.

Williams, Terry. *Crackhouse. Notes from the End of the Line*. New York: Addison-Wesley, 1992.

Williams, Terry. "Voices from the Tunnel." *Grand Street*, December 1994.

Williams, Terry. *Voices from the Underground*. Unpublished manuscript.

Western Regional Advocacy Project (WRAP). *Without Housing: Decades of Federal Housing Cutbacks, Massive Homelessness, and Policy Failures*. San Francisco: 2006.

ACKNOWLEDGEMENTS

This book would not have been possible without the cooperation and incredible kindness of many people. Of course, I am mostly indebted and extremely grateful to the tunnel people who allowed me inside their lives: Bernard, Bob, Tony, Frankie, Ment, Fatima, Maria, Joe, Kathy, Hugo, Poncho, Estoban, Getulio, and Ozzy. Marcus, Lee, Julio, and José: rest in peace and may you find up in Heaven the tranquility and peace you tried so hard to find down in the tunnels...

Captain Bryan Henry from Metro North Police; Guy Polhemus from WeCan; Perry Chester Taylor from MTA; Mike Harris from the Coalition for the Homeless; Eric Roth from Bowery Residents Committee; Victoria Mason-Ailey and Sharry Siegel from MTA/Connections; Doris Combs and Richard Rubel from Amtrak; Dov Waisman, Stephanie Cowles and Ivy Raff from Project Renewal; Keith Cylar from Housing Works; Helen Greer and Shari Blackmon from Project HELP; Rev. William Robinson from Pete's Place; Thomas Main from Baruch University, thanks for all your help and sharing your expertise with me.

My fellow tunnel scholars Terry Williams, Marc Singer, Margaret Morton, Jennifer Toth, Sabine Guez and Chris Pape, thanks for all the inspiration and encouragement. Andrew Lichtenstein, Matthew Septimus, Robert Pledge, Louis Zaal, Marc de Haan, Jane Welna, Marcia Dover, thanks so much for your photographic advice. Richard, Christine, Arnold and Maryze, Nasser, Sebastian and Daniela, Pierre and Abi, Maria, Nancy, Jackie and Meredith, Keith and Katrin, all the folks at the Carlton Arms Hotel, thanks for making my New York life a bit easier...

Gert Van Langendock, Linda Polman and Charlotte Zwemmer were instrumental in cleaning the first, very sloppy draft of the manuscript. The Dutch Foundation for Special Journalistic Projects supported the first edition of the book—so did the unflappable Mrs. Zwemmer! And it was Emile Brugman from Atlas Publishers who pushed me actually to write a book. The Foundation for the Production and Translation of Dutch Literature helped me with this American edition.

I want to thanks all the folks from PM Press who had the courage—and hopefully the wisdom—to take on my book in the American edition. Andrea Gibbons put an amazing amount of time in the book and brilliantly transformed my Dutch-English into American-English...

I want to thank my son Sebastian for his patience while I was working on the translation instead of paying attention to him. I want to thank my parents, Ad and Marieke for always stimulating my curiosity, although I realize it sometimes must have driven them crazy...

Brussels and New York, 1996 and 2010.

ABOUT THE AUTHOR

Teun Voeten, who originally studied Cultural Anthropology and Philosophy in the Netherlands, is an award-winning photo-journalist and author. He has worked covering the conflicts in the former Yugoslavia, Rwanda, Sudan, Angola, Sierra Leone, Liberia, Afghanistan, Colombia, Iraq, Lebanon and Gaza. His work has been published in *Vanity Fair*, *Newsweek*, *The New Yorker*, and *National Geographic*, among others. Voeten is also a contributing photographer for organizations such as the International Red Cross, Doctors Without Borders, Human Rights Watch and the United Nations.

He has published three books: *Tunnel People*, which originally appeared as *Tunnelmensen* in Amsterdam, 1996; *A Ticket To*, a collection of Voeten's hard-hitting war photography along with a much-cited essay on war photography was released in 1999; *How de Body? Hope and Horror in Sierra Leone*, was published by Meulenhoff, Amsterdam in 2000 and came out in translation at St. Martin's Press, 2002. It is a book about his first trip to Sierra Leone to photograph a project on child soldiers that nearly ended in disaster when he was hunted down by rebels intent on killing him. Currently, Voeten is working on a photo book and a video documentary about the drug violence in Mexico. He lives alternately in New York and Brussels.

From Here to There

The Staughton Lynd Reader

From Here To There collects unpublished talks and hard-to-find essays from legendary activist historian Staughton Lynd.

The first section of the Reader collects reminiscences and analyses of the 1960s. A second section offers a vision of how historians might immerse themselves in popular movements while maintaining their obligation to tell the truth. In the last section Lynd explores what nonviolence, resistance to empire as a way of life, and working class self-activity might mean in the 21st century. Together, they provide a sweeping overview of the life, and work—to date—of Staughton Lynd.

Both a definitive introduction and further exploration, it is bound to educate, enlighten, and inspire those new to his work and those who have been following it for decades. In a wide-ranging Introduction, anarchist scholar Andrej Grubacic considers how Lynd's persistent concerns relate to traditional anarchism.

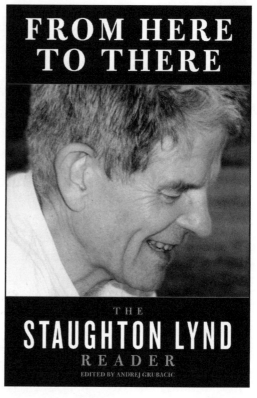

Staughton Lynd
edited by Andrej Grubacic
PM Press
978-1-60486-215-7
320 pages
$22.00

PM PRESS, PO BOX 23912, OAKLAND, CA, 94623
info@pmpress.org • www.pmpress.org

From the Bottom of the Heap

The Autobiography of Black Panther Robert Hillary King

In 1970, a jury convicted Robert Hillary King of a crime he did not commit and sentenced him to 35 years in prison. He became a member of the Black Panther Party while in Angola State Penitentiary, successfully organizing prisoners to improve conditions. In return, prison authorities beat him, starved him, and gave him life without parole after framing him for a second crime. He was thrown into solitary confinement, where he remained in a six by nine foot cell for 29 years as one of the Angola 3. In 2001, the state grudgingly acknowledged his innocence and set him free.

The conditions in Angola almost defy description, yet King never gave up his humanity, or the work towards justice for all prisoners that he continues to do today. His story strips bare the injustices inherent in our society, while continuing to be a powerful literary testimony to our own strength and capacity to overcome.

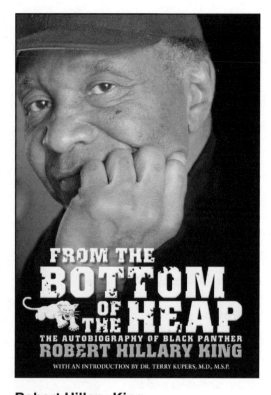

Robert Hillary King
introduction by Terry Kupers
PM Press
978-1-60486-039-9
224 pages
$24.95

PM PRESS, PO BOX 23912, OAKLAND, CA, 94623
info@pmpress.org • www.pmpress.org

I-5

A Novel of Crime, Sex, and Transport

A novel of crime, transport, and sex, *I-5* tells the bleak and brutal story of Anya and her journey north from Los Angeles to Oakland on the interstate that bisects the Central Valley of California.

Anya is the victim of a deep deception. Someone has lied to her; and because of this lie, she is kept under lock and key, used by her employer to service men, and indebted for the privilege. In exchange, she lives in the United States and fantasizes on a future American freedom. Or as she remarks to a friend, "Would she rather be fucking a dog...or living like a dog?" In Anya's world, it's a reasonable question.

Much of *I-5* transpires on the eponymous interstate. Anya travels with her "manager" and driver from Los Angeles to Oakland. It's a macabre journey: a drop at Denny's, a bad patch of fog, a visit to a "correctional facility," a rendezvous with an organ grinder, and a dramatic entry across Oakland's city limits.

Summer Brenner
PM Press
978-1-60486-019-1
256 pages
$15.95

PM PRESS, PO BOX 23912, OAKLAND, CA, 94623
info@pmpress.org • www.pmpress.org

FRIENDS OF PM PRESS

These are indisputably momentous times—the financial system is melting down globally and the Empire is stumbling. Now more than ever there is a vital need for radical ideas.

In the three years since its founding—and on a mere shoestring—PM Press has risen to the formidable challenge of publishing and distributing knowledge and entertainment for the struggles ahead. With over 100 releases to date, we have published an impressive and stimulating array of literature, art, music, politics, and culture. Using every available medium, we've succeeded in connecting those hungry for ideas and information to those putting them into practice.

Friends of PM allows you to directly help impact, amplify, and revitalize the discourse and actions of radical writers, filmmakers, and artists. It provides us with a stable foundation from which we can build upon our early successes and provides a much-needed subsidy for the materials that can't necessarily pay their own way. You can help make that happen— and receive every new title automatically delivered to your door once a month—by joining as a Friend of PM Press. And, we'll throw in a free T-Shirt when you sign up. Here are your options:

• **$25 a month** Get all books and pamphlets plus 50% discount on all webstore purchases
• **$25 a month** Get all CDs and DVDs plus 50% discount on all webstore purchases
• **$40 a month** Get all PM Press releases plus 50% discount on all webstore purchases
• **$100 a month** Superstar—Everything plus PM merchandise, free downloads, and 50% discount on all webstore purchases

For those who can't aff ord $25 or more a month, we're introducing **Sustainer Rates** at $15, $10 and $5. Sustainers get a free PM Press t-shirt and a 50% discount on all purchases from our website.

Your Visa or Mastercard will be billed once a month, until you tell us to stop. Or until our eff orts succeed in bringing the revolution around. Or the financial meltdown of Capital makes plastic redundant. Whichever comes first.

ABOUT PM PRESS

PM Press was founded at the end of 2007 by a small collection of folks with decades of publishing, media, and organizing experience. PM Press co-conspirators have published and distributed hundreds of books, pamphlets, CDs, and DVDs. Members of PM have founded enduring book fairs, spearheaded victorious tenant organizing campaigns, and worked closely  with bookstores, academic conferences, and even rock bands to deliver political and challenging ideas to all walks of life. We're old enough to know what we're doing and young enough to know what's at stake.

We seek to create radical and stimulating fiction and non-fiction books, pamphlets, t-shirts, visual and audio materials to entertain, educate and inspire you. We aim to distribute these through every available channel with every available technology—whether that means you are seeing anarchist classics at our bookfair stalls; reading our latest vegan cookbook at the café; downloading geeky fiction e-books; or digging new music and timely videos from our website.

PM Press is always on the lookout for talented and skilled volunteers, artists, activists and writers to work with. If you have a great idea for a project or can contribute in some way, please get in touch.

PM Press
PO Box 23912
Oakland, CA 94623
www.pmpress.org